Managing Ego Energy

Ralph H. Kilmann
Ines Kilmann
and Associates

Managing
Ego
Energy

*The Transformation of
Personal Meaning into
Organizational Success*

Jossey-Bass Publishers · San Francisco

Substantial discounts on bulk quantities of Jossey-Bass books are available to corporations, professional associations, and other organizations. For details and discount information, contact the special sales department at Jossey-Bass Inc., Publishers. (415) 433-1740; Fax (415) 433-0499.

For sales outside the United States, contact Maxwell Macmillan International Publishing Group, 866 Third Avenue, New York, New York 10022.

Manufactured in the United States of America. Nearly all Jossey-Bass books and jackets are printed on recycled paper containing at least 10 percent postconsumer waste, and many are printed with either soy- or vegetable-based ink, which emits fewer volatile organic compounds during the printing process than petroleum-based ink.

Library of Congress Cataloging-in-Publication Data

Kilmann, Ralph H.
    Managing ego energy : the transformation of personal meaning into organizational success / Ralph H. Kilmann, Ines Kilmann, and Associates.
        p.   cm. — (Jossey-Bass management series)
    Includes bibliographical references and index.
    ISBN 1-55542-618-2 (alk. paper)
    1. Employee morale. 2. Self-esteem. 3. Employee motivation.
4. Psychology, Industrial. 5. Organizational effectiveness.
I. Kilmann, Ines. II. Title. III. Series.
HF5549.5.M6K466   1994
158.7—dc20   93-41803
                                                      CIP

FIRST EDITION
HB Printing   10 9 8 7 6 5 4 3 2 1   *Code 9415*

The Jossey-Bass
Management Series

Consulting Editors
Organizations and Management

Warren Bennis
University of Southern California

Richard O. Mason
Southern Methodist University

Ian I. Mitroff
University of Southern California

Contents

Contents

To our special ego energy friends:
Colleen Carney, Christine Fischetti,
and Elaine Portner

Preface

TODAY'S INCREASINGLY DYNAMIC WORLD produces uncertainty, anxiety, and fear—making it easy for organizations to deactivate their human resources and drive performance and morale to low levels. Especially during turbulent times, people need a clear sense of direction and personal meaning if they are to risk their energies and abilities on the success of their organization. Moreover, constant pressure for continuous improvement can take a great toll on the human ego, since people prefer stability over change. There is an urgent need, therefore, to help people make sense of the incessant change and constant pressure around them.

Self-esteem, self-regard, self-respect, self-worth, self-confidence, and self-efficacy are just some of the terms we use to examine what people think of themselves, how they define the world around them, and why these crucial judgments affect everything they do. In particular, *ego energy* is each person's primitive struggle to know, both consciously and accurately, his or her

- Identity: Who am I?
- Competency: How effective am I? Are my decisions, actions, and investments ethical?
- Value: Have I contributed what others need or want? Is my organization benefiting from my decisions, actions, and investments?
- Worth: Am I a good or bad person? Do I deserve to be happy?
- Responsibility: Who controls who I am, what I do, and whether I am good or bad, happy or sad?

The ongoing struggle to define these self-concepts and to answer these age-old questions unleashes vast amounts of ego energy.

But how well do organizations and their managers mobilize and channel ego energy for the purposes of achieving organizational goals? Does this ego energy remain largely untapped, deactivated, or defused—to be utilized, perhaps, off the job? Or, worse yet, is this ego energy working not only against the personal goals of each member but also against the strategic goals of the organization? If the essential person-to-organization relationships have not been properly nurtured and established, day-to-day decisions will be based primarily on personal preferences, narrow departmental agendas, and office politics. In time, employees learn to take care of themselves first, their departments second, and the customer third. This ordering of priorities does not lead to long-term organizational success. But if we can channel employees' ego energy into worthwhile pursuits, both personal meaning and organizational success can be achieved.

The major premise of *Managing Ego Energy* is that the effective management of ego energy will enable organizations and their members to cope more effectively with our fast-paced, dynamic, competitive world—where the traditional, rational, technical, and economic approaches to organizational success are no longer sufficient. The human spirit—perhaps the final frontier of the human cosmos—must also be explicitly and thoroughly managed. In essence, if we wish to achieve both personal meaning and organizational success, we must come to grips with ourselves. Not surprisingly, we will then discover that the attributes and processes of healthy, well-functioning individuals closely parallel the systems and practices of healthy, adaptive organizations. Both individuals and organizations must be in close touch with their inner being and the outside world, in order to devote all their energies and abilities to the problems and opportunities that come their way.

Background

The Program in Corporate Culture at the University of Pittsburgh was founded in September 1983 to develop new knowledge about the impact of culture on organizational success and to disseminate this knowledge so that managers could increase the competitiveness of their organizations. The first major event sponsored by the program was a conference, held in 1984, on the topic of managing corporate culture, which resulted in the book *Gaining Control of the Corporate Culture* (1985). The second major conference took place in 1986 on the topic of managing organization-wide transformation, which also resulted in a book, *Corporate Transformation* (1988). The third conference took place in 1988 on the topic of competing in a global economy and resulted in the book *Making Organizations Competitive* (1991). The fourth major project of The Program in Corporate Culture, as noted above, focuses on the essence of the human ego and the relationship between ego energy and organizational success. Since this area of study has been somewhat fragmented across the academic disciplines and largely ignored by the practitioner community, we set out to learn from the professionals in the field.

The experts who wrote the chapters for *Managing Ego Energy* were chosen in two ways. First, we made a list of those who, in our view, had demonstrated a keen understanding of the topic through academic research or by direct involvement in organizational efforts at managing ego energy. In this way, eight experts were invited to write chapters for the book. Second, we mailed a call for papers to more than thirty thousand members of professional organizations and corporations: the Academy of Management, the American Society of Training and Development, and the American Psychological Association; subscribers to *Administrative Science Quarterly, California Management Review,* and *Journal of Applied*

Psychology; and executives of the thousand largest organizations in the United States. Our objective was to uncover important research and reports that were not yet published. And our expectations were realized: thirty papers covering a wide range of material on understanding and managing ego energy were submitted.

These papers were then subjected to a thorough review. Each paper received at least two independent reviews and was evaluated on the basis of four criteria: innovativeness in approach to the topic, quality in developing the approach, usefulness in guiding management action, and clarity of expression for a broad audience. In cases of disagreement, the paper was reviewed by a third person, and a discussion among the editors resolved any differences in opinion. (All the submitted papers were also discussed and evaluated in several meetings by the Ego Energy Group, which is made up of nine doctoral students majoring in a variety of social science disciplines.) The entire review process allowed the editors to select the best of the submitted papers. Editorial recommendations for revision were then sent to all authors. The invited authors' papers were subjected to a similar review procedure to help them fine-tune their ideas and improve their style as well. As a result of this comprehensive review process, the chapters in the book offer original ideas whose arguments are clearly conceived and well developed.

Audience

We expect that both academics and practitioners will find this book an invaluable resource. The practitioners who may be especially interested in the book include chief executive officers; senior operating executives; vice presidents of corporate organization, planning, and development; general managers; human resource managers; marketing managers; quality control managers; management consultants; organizational development experts; management training and development experts; and administrators and directors of nonprofit organizations. The academics who may be especially interested in *Managing Ego Energy* include faculty specializing in organizational theory, organizational behavior, organizational development, industrial psychology, strategic planning, information systems, marketing, industrial engineering, education, and public administration.

Overview of the Contents

Managing Ego Energy consists of eleven chapters organized into four major parts, plus an introductory chapter and a concluding chapter by the lead authors. The introductory chapter explores five fundamental themes that are addressed throughout this book: What is ego energy? What is its source? What is positive versus negative ego energy? How can positive ego energy be channeled to achieve organizational goals? Why must ego energy be managed now?

Part One, "The Significance of Ego Energy," comprises three chapters that provide important insights into the underlying concepts and radical perspectives on the topic. In Chapter Two, Nathaniel Branden offers a penetrating look into the core concept of self-esteem and the essential ingredients of a high–self-esteem organization. Lee L. Holmer draws attention in Chapter Three to a largely overlooked element in the mainstream (rational and technical) approaches to studying organizations: how employees and their organizations respond to emotional challenge. In Chapter Four, Terrence E. Deal and Pamela C. Hawkins continue with this unconventional approach by examining the importance of the human spirit—both for individuals and for their organizations. These chapters thus lay the groundwork for the detailed discussions of theory and action in the rest of the book.

Part Two, "Basic Theory and Action Implications," consists of three chapters that review the theory and research on ego energy. In Chapter Five, Mark A. Mone and Dawn Kelly review the literature on the two core concepts of self-esteem and self-efficacy, including the causes and consequences of these self-evaluations in organizational settings. In Chapter Six, James R. Bailey, Michael J. Strube, John H. Yost, and Michael Merbaum review additional literature on the process and the effects of self-appraisal: why and how employees gather diagnostic information in order to learn about their abilities—information that, ironically, can interfere with the actual performance of their work. Seth Allcorn summarizes the abundant literature on ego psychology in Chapter Seven, which includes a review of such basic concepts as id, ego, and superego along with a discussion on the defense mechanisms and dysfunctional interpersonal solutions that people habitually use to cope with basic and neurotic anxiety. Even though these chapters review the basic theory and research on ego energy, they also discuss numerous action implications that derive from this substantial body of scholarly knowledge.

Part Three, "Managerial Programs and Practices," contains three chapters that explain various ways to unleash, mobilize, and channel ego energy toward the achievement of both personal and organizational goals. In Chapter Eight, Robert E. Kaplan concentrates on the special problem of senior executives who have excessive self-esteem and tells how special programs can redirect their intense, dysfunctional energy toward greater balance in life and more effective interpersonal relationships. William P. Ferris presents in Chapter Nine a systematic and comprehensive framework for providing a wide array of management practices that promote positive ego energy to achieve organizational as well as personal goals. In Chapter Ten, Mary Cianni and Beverly Romberger focus on the special problem of a diverse workforce and offer a number of ways in which the ego energy of women and minorities can be used more effectively. While these chapters provide numerous action guidelines for managing ego energy, they also expand on some of the basic theories and concepts.

Part Four, "Organizational Transformations," consists of two case studies that make use of what is currently known about ego energy in order to ease the difficulties of conducting large-scale change. In Chapter Eleven, Robert B. Marshall, Jo-Anne I. Pitera, Lyle Yorks, and Stephen T. DeBerry present the case of fifteen thousand employees at an electric utility company who experienced a major redeployment of jobs and work units. Some eight thousand positions were redefined in the process of zero-based staffing, which deeply affected people's ego attachments to their "old" organization. Designing and managing this process with a deep understanding of positive versus negative ego energy, however, seems to have made the big difference in conducting this process effectively and compassionately. Herbert A. Marlowe, Jr. and Ronald C. Nyhan present in Chapter Twelve the case of a large county government that, like many other public organizations, had been losing the confidence of its citizens and was being faced with increasing fiscal pressures to do more and more with fewer and fewer resources.

Again, with an understanding of the basic concepts and practices of ego energy, this case illustrates how the fear and pain of change can be managed for the benefit of the employees, the organization, and its citizens (customers). Although the concept of ego energy is still new to most organizations, these two cases convey the tremendous potential for managing people more effectively whenever life in an organization is severely threatened or challenged.

Chapter Thirteen, the concluding chapter of this book, considers new directions for both research and practice in order to improve our understanding of ego energy and how to manage it. Since uncertainty, anxiety, and fear are all likely to increase in this dynamically complex world, we need to learn more about ego energy so that people can make rapid and effective adjustments to changed circumstances with an accurate sense of who they are and what their organizations need for long-term success.

Acknowledgments

Many people played a key role in making this book possible. Dean H. J. Zoffer and former Executive Associate Dean Andrew R. Blair at the Joseph M. Katz Graduate School of Business at the University of Pittsburgh provided the impetus to form The Program in Corporate Culture and to embark on these major projects. Camille D. Burgess, administrative assistant to The Program in Corporate Culture, managed all the logistical details with great care and proficiency. A special acknowledgment is given to the Ego Energy Group: Robert R. Albright, Darlene Y. Gambill, Nancy Kurland, Reg Litz, Kevin Pitts, Louise Serafin, Diane Swanson, and Gilbert Tan. These dedicated professionals helped in defining ego energy and designing this project. Last, we would like to express our sincere appreciation to all the authors who contributed to this project. It seems clear to us that these people have a special place in their hearts for the topic of ego energy and, therefore, they contributed their spirit as well as their ideas.

December 1993   RALPH H. KILMANN
Pittsburgh, Pennsylvania   INES KILMANN

The Authors

Ralph H. Kilmann holds the George H. Love Chair in Organization and Management and is director of The Program in Corporate Culture at the Joseph M. Katz Graduate School of Business, University of Pittsburgh. He received both his B.S. and M.S. degrees in industrial administration from Carnegie Mellon University and his Ph.D. degree in management from the University of California, Los Angeles. Since 1975, Kilmann has served as president of Organizational Design Consultants, a Pittsburgh-based firm specializing in the five tracks to organizational success. Kilmann has published more than one hundred articles and fifteen books on topics such as organizational design, strategy and structure, problem management, and organizational change and development. He is the developer of the MAPS Design Technology and co-developer of several diagnostic instruments, including the Thomas-Kilmann Conflict Mode Instrument and the Kilmann-Saxton Culture-Gap Survey. His recent books include *Gaining Control of the Corporate Culture* (1985, with M. J. Saxton, R. Serpa, and Associates), *Corporate Transformation* (1988, with T. J. Covin and Associates), *Managing*

Beyond the Quick Fix (1989), *Making Organizations Competitive* (1991, with I. Kilmann and Associates), *Workbook for Implementing the Five Tracks: Volumes I and II* (1991), and *Workbook for Continuous Improvement* (1993).

INES KILMANN is vice president of Organizational Design Consultants, a management consulting firm specializing in the five tracks to organizational success. She received her B.B.A. in management from Bernard M. Baruch College and her M.P.A. in public administration from the University of Pittsburgh. Currently she is studying for her Ph.D. degree at the University of Pittsburgh's Graduate School of Public and International Affairs. Her current research is focused on the integration of human resources, planned change, quality management, and ego energy. Prior to her consulting work, Kilmann spent fifteen years in various management positions with The Equitable in New York. Her publications include *Making Organizations Competitive* (1991, with R. H. Kilmann and Associates).

SETH ALLCORN is associate dean for fiscal affairs at Stritch School of Medicine, Loyola University, Chicago. He received his Ph.D. degree from the University of Missouri at Columbia. He has been the administrator of departments of medicine at the University of Missouri at Columbia and the University of Rochester. His research has focused on the psychodynamics of organizations and leadership, health sciences center and hospital administration, and medical group management. His consulting work is in the area of facilitating organizational change. He is the author of over fifty books and articles, including *Workplace Superstars in Resistant Organizations* (1991) and *Codependency in the Workplace* (1992).

JAMES R. BAILEY is assistant professor of organization management and director of the behavioral research laboratory at the Graduate School of Management, Rutgers University. He received his Ph.D. degree from Washington University, St. Louis. In addition to research on the interface of the self and the organization, Bailey's interests include psychological decision theory, particularly how decision making influences one's representation of the problem. He has published on a range of topics, including personality psychology, metaphors in scientific inquiry, and the intellectual history of the social and behavioral sciences. He has served as a psychometric consultant on large-scale organizational testing projects, and is the author of the American Assembly of Collegiate Schools of Business's *Outcome Measurement Project: The Final Report* (1986).

NATHANIEL BRANDEN is a private psychotherapist who also advises business organizations on the application of self-esteem principles and technology to improve performance in the workplace. He received his Ph.D. degree from California Graduate Institute, Los Angeles, in psychology. Branden developed an innovative approach to psychotherapy and began offering training through his institute to psychologists, psychiatrists, and other mental health professionals. The central focus of his therapeutic innovations is raising self-esteem and thereby stimulating the capacity for self-healing. His first major work was *The Psychology of Self-Esteem* (1969), now in its twenty-seventh printing. Branden is the author and coauthor of numerous other publications which have been published in French, German, Japanese, Spanish, Portuguese, Dutch, Hebrew, Greek, Norwegian, and Italian. His most recent works are *The Power of Self-Esteem* (1992) and *The Six Pillars of Self-Esteem* (1993).

MARY CIANNI is assistant professor of management at the Sigmund Weis School of Business at Susquehanna University. She received her Ph.D. degree from Pennsylvania State University in counseling psychology. In 1992 she was awarded the Lindback Distinguished Teaching Award. Cianni has worked as a consultant since 1980 and focuses on the design of management and professional development programs for a variety of organizations. Her primary research projects include the differential impact of corporate culture on women and minorities and the link between management development and corporate strategy. She has a dozen scholarly publications on workforce diversity, management development and corporate strategy, career development, and assertiveness training.

TERRENCE E. DEAL is professor of education at Peabody College, Vanderbilt University. He received his Ph.D. degree from Stanford

University in educational administration and sociology. He has coauthored nine books, including *Corporate Cultures: The Rites and Rituals of Corporate Life* (1982, with A. Kennedy) and *Reframing Organizations: Artistry, Choice, and Leadership* (1991, with L. Bolman).

STEPHEN T. DEBERRY is the director of psychology at Broughton State Hospital, Morganton, North Carolina. He received his Ph.D. degree from Long Island University in clinical psychology. He is a board-certified clinical psychologist and has maintained a private practice for twelve years in New York State. For thirteen years, DeBerry was an assistant clinical professor of psychiatry at the Albert Einstein College of Medicine. He has published numerous articles in academic journals pertaining to psychotherapy, community, and culture.

WILLIAM P. FERRIS is associate professor of management in the School of Business at Western New England College in Springfield, Massachusetts. He received his Ph.D. degree from Rensselaer Polytechnic Institute in communication. He is past president of the Eastern Academy of Management and holds a variety of elected positions in various professional organizations. Ferris has written articles and presented papers on such topics as team building, conflict resolution, leadership, interpersonal communication, and promotability as well as the use of case study and experiential exercise methodologies in teaching management subjects in schools of business.

PAMELA C. HAWKINS is executive assistant for the Office of University Relations and General Counsel at Vanderbilt University. She received her M.S. degree from Vanderbilt University in clinical audiology and early language intervention. She is currently in the graduate program of Vanderbilt Divinity School. Her present areas of interest include organizational spirituality, educational and administrative ethics, and organization conversion. Hawkins's professional experience includes work in special education, family counseling, and human resource services.

LEE L. HOLMER is the principal associate of Worklife Consultation Services, a Columbus, Ohio, consulting firm specializing in team building, conflict resolution, and strategic management. She is a Ph.D. candidate in the School of Public Policy and Management at Ohio State University. Prior to starting her consulting business in 1988, Holmer served as director of budget and finance for the Ohio Bureau of Employment Services, as budget director for the Ohio Department of Development, and as manager of planning for the City of Columbus Department of Finance. She has also served a number of leadership roles in community organizations concerned with urban problems, human services, and recovery issues.

ROBERT E. KAPLAN is a consultant and researcher specializing in executive leadership and development. He is co-president of Kaplan DeVries Inc., based in Greensboro, North Carolina. He has been at the Center for Creative Leadership for twelve years. Kaplan received his Ph.D. degree from Yale University in organizational behavior. In addition to various articles on management, individual and team development, and organizational change, he is author of *Beyond Ambition: How Driven Managers Can Lead Better and Live Better* (1991, with W. H. Drath and J. R. Kofodimos).

DAWN KELLY is a visiting associate professor of organization behavior at Northwestern University. She received her Ph.D. degree from Northwestern University. Her present research interests focus on models of organizational citizenship and diversity, organizational learning, and organizational change. Her most recently published articles can be found in *Research in Personnel and Human Resources Management* and *Academy of Management Journal.*

HERBERT A. MARLOWE, JR., is assistant research scholar at the Institute for Higher Education of the University of Florida. He received his Ph.D. degree from the University of Florida in counselor education. Marlowe's principal area of specialization is organizational design, change, and development. Recently he has been assisting Florida governments in "rightsizing" processes. He is the author or editor of numerous papers and books, including *Compe-*

tence Development (1985) and *Redesigning Local Government* (forthcoming).

ROBERT B. MARSHALL is founder and principal of The Marshall Group, which specializes in major organizational change carried out under the technology known as redeployment. He received his M.B.A. degree from New York University. Before starting The Marshall Group, he was executive vice president of Drake Beam Morin, Inc., where he directed the consulting resources to serve major corporate clients undergoing extensive change. Marshall has also held executive positions with Bendix International and the Edison Electric Institute and was a nuclear test engineer for Newport News Shipbuilding and Dry Dock Company.

MICHAEL MERBAUM is professor of psychology at Washington University, St. Louis. He received his Ph.D. degree from the University of North Carolina. He has served as senior vice president and director of assessment services for Psychological Associates and is currently the consulting psychologist for Wetterau International. Merbaum's research is concerned with therapist/patient interactions, and he is considered an expert in the use of the Minnesota Multiphasic Personality Inventory (MMPI).

MARK A. MONE is assistant professor of organizations and strategic management at the University of Wisconsin, Milwaukee. He received his Ph.D. degree from Washington State University in organizational behavior and organization theory. Mone spent ten years opening and managing properties in the hospitality industry and has been a consultant for Holiday Inns and other service-sector firms. His research examines different aspects of work motivation, including self-regulation and goal mechanisms. His publications include articles in *Human Performance* and *Hospitality Education and Research Journal.*

RONALD C. NYHAN has been a principal with Booz, Allen, Hamilton and CEO of an international management services corporation. He is a Ph.D. candidate in public administration at Florida Atlantic University. Nyhan has over fifteen years of consulting experience in organizational development and management systems design. His recent publications concern productivity enhancement and motivation theory.

Jo-Anne I. Pitera is director of corporate education and training at Florida Power and Light Company. She received her Psy.D. degree from the Florida Institute of Technology in clinical psychology. A trainer, presenter, and consultant for more than fifteen years, Pitera was awarded the American Psychological Association's prestigious "National Psychological Consultants to Management Award for Excellence in Consulting Psychology" in 1988 for her development of a managerial/supervisory training program.

Beverly Romberger is associate professor of speech communication at Susquehanna University. She received her Ph.D. degree from Pennsylvania State University, where she specialized in interpersonal, group, and organizational communication. She has used oral history as a methodology since 1983 and has gathered oral histories from rural, elderly women over the age of seventy-five and from women faculty about their everyday experiences in academe. She has published in scholarly journals and presented numerous papers on her findings and methodology at scholarly conferences.

Michael J. Strube is professor of psychology at Washington University, St. Louis. He received his Ph.D. degree from the University of Utah. His research on how people attempt to control their psychological and social environment has been applied to a variety of domains, including health psychology, behavioral medicine, and, most recently, organizational behavior. He has served on the editorial board of several psychology journals, and his work can be found in such periodicals as *Psychological Bulletin, Journal of Personality and Social Psychology,* and *Journal of Applied Psychology.*

Lyle Yorks is professor of management and coordinator of the Master of Science Program in Organizational Relations at Eastern Connecticut State University. He is also a principal of The Marshall Group, Scottsdale, Arizona. Yorks is currently completing his Ed.D. degree at Teachers College, Columbia University. He is author or coauthor of seven books, the most recent of which are *Scenarios of Change* (1989, with D. Whitsett) and *Dismissal* (1990, with W. Morin). His articles have been published in *Academy of Management Review, California Management Review, Personnel Planning Review,* and other professional journals.

JOHN H. YOST is a National Institute of Mental Health postdoctoral fellow in the psychology department of Ohio State University. He received his Ph.D. degree from Washington University, St. Louis. His research has examined the role of the self in goal setting, social facilitation, and a variety of performance arenas. In *Current Psychology: Research and Reviews,* he has advanced a major theory of self-construction that integrates psychology, evolutionary theory, and pragmatic philosophy. He has also designed marketing surveys for large organizations.

Managing Ego Energy

1

Introduction: The Personal Struggle for Identity, Competency, Value, Worth, and Responsibility

Ralph H. Kilmann and the Ego Energy Group
(Robert R. Albright, Darlene Y. Gambill, Ines Kilmann,
Nancy Kurland, Reg Litz, Kevin Pitts, Louise Serafin,
Diane Swanson, Gilbert Tan)

SINCE THE TIME OF SIGMUND FREUD in the nineteenth century, many terms have been used to describe and understand the human ego—how it forms, develops, and affects every aspect of human existence. Consider just some of the frequently used *self* concepts: self-esteem, self-regard, self-respect, self-worth, self-confidence, self-efficacy, self-identity, self-definition, self-differentiation, self-expression, self-enhancement, self-evaluation, self-appraisal, self-verification, self-awareness, self-knowledge, self-responsibility, self-pride, self-reflection, self-assertiveness, and self-reliance. While many of these terms are used synonymously and interchangeably, there are also some important differences among them that address the many subtle and mysterious aspects of the human mind and spirit.

As the editors of this book, we felt that it was essential to focus every author's effort on using a common language for examining the impact of the human ego in work organizations. Consequently, we asked all of them to define the term *ego energy* explicitly and indicate how their perspective adds to our understanding of organizational life. While their definitions and perspectives vary widely (according to the concepts they use to examine ego energy), their efforts at consistency and focus certainly help us to integrate the emerging knowledge and practices in this field of study. As a result of their efforts, we can say much more about the many ways in which an understanding of ego energy offers additional and different—even fascinating—approaches for improving the functioning of people and their organizations.

This chapter presents an overview of the key themes addressed throughout this book and therefore serves as a general introduction to the topic of ego energy. We have organized our overview according to five fundamental questions: What is ego energy? What is its source? What is positive versus negative ego energy? How can positive ego energy be channeled to achieve organizational goals? Why must ego energy be managed now?

What Is Ego Energy?

Since the use of self-concepts for describing and understanding work organizations has been rather fragmented across the social science disciplines (and largely ignored by the practitioner community), there is considerable freedom in proposing definitions. Yet, surprisingly, there is considerable agreement among the authors in this book.

Two components of ego energy are discussed more than any others: self-efficacy and self-esteem. Branden (Chapter Two) views self-efficacy as confidence in one's ability to master challenges and manage change, while he defines self-esteem as a combination of both self-efficacy and self-respect (one's right to be happy). Mone and Kelly (Chapter Five) divide their review of the research into self-efficacy (one's belief regarding one's ability to perform specific tasks) and self-esteem (a general sense of self-worth that includes self-respect). Bailey, Strube, Yost, and Merbaum (Chapter Six) use the term self-knowledge to describe the ability component of ego energy and the term self-esteem as a desire to hold oneself in a positive regard (similar to self-respect). Kaplan (Chapter Eight) is concerned with people's desire for mastery (being on top of their jobs in terms of competence and control) and a sense of personal worth (self-esteem) that comes from their mastery of tasks. Although

Cianni and Romberger (Chapter Ten) build their approach to ego energy primarily around the concept of self-efficacy, they do acknowledge the role of self-respect. Thus people's confidence in their abilities (self-efficacy) and people's regard for themselves (self-esteem) are two recurring components of ego energy.

Mone and Kelly (Chapter Five) integrate these two components by examining four levels of self-esteem: global self-esteem, organizationally based self-esteem, role-specific self-esteem, and situation-specific self-esteem. The latter form, situation-specific self-esteem, is based on a person's belief about his or her ability to perform a particular task—and thus is identical to self-efficacy. The components of self-esteem and self-efficacy can therefore be viewed as representing two ends of a continuum ranging from global self-esteem (general self-regard that is independent of context) to self-efficacy (specific beliefs in one's ability to perform a given task). Mone and Kelly also demonstrate how these four levels of self-esteem operate as both causes and consequences for the cognitive, emotional, and behavioral life of people in organizations.

Several authors, however, suggest additional components of ego energy. While Holmer (Chapter Three) cites two components, she defines them as self-esteem and *self-awareness*—whether people stay open to threatening emotional experiences or shut down and deny what they see, think, or feel. Denial and self-deception play a major role in Holmer's concept of ego energy, since people cannot address (in themselves and others) what they are not willing to see. Although Ferris (Chapter Nine) considers self-competence (self-efficacy) and regard (received from others) in his discussion of ego energy, he builds his comprehensive framework around four detailed components of the ego: sense of self (awareness, self-identity), sense of pride (being unique and valued), sense of achievement (similar to self-efficacy but including actual accomplishment), and sense of justice (including ethics, ideals, morals, equity, and fairness). Branden (Chapter Two) similarly expands the two components of ego energy (self-efficacy and self-regard) into what he calls the six pillars of self-esteem: living consciously (self-awareness), self-acceptance (refusing to fight with oneself), self-responsibility (for thoughts, feelings, behavior, and self-esteem), self-assertiveness (authenticity), living purposely (setting and achieving goals), and integrity (matching one's behavior to one's ideals and rhetoric).

Allcorn (Chapter Seven) examines the ingredients of ego energy by making use of Freud's (1960) three intrapsychic components: id, ego, and superego. The id's unconscious feelings, desires, and needs are in perpetual conflict with the superego's unconscious false self (extra good or extra bad)—which generates two kinds of anxiety (Horney, 1950): *basic anxiety* (which stems from being generally anxious about the self and the outside world) and *neurotic anxiety* (which stems not only from conflicts in using psychological defenses for distorting reality in the intrapsychic world but also from conflicts in using these defense mechanisms and other dysfunctional behavioral solutions in the interpersonal world). The ego represents the conscious, conflict-free, reality-based functioning of the true self—which can effectively cope with normal anxiety.

Building on aspects of this Freudian model, Marshall, Pitera, Yorks, and DeBerry (Chapter Eleven) add the dimensions of locus of control (Do people believe what happens to them is determined by what they do—or by outside forces?) and ego attachment (Do people believe their attachments in a work setting will be severed— or nurtured?). Marlowe and Nyhan (Chapter Twelve) also build on this attachment theme by considering the cognitive and emotional investments that people make in an organization—and particularly how these investments are affected by the external environment of an organization.

Perhaps the most provocative discussion on the nature of ego energy is presented by Deal and Hawkins (Chapter Four). For these authors, the essential component of ego energy is human spirit. Although the substance and form of spirit is tough to pin down, it is undeniably real—especially when a spiritual undertaking touches the souls of people in an organization and enables them to accomplish what no one thought possible. Deal and Hawkins's entire discussion on ego energy focuses on the elusive qualities of spirit.

We will return to the separate components of ego energy throughout this chapter (and the rest of the book). But now let us see how the various authors answer the question: What is ego energy? Branden (Chapter Two) focuses on the human impulse toward achievement, self-expression, and self-assertion (key aspects of his six pillars of self-esteem). Holmer (Chapter Three) defines ego energy as the extent to which people are able to direct energy to rational and constructive purposes (as opposed to irrational and destructive purposes) by effectively responding to emotional challenge. Deal and Hawkins (Chapter Four) see ego energy as human spirit that is set free so that people and their organizations can be converted to a new spiritual faith—for competitive advantage. As suggested by Deal and Hawkins, when all these ego energies are mobilized and channeled in the same spiritual direction, a collective ego energy is released—which may be the common ingredient of strong corporate cultures (whether functional or dysfunctional).

Mone and Kelly (Chapter Five) define ego energy as a composite of the cognitive energies that people exert toward affective reactions, choices, and behavior. Bailey, Strube, Yost, and Merbaum (Chapter Six) view ego energy as the process by which people learn about, promote, and protect themselves—using a self-appraisal process that allows them to maintain their self-regard. Allcorn (Chapter Seven) discusses the net energy that remains for a person's conscious, reality-based intrapsychic and interpersonal functioning (for dealing with normal anxiety) after wasting energy on intrapsychic defenses and dysfunctional lifestyle solutions (for addressing basic and neurotic anxiety). Kaplan (Chapter Eight) defines ego energy along the same lines as Allcorn by considering the dysfunctional—excess—energy that executives use to compensate for their feelings of low self-esteem.

Ferris (Chapter Nine) views ego energy as the chronic desire to define oneself through one's behavior in a way that demonstrates to others that one is valuable and unique. Cianni and Romberger (Chapter Ten) define ego energy as the power to maintain control over one's inner world and to sustain a level of self-confidence (self-efficacy) and belief in oneself (self-regard, respect, and esteem)—especially during periods of chaos and massive change. Marshall, Pitera, Yorks, and DeBerry (Chapter Eleven) discuss ego energy as the psychological investments a person imparts to work—an investment that depends on the variables of ability (self-efficacy), self-esteem, locus of control, and attachment. Finally, Marlowe and Nyhan (Chapter Twelve) consider ego energy as a person's interior perceptions and feelings of hope, agency, worth, and potentiality.

Certainly there is more consensus on the basic components of ego energy than on its meaning for people and their organizations. Nevertheless, certain themes do emerge and suggest a working definition of the concept. It seems evident that ego energy can be used individually and collectively, consciously and unconsciously, constructively and destructively. Indeed, ego energy can be drained by dysfunctional use (on oneself and toward others)—which limits what can then be used for achieving personal and organizational goals. Furthermore, ego energy enables people to make strong psychological attachments and emotional investments in their organization—which an organization can either damage or nurture. Finally, since the ego can be viewed as a dynamic solution to the perpetual tug of war between the id and the superego, the challenge of being driven by one's desires and fears versus what is desirable or ideal (or, alternatively, what is punitive or bad) leads to many difficult questions about ethics, morals, and justice for every organization and its many stakeholders. As Ferris (Chapter Nine) clearly states, the surest way to immobilize ego energy is to violate people's sense of justice—the superego.

The following definition of ego energy integrates most of the foregoing perspectives: *Ego energy* is a person's primitive struggle to know (both consciously and accurately) his or her *identity* (Who am I? What emotional investments should I make?); *competency* (How effective am I at being who I am? Are my decisions, actions, and investments ethical?); *value* (Have I contributed what others need or want? Is my organization benefiting from my decisions, actions, and investments?); *worth* (Am I a good or bad person? Do I deserve to be happy?); and *responsibility* (Who controls who I am, what I do, what emotional investments I make, and whether I am good or bad, happy or sad?). Although the source of ego energy is within each person, it can be unleashed, mobilized, and channeled for the collective good (or bad) of an organization. Thus each person's struggle with identity, competency, value, worth, and responsibility affects the achievement of both personal and organizational goals—and the satisfaction derived from these pursuits.

What Is the Source of Ego Energy?

Knowing the source of ego energy helps us to create and mobilize it in beneficial ways; knowing the amount of ego energy suggests what is available to channel for the achievement of personal and organizational goals. While the authors address these issues within their different frameworks, there is still considerable agreement on where ego energy comes from and how much of it is available for productive use.

Based on the Freudian model (and its subsequent refinements), Allcorn (Chapter Seven) devotes considerable attention to the question of source. He equates the big bang theory of the origin of the universe to the big bang theory of the origin of the ego: at birth, the id, ego, and superego are undifferentiated and fused, but these three intrapsychic elements become differentiated and detached as the infant separates from the mother (and the rest of the world). Thereafter the child experiences inherent tensions between the id and the superego (in the inner world) and between the ego and others (in the outer world). These tensions derive from fears of abandonment (being completely separate from others and, hence, not fused) and engulfment (being completely fused with others and, hence, not being separate). Such countervailing forces in the ego generate anxiety. The ego must then tap biochemical, neurological, and biomechanical energy in order to cope with this anxiety. An intrapsychic chain reaction creates ego energy: the ongoing tension among the id, superego, ego, and the outer world; the basic and neurotic anxiety that a person experiences from all this tension; and the biochemical, neurological, and biomechanical energy that the ego activates in order to manage this anxiety.

People may differ significantly with respect to the potential amount of ego energy available to them—due to various environmental, genetic, and developmental factors that create different tensions, anxieties, and reservoirs of biochemical, neurological, and biomechanical energy. For example. Allcorn suggests how different kinds of family pathology (resulting from parents who are physically, sexually, or emotionally abusive; cold, unpredictable, uncaring, unnurturing, and unavailable) affects not only the amount of anxiety that people experience but also the particular mix of psychological defenses (such as denial, projection, identification, and regression) and interpersonal solutions (expansive, self-effacing, or resignation) they habitually use to cope with their anxiety. It would be mere speculation, however, to suggest the extent of such differences in the potential ego energy among the members of an organization. But one thing is clear: the more that psychological defenses and dysfunctional interpersonal solutions are used to manage basic and neurotic anxiety, the less ego energy is available to people for consciously and accurately determining their identity, competency, value, worth, and responsibility in their organizations.

A key question: how much ego energy is actually available for conscious (reality-based) functioning once basic and neurotic anxiety have been addressed? Instead of trying to expand (let alone measure) the total amount of potential ego energy in organizational members, it might be more productive to find ways to increase the *actual* ego energy available for reality-based solutions (for normal anxiety) versus reality-hiding solutions (for basic and neurotic anxiety). And besides, as we will see in a moment, generating more and more ego energy—at its source—is not necessarily a good thing, especially if it will be used excessively and, therefore, dysfunctionally.

Kaplan (Chapter Eight) believes that the source of ego energy is basic desires and fears—specifically, the desire to succeed and the fear of failing. Kaplan is particularly concerned about the excess energy that some senior executives have—and use in dysfunctional ways—thereby equating excess energy with energy spent on psychological defenses and dysfunctional interpersonal solutions (what he calls "extremely expansive" solutions) versus energy spent on balanced interpersonal solutions. Of course, some executives (and people in general) use "underexpansive" solutions, because their ego energy is somehow blocked, inhibited, or deactivated—which also results in dysfunctional behavior and outcomes. The ideal case for a person, according to both Kaplan and Allcorn, is having—and using—adequate ego energy: a moderate amount of energy that is readily available for productive use (and hence is not deactivated) but does not overwhelm the self or others (and hence is not being used excessively for defense mechanisms and dysfunctional interpersonal solutions). Ironically, perhaps, it might be better for people to *reduce* their total supply of ego energy if this reduction would remove their excessive, dysfunctional energy—leaving them a greater share of conscious ego energy for reality-based functioning.

Ferris (Chapter Nine) also believes that the primary source of ego energy is the anxiety of separation from the mother (by the infant) and a general fear of further separations throughout life. The conflicting fears of abandonment (separation) versus suffocation (fusion) drive ego development and self-identity: Who am I? What makes me unique? What makes me valuable? Marshall, Pitera, Yorks, and DeBerry (Chapter Eleven) also see the primary source of ego energy as a fear of abandonment (becoming detached, betrayed, and violated), but they include the additional fear of not being in control (when, for example, other people are in a position to make decisions that can result in separation and abandonment).

Bailey, Strube, Yost, and Merbaum (Chapter Six) discuss the source of ego energy as an instinct or desire to discover self-knowledge while maintaining self-regard—especially when a person is confronted with uncertainty about his or her abilities. These authors view uncertainty in the work environment as generating anxiety, which then motivates people to appraise their abilities (so long as the information they acquire does not undermine their self-concepts). Holmer (Chapter Three) also addresses the desire for self-awareness (similar to self-knowledge) as the primary source of ego energy—and considers whether people are capable of receiving feedback without distortion, a trait that she calls emotional capacity.

Probably the most elusive, yet the most provocative, source of ego energy is *spirit*. Deal and Hawkins (Chapter Four) offer many examples of how individuals, groups, and organizations have been able to mobilize huge amounts of their spirit by various expressive acts: rituals, rites, stories, myths, legends, ceremonies, music, art, theater, festivity, poetry, and song. Whatever latent spirit resides within people (arriving there by whatever means), it is these collective—cultural—forums that seem to release a spiritual substance that can then be channeled into either functional or dysfunctional uses.

In sum, then, several authors concur that the original source of ego energy (much like original sin) stems from each human being's primitive fears of being abandoned versus being suffocated, fears that result in a lifelong struggle to define and verify the generic self-concepts: identity, competency, value, worth, and responsibility. Furthermore, these conflicting fears result in various types of anxiety—which can be generated internally (tensions between the id and the superego) or externally (tensions between the ego and the interpersonal world). Externally generated sources of ego energy, incidentally, not only stem from uncertainties and emotional challenges originating in the external environment; they may also result from both planned and unplanned expressive acts that can release the latent spiritual energy that exists in everyone.

Moreover, while it is difficult (perhaps impossible) to know just how much ego energy is potentially—or actually—available for people and organizations, most of these authors believe we have a long way to go before we fully unleash, mobilize, and channel all the latent ego energy in organizational members. But if people rely too heavily on psychological defenses and dysfunctional lifestyle solutions to manage their excess anxiety (or to keep their available energy suppressed), they may not have much ego energy left over to achieve their personal and organizational goals.

What Is Positive vs. Negative Ego Energy?

We have already suggested what ego energy is and where it comes from—as well as how much is potentially and actually available for use. Now we must say more about its consequences. While the usefulness of ego energy (like most other qualities) can range across a wide spectrum of outcomes (benefits and costs for internal and external stakeholders), for convenience we will simplify our discussion by speaking in terms of constructive versus destructive, functional versus dysfunctional, and positive versus negative.

Most of the contributors examine the consequences of ego energy and consider whether these effects are positive or negative for both individuals and their organizations. Branden (Chapter Two) boldly asks whether the workplace supports a person's self-esteem— or does violence to it. He views positive ego energy as representing an immune system of consciousness that enables people to respond to life's adversities in an adaptive way. Negative ego energy, in contrast, is evident when this psychological immune system is either insufficient or nonexistent—so that people crumble before inconsequential obstacles (at home and at work).

Similar to this intrapsychic immune system, Holmer (Chapter Three) defines the concept of "orientation and response to emotional challenge" (OREC) for the purpose of identifying those who can receive feedback with minimal distortion and denial—even though an experience is threatening. Those people who have an emotional capacity to "stay open" to the outside world will be able to perform rationally and constructively by making full use of their mental abilities despite the anxiety and threat in the situation. But those without this emotional capacity will "shut down" in the face of adversity, deny what they see, and thereby deceive themselves—resulting in irrational and destructive outcomes. Naturally, if management practices encourage and develop the emotional capacity of the membership, the organization will be more rational and adaptive to difficult challenges. But if an organization's formal and informal systems discourage or, worse yet, demean the emotional capacity of its members, the organization will similarly distort or deny vital aspects of its external environment—to its own eventual demise.

Deal and Hawkins (Chapter Four) note the constructive versus destructive aspects of spirit when they distinguish between hope and despair. When spirit is either purposely suppressed or inadvertently deactivated, it puts an anchor on performance—to the detriment of both individuals and their organizations. In contrast, when leadership is able to provide a nourishing environment in which people can utilize their talents while connecting with the souls of others, a large amount of both individual and collective ego energy can be unleashed and mobilized for constructive purposes. According to Deal and Hawkins, encouraging members to engage in expressive activity (meaningful spiritual ceremonies, for example) not only creates an energized and committed membership but also enhances consciousness (being in touch with one's self, other people, and the world at large).

While Mone and Kelly (Chapter Five) and Bailey, Strube, Yost, and Merbaum (Chapter Six) do not explicitly address the distinction between positive and negative ego energy, it can easily be inferred from their review of the research literature. For Bailey and colleagues, positive ego energy results when each job in the organization is designed (and then assigned) to fit with the jobholder's need to self-appraise his or her ability to perform—and to maintain a favorable image of the self. Indeed, if members feel confident in their ability to perform their jobs because they regularly receive the information they want and need about their abilities, they do not have to waste energy by designing and conducting self-appraisals: they can use all their ego energy to achieve organizational goals. Yet if the job situation is highly uncertain, rapidly changing, and the information that members need to assess their abilities is not readily available, they will purposely withhold their energy to see how their abilities affect job performance (relative to all the other contributing factors in the situation). But withholding energy for the purpose of assessing the effects of one's abilities also lowers job performance. Thus negative ego energy results when members either do not have the ability to perform their job (which negatively affects their self-image) or do not have the information they desire to see the results of their effort (which wastes valuable energy as they collect this information and appraise their abilities).

As Bailey and colleagues caution us, however, some people, particularly those with low self-esteem, may only desire information that positively confirms their abilities: they do not want information that points out any deficiencies. If these people (who have a low desire for self-appraisal) are automatically given the negative information they do not want, their self-image will be negatively affected—which will reduce their ego energy during the next cycle of job performance. Again, as Mone and Kelly also propose, jobs should be designed to match not only people's ability to perform but also their self-concepts (identity, competency, value, worth, and responsibility)—which may vary from one person to another.

Allcorn (Chapter Seven) implies a somewhat different slant on functional versus dysfunctional ego energy. As noted earlier he focuses on the dynamic interplay among the id, ego, and superego. Negative ego energy results when people frequently, rigidly, and compulsively use psychological defenses and dysfunctional interpersonal approaches to ward off basic and neurotic anxiety. But when these solutions fail to work (especially for satisfying *other* people's needs and managing complex business problems), even more anxiety is generated—which is then followed by more of the same ineffective solutions that further disconnect people from their true self and the outside world. As a result of these vicious cycles, most of the ego's energy is shifted toward maintaining a false self (extra good or extra bad) that is not allowed to be questioned by others—which therefore prevents the conflict-free, reality-based portion of the ego from performing effectively in the interpersonal world.

For Allcorn, positive ego energy occurs when people use adaptive, flexible, and well-reasoned solutions for coping with normal anxiety. In this case, a large portion of the ego is available for conscious functioning—with minimal energy being used to deny or distort personal and interpersonal reality. While Allcorn suggests that not much can be done (in an organizational setting) to make chronically low-esteem people feel better about themselves (other than to be aware, sensitive, and compassionate about their predicament—and not to get caught in their emotional traps), supportive and consistent management practices can enhance the functioning of people who have adequate self-esteem.

Kaplan's approach (Chapter Eight) is completely consistent with Allcorn's use of ego psychology. For Kaplan, negative ego energy is released when a person relies on either an overexpansive (excessive) or underexpansive (inhibited) solution to organizational life. The overexpansive solution is based on an idealized false self (extra good); the underexpansive solution is based on a punitive false self (extra bad). In contrast, positive ego energy is demonstrated when people are more relaxed, open, balanced, sensitive, flexible, tolerant, reasonable, patient, trusting, and accepting of themselves and others—traits rooted in adequate self-esteem (neither too much nor too little). Kaplan tries to help people (especially senior executives) redirect their negative ego energy to positive ego energy—primarily through a comprehensive, customized, personalized management development program.

The most explicit treatment of positive versus negative ego energy is provided by Ferris (Chapter Nine). He distinguishes ego energy as either a powerful asset or a ruinous liability and puts the burden on management for either helping employees to alleviate their anxiety or exacerbating it. On the one hand, if management practices (and the design and administration of formal organizational systems) foster employees' natural ego-defining behavior by enabling them to enhance their sense of self, pride, achievement, and ethics (or, in terms of our self-concepts, their identity, competency, value, worth, and responsibility), members will be energized to achieve organizational goals along with their personal goals. On the other hand, if various management practices violate employees' ego-defining behavior by expecting them to succeed at the expense of one another (or at the expense of external stakeholders), they will be energized to accomplish their personal goals *instead* of organizational goals. Or, worse yet, members may sabotage their work because, as Ferris suggests, they experience the organization as the enemy of their ego.

Cianni and Romberger (Chapter Ten), while primarily concerned about the self-efficacy (competency) component of ego energy, also see management practices as either sustaining members' beliefs in their ability to accomplish personal and organizational goals or, alternatively, losing their self-confidence and belief in themselves. Mone and Kelly (Chapter Five), who review the extensive research on self-efficacy, come to the same general conclusions and implications for action. If people do not *believe* they can succeed on the job, they probably will not try. While Cianni and Romberger concentrate on developing and sustaining the self-efficacy of women and minorities during periods of prolonged stress from organizational restructuring, it is clear that their discussion applies to everyone when uncertainty and anxiety are present. Management practices such as furnishing job mastery experiences, providing effective role models, giving emotional support, and reducing stress levels—for all organizational members—will develop self-efficacy and thus mobilize positive ego energy. But if management fails to provide what is needed for nurturing the self-concepts or does not offer developmental experiences (and encouragement) to all employees on an equal basis, people's self-efficacy will deteriorate and their sense of ethics will be violated. Under these circumstances, employees will have little ego energy (or belief in themselves) to perform their jobs to the best of their ability.

Marshall and colleagues (Chapter Eleven) make clear distinctions between positive and negative ego energy as they consider the trauma of organizational transformation for fifteen thousand employees at Florida Power and Light. For these authors, two primary experiences lead to massive anxiety during restructuring, downsizing, redeployment, and job abolishment. First, employees can easily feel out of control (which fosters belief in external control), since these corporate decisions are usually out of their hands and little formal communication is provided as senior management secretly makes these decisions and plans their implementation; second, major organizational change usually severs the psychological bonds among the members of work groups—as existing jobs are eliminated while new jobs and departments are formed. In most system-wide transformations, members probably feel violated on both counts: not only are their self-identity, competency, value, worth, and responsibility being negatively affected (or at least threatened) by someone else, but their attachments to the organization are being torn apart without anything (at least for the moment) to replace them—a powerful replay, perhaps, of abrupt separations at birth and thereafter (which generates massive anxiety).

The good news is that Marshall and colleagues illustrate how, under the difficult and anxiety-producing process of large-scale change, an organization can not only minimize the trauma but also mobilize positive ego energy: employees can be encouraged to participate actively in the transformation process (which fosters belief in the *internal* control of their self-concepts) and, at the same time, to reattach themselves securely to new work groups and new jobs designed with their abilities and needs in mind. Thus, rather than violating members' self-concepts and thereby mobilizing negative ego energy against the (villainous) organization, fostering active involvement in the change process and keeping everyone informed of what is happening (and thereby activating positive ego energy) will help members take care of both themselves and their organization.

In another case of organizational transformation (for four thousand employees of a county government in the United States), Marlowe and Nyhan (Chapter Twelve) make the distinction between ego energy that is activated and ego energy that is enervated. While they address the differences in positive and negative ego energy much like many of the other authors (via the impact of the formal and informal systems in the organization), these authors discuss an additional perspective: the effect of the external environment (and not just internal management practices) on the mobilization of ego energy. Marlowe and Nyhan suggest at least three environmental factors (which we have generalized from their focus on county government) that affect the self-concepts of organizational members: a negative image of the organization and its members held by the public at large or other external stakeholders, which includes diminished expectations about the quality of the organization's products or services; a fiscal crisis driven largely by external conditions in the region, industry, nation, or global economy; and the growing complexity of the external problems and opportunities facing the organization. These outside factors can significantly drain the ego energy of members—above and beyond what may be occurring inside the organization. But an improvement process that actively involves members in reinventing their organization (and takes into account how every decision and action might raise or lower their ego energy) can succeed in mobilizing positive ego energy—not only to achieve personal and organizational goals but also to create (or select) a more benign external environment.

In sum, much like the discussions on what ego energy is and where it comes from, there is considerable agreement here concerning the mobilization of positive (constructive) versus negative (destructive) ego energy: when organizational systems and management practices enable members to define their self-concepts (identity, competency, value, worth, and responsibility) proactively and positively, members will invest abundant ego energy in the achievement of organizational goals. They will consistently apply their unique and valued abilities to their well-designed jobs—which provide just the right amount and kind of information to appraise their abilities while maintaining their self-image. In the opposite case, if systems and practices rely on external control, produce unannounced—radical—disruptions in ego attachments, violate members' self-concepts, and otherwise threaten their self-image, members will spend most of their energy taking care of their anxiety with psychological defenses and dysfunctional interpersonal solutions. And even if members do not need to use their energy for maintaining an extra good or bad false self (because they have adequate self-esteem), their ego energy will be primarily devoted to achieving personal goals—while they either ignore or undermine organizational goals.

How Can Positive Ego Energy Be Channeled
to Achieve Organizational Goals?

In the process of summarizing each author's distinction of positive versus negative ego energy, we mentioned a number of management practices that facilitate the positive—functional—side of the equation: helping employees to stay open during crises so they can apply reality-based approaches to these anxiety-ridden surprises; encouraging the active participation of all employees in transformational change (for reinventing the organization while redefining their self-concepts and reattaching themselves to new surroundings); designing and assigning jobs to fit with employees' ability and their need for self-appraisal and self-regard; providing all employees with job mastery experiences, role models, emotional encouragement, and stress reduction so they continue to believe in their abilities and themselves; endorsing expressive activities (ceremonies, rites, rituals, stories, theater, song, and dance) so that employees can release—and then effectively channel—their collective spirit; counseling employees to help them redirect their excessive self-esteem toward more balanced, adaptive, and flexible behavioral solutions to complex problems.

This brief listing of management practices does not do justice to the extensive discussions provided by the authors themselves. Several contributors, in fact, devote most of their attention to various action implications and specific management practices that unleash, mobilize, and channel positive ego energy. Rather than restate all their observations here, we offer a general classification scheme that summarizes the wide range of organizational systems, management practices, and leadership behavior that can channel ego energy toward the achievement of organizational goals.

Kilmann (1989) classifies all the formal and informal systems in an organization into these categories: the setting (dynamic complexity and external stakeholders), the organization (strategy-structure and the reward system), the individual (interpersonal styles and skills for managing people and problems), the group (collective decision making and action taking), and, at center stage, the informal organization (cultural norms, values, beliefs—and collective spirit).. The key question is whether these systemic elements are barriers or channels to achieving the desired results: the ongoing satisfaction of customers and other key stakeholders.

It should be apparent that the "prime directive" for this project is to learn how to unleash, mobilize, and channel *positive* ego energy in order to improve the functioning of people and their organizations. But for the purpose of clarifying the key distinctions, the next few paragraphs summarize the two extremes: how organizational systems and their management practices can generate either negative or positive ego energy—depending on how they are designed and conducted throughout an organization.

Organizational systems that are systemic barriers to success (and, hence, promote *negative* ego energy) are evidenced when the culture fosters mistrust and dysfunctional behavior among members: employees exhibit defensive communication and deficient problem-solving skills; they show little cooperation and teamwork both within and across their work groups; they receive conflicting strategic signals that have been translated into confusing goals, objectives, and jobs; formal work units are divided by steep functional walls—which prevent employees from obtaining the essential resources (and information) to perform their jobs (and define their self-concepts); the reward system overemphasizes measures of short-term financial results, downplays the various behavioral contributions needed to manage complex problems and improve business processes, and, in the worst cases, promotes unhealthy competition among employees.

Management practices (guided by barriers to success) that promote negative ego energy are evidenced as discouraging employees from enacting their natural ego-defining behavior (with respect to all the self-concepts)—and thereby maintaining external control over the ego energy of employees and, correspondingly, being insensitive to their ego attachments. As might be expected, these management practices do not question the systemic barriers to success and, therefore, do not even consider the option of changing the formal and informal systems so they will foster more authentic, constructive, and satisfying human relationships.

Organizational systems that are systemic channels to success (and, hence, promote *positive* ego energy) are evidenced when the culture fosters trust, candor, information sharing, and a willingness to change and improve: employees have the appropriate styles and skills to communicate effectively with one another, identify and solve complex problems, and manage themselves; a spirit of cooperation and teamwork flourishes within and across all work units; employees have a clear understanding of how their daily jobs (and their self-concepts) align with the strategic direction of their organization and have the resources to perform efficiently and effectively; the reward system motivates high individual—and team—performance according to external (benchmarked) standards of excellence (versus internal social comparisons among employees) and explicitly appraises behavioral contributions to long-term organizational success (such as fostering positive ego energy among employees and improving complex business processes).

Management practices (guided by channels to success) that promote positive ego energy are evidenced as actively encouraging the meaningful involvement of all employees in their natural ego-defining behavior and being especially sensitive to their ego attachments—especially during periods of transformation, anxiety, and uncertainty. In fact, these management practices regularly examine (akin to the self-appraisal process) the functionality of the formal and informal organizational systems and proceed to transform barriers to success into channels for success. In essence, these practices encourage all people and systems to stay open to reality—despite ongoing threats to members' self-concepts (Holmer, Chapter Three).

Besides these organizational systems and management practices for unleashing and mobilizing positive (versus negative) ego energy, we must also consider the influence of the external environment on the organization as suggested by Marlowe and Nyhan (Chapter Twelve): dynamic complexity in general (which can generate considerable anxiety via fiscal crises, for example) and external stakeholders in particular (whose unfavorable opinions of the organization can erode members' self-concepts and stimulate psychological defenses and dysfunctional interpersonal solutions). But the more the organization has developed functional systems and practices, the more it can be proactive in influencing (and selecting) its external setting (Bailey, Strube, Yost, and Merbaum, Chapter Six).

And besides systems, practices, and proactively managing the external setting, it is clear that leadership (creating and changing systems) and not just management (administering the existing systems) has a fundamental effect on channeling positive ego energy. Several contributors place a special burden on the organization's senior executives. Branden (Chapter Two), Kaplan (Chapter Eight), and Ferris (Chapter Nine), for example, suggest that the major task for leaders is to enhance their own self-esteem before they can expect to foster the self-esteem of anyone else in their organization. Kaplan, as noted previously, conducts specially designed programs to redirect the ego energy of senior executives—from overexpansive (or underexpansive) to a more functional use of ego energy. And Deal and Hawkins (Chapter Four) speak of "leaders of spirit" and the crucial role they play in tapping the vast amount of ego energy that lies dormant in their organizations.

Not everyone can benefit from the organizational systems, management practices, and leadership efforts that attempt to foster positive ego energy. Both Branden (Chapter Two) and Allcorn (Chapter Seven) remind us that people with chronically low self-esteem are too engrossed with their intrapsychic survival to receive feedback and then respond in a functional manner. Or in Holmer's terms (Chapter Three), some people have not developed a sufficient emotional capacity to respond adaptively when faced with considerable anxiety and threat. (Nor might senior executives with chronically low self-esteem be able to handle the intense feedback and discussions that take place in Kaplan's programs.) But if people with low self-esteem wish to pursue their personal growth and development, they can get professional help outside the immediate workplace (for example, through an employee assistance program or in another therapeutic setting), since a business organization, as Branden notes, is not a psychological clinic.

The external environment, organizational systems, management practices, leadership behavior—all play an important role in channeling positive ego energy to achieve organizational goals (especially for people with adequate self-esteem). Likewise, the key ingredients that keep people in touch with their inner being and their interpersonal world (so they can make constructive use of their abundant energy and abilities) are the same ingredients that enable an organization to satisfy its internal and external stakeholders. The ultimate win/win scenario: it takes well-functioning people to sustain a well-functioning organization—and vice versa.

Why Must Ego Energy Be Managed Now?

The fifth and last question could just as well have been the first—since it concerns the timeliness of these discussions and this book. Indeed, several authors recognize a particular confluence of circumstances and events that make ego energy more important now than ever before: rapid technological, political, economic, and social change generates massive anxiety, uncertainty, turbulence, and fear. In today's world, people's identity, competency, value, worth, and responsibility are constantly being challenged and threatened—especially since organizations have to implement major transformations and frequent restructuring in order to survive. More than ever before, people must minimize the use of reality-avoiding psychological defenses and dysfunctional interpersonal solutions and, instead, rely on more adaptive—functional—solutions. Mental health and organizational health are now at stake.

Branden (Chapter Two) argues that the human mind has become the dominant factor in our global marketplace—given the economic imperative to rapidly create and market better products and services. And as the mind has become more important, so too has self-esteem—since without adequate self-esteem, people cannot use their minds for creative and constructive purposes. Similarly, Holmer (Chapter Three) recognizes that mental processes are severely affected by people's emotional capacity: if people deny what they see and feel in the face of threat and anxiety, their minds cannot manage reality or complexity.

Holmer also believes that the development of rational technology (computer technology, robotics, artificial intelligence, telecommunications) has far exceeded the development of people's emotional capacity to use this technology as intended. Thus there may be a large gap between what organizations have the potential to do (rationally, technically, and economically) and what they can actually do—given people's undeveloped emotional capacity to cope with anxiety-producing situations (including transformations and restructurings). Deal and Hawkins (Chapter Four) argue the same essential point: the traditional, rational approaches for improving organizations have not worked—because they routinely ignore the spiritual side of collective action. Therefore, the gap between the rational/technical and the emotional/spiritual approaches must now be closed; otherwise, organizations will not succeed in increasingly competitive environments.

The advent of greater environmental complexity (and not just competitiveness) also argues for a better understanding and use of ego energy. Complex problems (and business processes) can only be managed by integrating the wisdom and abilities of diverse experts—since no one can possibly have all the knowledge and abilities to manage multidisciplinary, interconnected problems. Traditional external incentives to ensure compliance with formal rules and regulations (external control) do not seem to work very well for motivating creative exchanges among diverse experts. Instead, internal incentives are needed to stimulate complex mental processes—which derive from the natural ego-defining behavior of organizational members. As Bailey, Strube, Yost, and Merbaum (Chapter Six) and Ferris (Chapter Nine) aptly propose, enabling people to define their self-concepts while they join together to solve complex problems is not only altogether natural. It is far more realistic than expecting external inducements to produce internal commitment among diverse experts. Incidentally, Kaplan's focus (Chapter Eight) on redirecting the ego energy of executives from intense solo efforts to balanced interpersonal relationships is consistent with this crucial need to make better use of diverse experts.

Besides having to use a diversity of experts for managing complexity, it is important to recognize the greater diversity of race, gender, and ethnic background among employees. What used to be an overwhelming majority of white males (particularly in management and technical positions) is quickly becoming a majority of women and minorities in the workforce. Yet, as suggested by Cianni and Romberger (Chapter Ten), women and minorities may still have greater difficulty in obtaining job mastery experiences, finding compatible role models (especially at the higher levels in the organization), receiving emotional support (outside the old boy network), and reducing stress levels (if they are not accepted by the white male establishment—which surely produces additional anxiety). As their belief in themselves and their ability to perform diminishes, their performance on the job also suffers. Making matters worse, according to Allcorn (Chapter Seven), women are socialized to rely on self-effacing (passive-dependent) solutions for managing anxiety, while men are socialized to use largely expansive (aggressive-independent) solutions. For men and women in the organization, therefore, these lifestyle solutions often result in a dysfunctional—codependent—relationship in which aggressive men hold the senior management positions while passive women occupy the lower-level jobs. But by knowing how to unleash, mobilize, and then channel ego energy for all employees on an equal basis, every organization can make full use of the latent energies and unique abilities of its diverse human resources.

In sum, then, we now need a deeper and richer understanding of the human mind and spirit if we are to meet the complex challenges in today's increasingly turbulent world. We must now recognize each individual's primitive struggle for personal meaning if the potential of human intelligence and adaptability is to be utilized for functional purposes. The emerging theories and methods of ego energy can now integrate the emotional/spiritual dynamics of organizational life with the mostly rational/technical approaches—to create the best of both worlds.

Conclusion

This introductory chapter has reviewed the key themes of the book according to five fundamental questions: What is ego energy? What is its source? What is positive versus negative ego energy? How can positive ego energy be channeled to achieve organizational goals? Why must ego energy be managed now? The following chapters examine these themes in much greater detail and depth—and thus provide the reader with comprehensive and useful knowledge for managing ego energy.

References

Freud, S. *The Ego and the Id.* New York: Norton, 1960. (Originally published 1923.)

Horney, K. *Neurosis and Human Growth.* New York: Norton, 1950.

Kilmann, R. H. *Managing Beyond the Quick Fix: A Completely Integrated Program for Creating and Maintaining Organizational Success.* San Francisco: Jossey-Bass, 1989.

Part One

The
Significance
of
Ego Energy

2

Creating High–Self-Esteem/ High-Performance Organizations

Nathaniel Branden

WE HAVE REACHED A MOMENT IN HISTORY when the need for self-esteem has achieved a new significance and urgency. Self-esteem has always been a profoundly important psychological need. Now it has become an imperative economic need. It is basic to our ability to adapt to a rapidly changing, fiercely competitive, global economy. It is needed, not only by leaders and managers, but by everyone who participates in the process of production.

What is the justification for this assertion? And if it is valid, how does one build a high–self-esteem organization to release the creative energy of the human ego? These are the questions I want to address here, for they relate intimately to the theme of this book. Ego energy is the energy of the human impulse toward achievement, self-expression, and self-assertion: it is the wellspring of all human progress. To inspire and coordinate this energy, in the service of organizational goals, is the great challenge of leaders and managers.

But there are other questions we must answer first. What is self-esteem? Why is it a basic human need? On what does its attainment depend?

Self-esteem is the experience of being competent to cope with the basic challenges of life and being worthy of happiness. It consists of two components: self-efficacy and self-respect. Self-efficacy is confidence in one's ability to think, learn, choose, and make appropriate decisions—by extension, to master challenges and manage change. Self-respect is confidence in one's right to be happy—by extension, confidence that achievement, success, friendship, respect, love, and fulfillment are appropriate to one (Branden, 1994).

By way of illuminating this definition, consider the following. If a person feels inadequate to face the challenges of life, if a person lacks fundamental self-trust, confidence in his or her mind, we recognize the presence of a self-esteem deficiency, no matter what other assets he or she possesses. Or if a person lacks a basic sense of self-respect, feels undeserving of the love or respect of others, unworthy of happiness, fearful of asserting thoughts, wants, or needs—again we recognize a self-esteem deficiency, no matter what other positive attributes he or she exhibits. Self-efficacy and self-respect are the dual pillars of healthy self-esteem; without either one, self-esteem is impaired. They are the defining characteristics of the term because they are fundamental. They represent not derivative or secondary meanings of self-esteem but its essence.

The Need for Self-Esteem

How we experience ourselves has an impact every moment of our existence. Our self-evaluation is the basic context in which we act and react, choose our values, set our goals, meet the challenges of life. Our responses to events are shaped by who and what we think we are—how competent and worthy we perceive ourselves to be. Of all the judgments we pass in life, none is more important than the judgment we pass on ourselves.

To say that self-esteem is a basic human need is to say that it makes an essential contribution to the life process; that it is indispensable to normal and healthy development; that it has survival value. Lacking positive self-esteem, our psychological growth is stunted. Positive self-esteem operates as, in effect, the immune system of consciousness, providing resistance, strength, and a capacity for regeneration. When self-esteem is low, our resilience in the face of life's adversities is diminished. We crumble before vicissitudes that a healthier sense of self could vanquish. We tend to be more influenced by the desire to avoid pain than to experience joy; negatives have more power over us than positives (Branden, 1983). If we do not believe in ourselves—neither in our efficacy nor in our goodness—the universe is a frightening place.

This does not mean that we are necessarily incapable of achieving any real values. Some of us may have the talent and drive to achieve a great deal in spite of a poor self-concept—like the highly productive workaholic who is driven to prove his worth to, say, a father who predicted he would amount to nothing. But it does mean that we will be less effective—less creative—than we have the power to be; and it means that we will be crippled in our ability to find joy in our achievements. Nothing we do will ever feel like "enough."

If we do have a realistic confidence in our mind and value, if we feel secure within ourselves, we tend to experience the world as open to us and to respond appropriately to challenges and opportunities. Self-esteem empowers, energizes, motivates. It inspires us to achieve and allows us to take pleasure and pride in our achievements. It allows us to experience satisfaction.

High self-esteem seeks the challenge and stimulation of worthwhile and demanding goals. Reaching such goals nurtures good self-esteem. Low self-esteem seeks the safety of the familiar and undemanding. Confining oneself to the familiar and undemanding serves to weaken self-esteem.

The more solid our self-esteem, the better equipped we are to cope with adversity in our personal lives or in our careers; the quicker we are to pick ourselves up after a fall; the more energy we have to begin anew. (Many successful entrepreneurs have two or more bankruptcies in their past; failure did not stop them.)

The higher our self-esteem, the more ambitious we tend to be—not necessarily in a career or financial sense, but in terms of what we hope to experience in life emotionally, intellectually, creatively, spiritually. The lower our self-esteem, the less we aspire to— and the less we are likely to achieve. Either path tends to be self-reinforcing and self-perpetuating.

The higher our self-esteem, the more open, honest, and appropriate our communications are likely to be. The lower our self-esteem, the more muddy, evasive, and inappropriate our communications are likely to be (because of uncertainty about our own thoughts and feelings as well as fear of the listener's response).

The higher our self-esteem, the more disposed we are to form nourishing rather than toxic relationships. The reason is that like is drawn to like, health is attracted to health. Vitality and expansiveness in others are naturally more appealing to persons of good self-esteem than are emptiness and dependency (Branden, 1980).

The healthier our self-esteem, the more inclined we are to treat others with respect, benevolence, goodwill, and fairness—since we do not tend to perceive them as a threat and since self-respect is the foundation of respect for others. With healthy self-esteem, we are not quick to interpret relationships in adversarial terms. We do not approach encounters with automatic expectations of rejection, humiliation, treachery, or betrayal. Contrary to the belief that an individualistic orientation inclines one to antisocial behavior, research shows that a well-developed sense of personal value and autonomy correlates significantly with kindness, generosity, social cooperation, and a spirit of mutual aid (Waterman, 1981, 1984). And, finally, research discloses that high self-esteem is one of the best predictors of personal happiness (Meyers, 1992). Low self-esteem, as one might expect, correlates with unhappiness.

The Six Pillars of Self-Esteem

On what does healthy self-esteem depend? There is reason to believe that we may come into this world with certain inherent differences that may make it easier or harder to attain healthy self-esteem— differences pertaining to energy, resilience, disposition to enjoy life, and the like. And certainly upbringing can play a powerful role. Research suggests that one of the best ways to have good self-esteem is to have parents who have good self-esteem and who model it (Coopersmith, 1981). If we have parents who raise us with love and respect, who allow us to experience consistent and benevolent acceptance, who give us the supporting structure of reasonable rules and appropriate expectations, who do not assail us with contradictions, who do not resort to ridicule, humiliation, or physical abuse

as means of controlling us, who project their belief in our competence and goodness—we have a decent chance of internalizing their
attitudes and thereby acquiring the foundation for healthy self-
esteem. But no research study has ever found this result to be inev-
itable. Coopersmith's study (1981), for one, clearly shows that it is
not. There are people who appear to have been raised superbly by
the standards cited here and yet are insecure, self-doubting adults.
And there are people who have merged from appalling backgrounds, raised by adults who did everything wrong, and yet they
do well in school, form stable and satisfying relationships, have a
powerful sense of their own value and dignity, and as adults satisfy
any rational criterion of good self-esteem.

While we may not know all the biological or developmental
factors that influence self-esteem, we know a good deal about the
specific (volitional) practices that can raise or lower it. We know
that an honest commitment to understanding inspires self-trust and
that an avoidance of the effort has the opposite effect. We know that
people who live mindfully feel more competent than those who live
mindlessly. We know that integrity engenders self-respect and that
hypocrisy does not (Branden, 1969).

Self-esteem is a consequence—a product of internally generated practices (Branden, 1994). If we understand what these practices
are, we can commit to initiating them within ourselves and to dealing with others in ways that encourage them to do likewise. To
encourage self-esteem in the workplace, for instance, is to create an
environment that reinforces the practices that strengthen self-esteem
(and thereby mobilize ego energy). What, then, are these practices?
More than three decades of study have convinced me that six are
crucial and fundamental.

The Practice of Living Consciously

If our lives and well-being depend on the appropriate use of our
consciousness, then the extent to which we honor sight over blind-
ness is the single most important determinant of our self-efficacy
and self-respect. We cannot feel competent in life while wandering
around (at work, dealing with bosses, subordinates, associates, customers, or in our marriages, or in our relations with our children)

in a self-induced mental fog. If we betray our basic means of survival by attempting to exist unthinkingly, or to evade discomfiting facts, our sense of worthiness suffers accordingly. We know our defaults, whether or not anyone else does. Self-esteem is the reputation we get with ourselves.

A thousand times a day we must choose the level of consciousness at which we will function. A thousand times a day we must choose between thinking and nonthinking. Gradually, over time, we establish a sense of the kind of person we are, depending on the choices we make, the degree of rationality and integrity we exhibit. That is the reputation of which I speak.

Living consciously entails:

- A mind that is active rather than passive
- An intelligence that takes joy in its own function
- Being "in the moment" without losing the wider context
- Reaching out toward relevant facts rather than withdrawing from them
- Noticing and confronting your impulses to avoid or deny painful or threatening realities
- Being concerned to know "where you are" relative to your various (personal and professional) goals and projects and whether you are succeeding or failing
- Being concerned to know if your actions are in alignment with your purposes
- Searching for feedback from the environment so that you can correct your course when necessary
- Persevering in the attempt to understand despite your difficulties
- Being receptive to new knowledge and willing to reexamine old assumptions
- Being willing to see and correct mistakes
- Seeking always to expand awareness—a commitment to learning and hence a commitment to growth as a way of life
- A concern to understand the world around you
- A concern to know not only external reality but also the internal reality of your needs, feelings, aspirations, and motives so that you are not a mystery to yourself

The Practice of Self-Acceptance

At the deepest level, self-acceptance is the virtue of commitment to the value of our own person—not the pretense at a self-esteem we do not possess, but rather the primary act of self-value that is the base of our dedication to achieving self-esteem. It is expressed, in part, through our willingness to accept—that is, to make real to ourselves, without denial or evasion—that we think what we think, feel what we feel, have done what we have done, and are what we are. It is the refusal to regard any part of ourselves—our bodies, our fears, our thoughts, our actions, our dreams—as alien, as "not me." Self-acceptance is our willingness to experience rather than to disown whatever may be the facts of our being at a particular moment.

Self-acceptance, in short, is our refusal to be in an adversarial relationship to ourselves. It is the willingness to say of any emotion or behavior: "This is an expression of me—not necessarily an expression I like or admire—but an expression of me nonetheless, at least at the time it occurred." It is the virtue of realism—that is, respect for reality—applied to the self. Thus if I am confronted with a mistake I have made, in accepting that it is mine I am free to learn from it and do better in the future. I cannot learn from a mistake I cannot accept having made. Self-acceptance is the precondition of change and growth.

The Practice of Self-Responsibility

To feel competent to live and be worthy of happiness, I need to experience a sense of control over my existence. This requires that I be willing to take responsibility for my actions and the attainment of my goals—which means that I take responsibility for my life and well-being. The practice of self-responsibility entails these realizations:

- I am responsible for the achievement of my desires.
- I am responsible for my choices and actions.
- I am responsible for the level of consciousness I bring to my work.
- I am responsible for the level of consciousness I bring to my relationships.

- I am responsible for my behavior with other people—co-workers, associates, customers, spouse, children, and friends.
- I am responsible for how I prioritize my time.
- I am responsible for the quality of my communications.
- I am responsible for my personal happiness.
- I am responsible for choosing the values by which I live.
- I am responsible for raising the level of my self-esteem.

The Practice of Self-Assertiveness

Self-assertiveness is the virtue of appropriate self-expression—honoring my needs, wants, values, and convictions and seeking rational forms of their expression in reality. Its opposite is surrender to timidity—consigning myself to a perpetual underground where everything that I am lies hidden or stillborn—in order to avoid confrontation with someone whose values differ from mine, or to please, placate, or manipulate someone, or simply to "belong."

Healthy self-assertion entails the willingness to confront rather than evade the challenges of life and to strive for mastery. When we expand the boundaries of our ability to cope, we expand self-efficacy and self-respect.

The Practice of Living Purposefully

All living action is goal-directed. Life itself has been defined as a process of self-sustaining and self-generated action. Thus purpose is at the very essence of the life process. Through our purposes we organize our behavior, giving it focus and direction. Through our purposes we create the sense of structure that allows us to experience control over our existence.

To live purposefully is to use our powers for the attainment of goals we have selected: the goal of studying, of raising a family, of earning a living, of starting a new business, of bringing a new product into the marketplace, of solving a scientific problem, of building a vacation home. It is our goals that lead us forward. It is our goals that call on the exercise of our faculties. It is our goals that energize our existence.

It is not the degree of a person's productive ability that matters, but the person's choice to exercise such ability as he or she possesses. It is not the kind of work selected that is important (provided the work is not intrinsically destructive), but whether a person seeks work that requires and expresses the full use of his or her intelligence if the opportunity to do so exists.

To observe that purposefulness is essential to fully realized self-esteem should not be understood to mean that the measure of a person's worth is his or her external achievements. We admire achievements—in others and in ourselves—and it is natural and appropriate for us to do so. But this is not the same thing as saying that my achievements are the measure of my self-esteem. The root of my self-esteem is not my achievements but those internally generated practices that, among other things, make it possible for me to achieve—all the self-esteem virtues we are discussing here.

The Practice of Integrity

As we mature and develop our own values and standards (or absorb them from others), the issue of personal integrity assumes increasing importance in our self-assessment. Integrity is the integration of ideals, convictions, standards, beliefs—and behavior. When our behavior is congruent with our professed values, when ideals and practice match, we have integrity.

When we behave in ways that conflict with our judgment of what is appropriate, we lose face in our own eyes. We respect ourselves less. If the policy becomes habitual, we trust ourselves less or cease to trust ourselves at all. When a breach of integrity wounds self-esteem, only the practice of integrity can heal it. At the simplest level, personal integrity entails such questions as: Am I honest, reliable, and trustworthy? Do I keep my promises? Do I do the things I say I admire and avoid the things I say are despicable?

To understand why lapses of integrity are detrimental to self-esteem, consider what a lapse of integrity entails. If I act in contradiction to a moral value held by someone else but not by me, I may or may not be wrong, but I cannot be faulted for having betrayed my convictions. If, however, I act against what I myself regard as right, if my actions clash with my own expressed values, then I act against my judgment, I betray my mind. Hypocrisy, by its very nature, is self-invalidating. It is mind rejecting itself. A default on integrity undermines me and contaminates my sense of self. It damages me as no external rebuke or rejection can damage me.

If I preach a concern with quality but indifferently sell my customers shoddy goods, if I unload bonds I know to be falling in value to a client who trusts my honor, if I pretend to care about my staff's ideas when my mind is already made up, if I outmaneuver a colleague in the office and appropriate his achievements, if I ask for honest feedback and penalize the employee who disagrees with me, if I ask for pay sacrifices from others on the grounds of hard times and then give myself a gigantic bonus—I may deny my hypocrisy, but the fact remains I launch an assault on my self-respect that no rationalization will dispel.

New Economic Realities—New Challenges to Self-Esteem

Everyone knows there have been major developments in the past few decades in the national and global economy. These developments have all contributed to making the need for self-esteem more urgent for everyone, from the leader of an enterprise to entry-level personnel. They include:

- The shift from a manufacturing to an information economy—entailing the diminishing need for manual or blue-collar workers and the rapidly growing need for knowledge workers with advanced verbal, mathematical, and social skills
- The escalating explosion of new knowledge, new technology, and new products and services, all of which keep raising the requirements of economic adaptiveness
- The emergence of a global economy of unprecedented competitiveness—yet another challenge to our ingenuity and belief in ourselves
- The increasing requirement at every level of a business enterprise, not just at the top but throughout the system, for self-management, personal responsibility, self-direction, a high level of consciousness, and a commitment to innovation and contribution

- The rise of the entrepreneurial model and mentality as central to our thinking about economic adaptiveness
- The emergence of *mind* as the dominant force in all economic activity

I want to elaborate on this last point. In an agricultural economy, wealth is identified with land. In a manufacturing economy, it is identified with the ability to make things: capital assets and equipment; machines and the various materials used in industrial production. In either of these societies, wealth is understood in terms of matter, not mind; physical assets, not knowledge and information. Intelligence is the guiding force behind economic progress in a manufacturing society, to be sure, but when people think of wealth they think of raw materials, such as nickel and copper, and physical property, such as steel mills and textile looms. Wealth is created by transforming the materials of nature to serve human purposes—transforming a seed into a harvest, transforming a waterfall into a source of electricity, transforming iron ore, limestone, and coal into steel and steel into the girders of apartment buildings.

If all wealth is the product of mind and labor, of thought directing action, then one way to understand the transition from an agricultural to an industrial society is to say that the balance between mind and physical effort is profoundly altered. Physical labor began to slide along a declining arc of importance, while mind began to climb. As an extension of human intelligence, a machine substitutes the power of thought for the power of muscles. While making physical labor less demanding, it makes it more productive. As technological development keeps evolving, the ratio keeps shifting in favor of mind. And as mind becomes more important, self-esteem becomes more important.

The climax of this process of development is the emergence of an information economy in which material resources count for less and less and knowledge and new ideas count for almost everything. The value of a computer, for instance, lies not in its material constituents but in its design—in the thinking and knowledge it embodies—and in the quantity of human effort it makes unnecessary. Microchips are made out of sand; their value is a function of the intelligence encoded within them. A copper wire can carry forty-

eight telephone conversations; a single fiber-optic cable can carry
more than eight thousand conversations; yet fiber-optic cables are
cheaper, more efficient, and much less energy-consuming to produce than copper.

Each year since 1979 the United States has produced more
with less energy than the year before. The worldwide drop in the
price of raw materials is a consequence of the ascendancy of mind
in our economic life. The mind always has been our basic tool of
survival. But for most of our history, this fact was not understood.
Today it is obvious to (almost) the whole world.

In an economy in which knowledge, information, creativity—and their translation into innovation—are clearly the source of
wealth and competitive advantage, there are distinct challenges
both to individuals and to organizations. To individuals, whether
as employees or as self-employed professionals, the challenges
include:

• Acquiring appropriate knowledge and skills and committing
  oneself to a lifetime of continuous learning—made mandatory
  by the rapid growth of knowledge
• Working effectively with other human beings, which includes
  skill in written and oral communication, the ability to participate in nonadversarial relationships, understanding how to
  build consensus through give and take, and willingness to assume leadership and motivate co-workers when necessary
• Managing change and responding appropriately to it
• Cultivating the ability to think for oneself, for without this
  ability innovativeness is impossible

Such challenges entail the need to bring a high level of consciousness to one's working life—to its demands in terms of knowledge
and skills and also its opportunities, the possibilities for growth and
self-development it offers. A commitment to lifelong learning is a
natural expression of the practice of living consciously.

In dealing with other people, one needs the self-respect that
underlies respect for others—as well as freedom from gratuitous
fear, envy, or hostility; the expectation of being dealt with fairly and
decently; and the conviction that one has genuine values to contrib-

ute. Again we are led to the importance of self-esteem. Moreover, cooperative endeavors rest on the willingness of participants to be accountable, which is a corollary of the practice of self-responsibility. Such endeavors rest on the willingness of people to keep their promises, honor their commitments, think about the consequences of their actions on others, and manifest reliability and trustworthiness—all expressions of the practice of personal integrity. Self-esteem is far from being the only asset one needs, of course—let there be no mistake about this—but without it one is severely impaired and is in effect at a competitive disadvantage.

To organizations, the challenges include:

- Responding to the need for a constant stream of innovation by cultivating a discipline of innovation and entrepreneurship into the mission, strategies, policies, practices, and reward system of the organization (Drucker, 1984)
- Going beyond paying lip service to "the importance of the individual" by designing a culture in which initiative, creativity, self-responsibility, and contribution are fostered and rewarded
- Recognizing the relationship between self-esteem and performance and implementing policies that support self-esteem—a challenge that demands recognizing and responding to the employees' need for a sane, intelligible, noncontradictory environment that a mind can make sense of; for learning and growth; for achievement; for being listened to and respected; for being allowed to make (responsible) mistakes.

When prospective employees ask themselves, "Is this an organization where I can learn, grow, develop myself, and enjoy my work?" they are implicitly asking, whether they recognize it or not, "Is this a place that supports my self-esteem—or a place that does violence to it?"

Conditions of a High–Self-Esteem Organization

An organization whose people operate at a high level of consciousness, self-acceptance (and acceptance of others), self-responsibility, self-assertiveness (and respect for the assertiveness of others), purposefulness, and personal integrity would be an organization of extraordinarily empowered human beings. These traits are supported in an organization to the extent that the following conditions are met:

- People feel safe: secure that they will not be ridiculed, demeaned, humiliated, or punished for openness and honesty or for admitting "I made a mistake" or for saying "I don't know, but I'll find out."
- People feel accepted: treated with courtesy, listened to, invited to express thoughts and feelings, dealt with as individuals whose dignity is important.
- People feel challenged: given assignments that excite, inspire, and test and stretch their abilities.
- People feel recognized: acknowledged for individual talents and achievements and rewarded monetarily and nonmonetarily for extraordinary contributions.
- People receive constructive feedback: they hear how they can improve performance in nondemeaning ways that stress positives rather than negatives and build on their strengths.
- People see that innovation is expected of them: their opinions are solicited, their brainstorming is invited, and they see that new ideas are welcomed.
- People are given easy access to information: not only are they given the information (and resources) they need to do their job properly, they are given information about the wider context in which they work—the company's goals and progress—so they can understand how their activities relate to the organization's overall mission.
- People are given authority appropriate to what they are accountable for: they are encouraged to take initiative, make decisions, exercise judgment.
- People are given clear-cut and noncontradictory rules and guidelines: they are provided with a structure their intelligence can grasp and count on, and they know what is expected of them.
- People are encouraged to solve as many of their own problems as possible: they are expected to resolve issues close to the action

rather than pass responsibility for solutions to higher-ups—and they are empowered to do so.

- People see that their rewards for success are far greater than any penalties for failure: in too many companies, the penalties for mistakes are much greater than the rewards for success and people are afraid to take risks or express themselves.
- People are encouraged to learn and rewarded for learning: they are encouraged to participate in internal and external courses and programs that will expand their knowledge and skills.
- People experience congruence between an organization's mission statement and professed philosophy, on the one hand, and the behavior of leaders and managers on the other: they see integrity exemplified and they feel motivated to match what they see.
- People experience being treated fairly and justly: they feel the workplace is a rational universe they can trust.
- People take pride in the value of what they produce: they perceive the result of their efforts as genuinely useful; they perceive their work as worth doing.

To the extent that these conditions are operative in an organization, it will be a place where people with high self-esteem will want to work. It will also be one in which people of more modest self-esteem will find their self-esteem raised.

Creating a High–Self-Esteem Organization

For executives who want to build a high-performance/high–self-esteem organization I would structure a different but inevitably overlapping list of proposals. These go to the heart of what such an organization requires:

- Work on your own self-esteem: commit yourself to raising the level of consciousness, responsibility, and integrity you bring to your work and your dealings with people—staff, subordinates, associates, higher-ups, customers, and suppliers.
- When you talk with your people, be present: make eye contact,

listen actively, offer appropriate feedback, give the speaker the experience of being heard.

- Be empathic: let the speaker know that you understand his or her feelings as well as statements—which is a way of giving the speaker an experience of being visible.
- No matter who you are speaking to, maintain a tone of respect: do not permit yourself a condescending, superior, sarcastic, or blaming tone.
- Keep work encounters task-centered, not ego-centered: never permit a dispute to deteriorate into a conflict of personalities. The focus needs to be on reality: What is the situation? What does the work require? What needs to be done?
- Give your people opportunities to practice self-responsibility: give them space to take the initiative, volunteer ideas, attempt new tasks, expand their range.
- Speak to your people's understanding: give the reasons for rules and guidelines (when they are not self-evident), explain why you cannot accommodate certain requests, do not merely hand down orders from on high.
- If you make a mistake in your dealings with someone, if you are unfair or short-tempered, admit it and apologize: do not imagine (like an autocratic parent) that it would demean your dignity to admit taking an action you now regret.
- Invite your people to give you feedback on the kind of boss you are: I agree with someone who once said that "you are the kind of manager your people say you are"—so check it out and let your people see that you are open to learning and self-correction, and set an example of nondefensiveness.
- Let your people see that it is safe to make a mistake or say "I don't know, but I will find out": to evoke fear of error or ignorance is to invite deception, inhibition, and an end to creativity.
- Let your people see that it is safe to disagree with you: convey respect for differences of opinion and do not punish dissent.
- Describe undesirable behavior without blaming: let someone know if his or her behavior is unacceptable, point out its consequences, communicate what kind of behavior you want instead—and refrain from character assassination.
- Let your people see that you talk honestly about your feelings:

if you are hurt or angry or offended, say so with honesty and dignity (and give everyone a lesson in the strength of self-acceptance).

- If someone does superior work or makes an excellent decision, invite him or her to explore how it happened: do not limit yourself simply to praise; by asking appropriate questions, help raise the person's consciousness about what made the achievement possible, and thereby increase the likelihood that others like it will occur in the future.

- If someone does unacceptable work or makes a bad decision, practice the foregoing principle: do not limit yourself to corrective feedback; invite an exploration of what made the error possible, thus raising the level of consciousness and minimizing the likelihood of a repetition.

- Give clear and unequivocal performance standards: let people understand your nonnegotiable expectations regarding the quality of work.

- Praise in public and correct in private: acknowledge achievements within the hearing of as many people as possible while letting a person absorb corrections in the safety of privacy.

- Let your praise be realistic: like parents who make compliments meaningless by praising everything extravagantly, you weaken your positive acknowledgments if they are overblown and not calibrated to the reality of what has been accomplished.

- When someone's behavior creates a problem, ask him or her to propose a solution: avoid handing down solutions; give the problem to the responsible party, thereby encouraging responsibility, self-assertiveness, and intensified awareness.

- Convey in every way possible that you are not interested in blaming—you are interested in solutions—and exemplify this policy personally: when we look for solutions, we grow in self-esteem; when we blame (or alibi), we weaken others' self-esteem.

- Give your people the resources, information, and authority to do what you have asked them to do: remember that there can be no responsibility without power, and nothing so undermines morale as assigning the first without giving the second.

- Remember that a great manager is not one who comes up with brilliant solutions but one who sees to it that his people come up with brilliant solutions: a manger, at his or her best, is a coach, not a problem solver for admiring children.

- Take personal responsibility for creating a culture of self-esteem: no matter what "self-esteem training" they might be given, subordinates are unlikely to sustain the kind of behavior I am recommending if they do not see it exemplified by higher-ups.

- Work at changing aspects of the organization's culture that undermine self-esteem: traditional procedures, originating in an older model of management, may stifle not only self-esteem but also any creativity or innovation (such as requiring that all significant decisions be passed up a chain-of-command, thus leaving those close to the action disempowered and paralyzed).

- Avoid overdirecting, overobserving, and overreporting: excessive managing ("micro-managing") is the enemy of autonomy and creativity.

- Plan and budget appropriately for innovation: do not ask for people's innovative best and then announce there is no money (or other resources)—creative enthusiasm may dry up and be replaced by demoralization.

- Find out the central interests of your people and, whenever possible, match tasks and objectives with individual dispositions: give people an opportunity to do what they enjoy most and do best; build on people's strengths.

- Ask your people what they would need in order to feel more in control of their work and, if possible, give it to them: if you want to promote autonomy, excitement, and a strong commitment to goals, empower, empower, empower.

- Reward such natural expressions of self-esteem as self-assertiveness, (intelligent) risk taking, flexible behavior patterns, and a strong action orientation: too many companies pay lip service to such values while rewarding those who conform, do not ask difficult questions, do not challenge the status quo, and remain essentially passive while going through the motions of their job description.

- Give assignments that stimulate personal and professional growth: without an experience of growth, self-esteem—and enthusiasm for the job—tend to be undermined.

- Stretch your people: assign tasks and projects slightly beyond their known capabilities.
- Educate your people to see problems as challenges and opportunities: this is one perspective clearly shared by high achievers and people with high self-esteem.
- Support the talented individualist: in spite of everything we can say about the necessity for effective teamwork, there should be a place for the brilliant hermit who is moving to different music—even team players benefit from seeing this respect for individuality.
- Teach that mistakes are opportunities for learning: "What can you learn from what happened?" is a question that promotes self-esteem; it also prevents repeating mistakes; and sometimes it points the way to a future solution.
- Challenge the seniority tradition and promote from any level on the basis of merit: recognition of ability is one of the great inspirers of self-respect.
- Reward generously for outstanding contributions, such as new products, inventions, services, and money-saving projects: profit-sharing programs, deferred compensation plans, cash or stock bonuses, and royalties can all be used to reinforce the signal that your organization wants innovation and respects intelligent self-assertion and self-expression.
- Write letters of commendation and appreciation to high achievers and ask the CEO to do likewise: when people see that their company values their *mind*, they are motivated to keep pushing at their limits.
- Set a standard of personal integrity: keep your promises, honor your commitments, deal with everyone fairly (not just insiders, but suppliers and customers as well), and acknowledge and support this behavior in others; give your people the pride of working for a moral company.

I doubt there is one principle listed here that thoughtful executives are not already aware of—in the abstract. The challenge is to practice them consistently and weave them into the fabric of daily procedures.

In conclusion, a few words about leaders. The higher the self-esteem of the leader, the more likely it is that he or she can inspire others. A mind that distrusts itself cannot evoke the best in the minds of others. Nor can leaders inspire the best in others if their primary need, arising from their insecurity, is to prove themselves right and others wrong.

It is a fallacy to say that a great leader should be egoless. A leader needs an ego sufficiently healthy that it does not feel itself on the line in every encounter—so that the leader is free to concentrate on tasks and results, not self-aggrandizement or self-protection.

If degrees of self-esteem are placed on a scale from 1 to 10, with 10 representing optimal self-esteem and 1 the lowest imaginable, then is a leader who is a 5 more likely to hire a 7 or a 3? Very likely this leader will feel more comfortable with the 3, since people often feel intimated by others more confident than themselves. Multiply this example hundreds or thousands of times and project the consequences for a business.

Warren Bennis, our preeminent scholar of leadership, tells us that the basic passion in the best leaders he has studied is the passion for self-expression (Bennis, 1989). Their work is clearly a vehicle for self-actualization. Their desire is to bring "who they are" into the world, into reality, the practice of self-assertiveness.

Leaders often do not fully recognize the extent to which "who they are" affects virtually every aspect of their organization. They do not appreciate the extent to which they are role models. Their smallest bits of behavior are noted and absorbed by those around them, not necessarily consciously, and reflected via those they influence throughout the organization. If a leader has unimpeachable integrity, a standard is set that others feel drawn to follow. If a leader treats people with respect—associates, subordinates, customers, suppliers, shareholders—that behavior tends to translate into company culture. For these reasons, a person who wants to work on "leadership ability" should work on self-esteem. Continual dedication to the six pillars and their daily practice is the very best training for leadership—as it is for life.

Can the right organizational environment transform a person of low self-esteem into one with high self-esteem? Not very likely—although I can think of instances where a good manager or supervisor drew out of a person what no one had ever drawn out before, and at least laid a foundation for improved self-respect. Clearly there are troubled individuals who need a more focused kind of professional help, and it is not the function of a business organization to be a psychological clinic. But for the person of average self-esteem, an organization dedicated to the importance of the individual has an immense potential for doing good at the most intimate and personal level—even though that is not, of course, its purpose for being. And in doing so, it contributes to its own life and vitality in ways that are not remote and ethereal but, ultimately, bottom line.

The policies that support self-esteem are also the policies that make money. They support and liberate ego energy. The policies that demean self-esteem are the policies that sooner or later cause a company to lose money—for when you treat people badly and disrespectfully, when you frustrate ego energy, you cannot possibly hope to get their best. And in today's fiercely competitive, rapidly changing, global economy, nothing less than their best is good enough.

References

Bennis, W. *On Becoming a Leader*. Reading, Mass.: Addison-Wesley, 1989.

Branden, N. *The Psychology of Self-Esteem*. Los Angeles: Nash Publishing, 1969; New York: Bantam Books, 1971.

Branden, N. *The Psychology of Romantic Love*. Los Angeles: Tarcher, 1980; New York: Bantam Books, 1981.

Branden, N. *Honoring the Self*. Los Angeles: Tarcher, 1983; New York: Bantam Books, 1984.

Branden, N. *The Six Pillars of Self-Esteem*. New York: Bantam Books, 1994.

Coopersmith, S. *The Antecedents of Self-Esteem*. 2nd ed. Palo Alto, Calif.: Consulting Psychologists Press, 1981.

Drucker, P. F. *Innovation and Entrepreneurship*. New York: Harper & Row, 1984.

Meyers, D. G. *The Pursuit of Happiness*. New York: Morrow, 1992.

Rand, A. *For the New Intellectual.* New York: Random House, 1961; New York: Signet, 1963.

Waterman, A. S. "Individualism and Interdependence." *American Psychologist,* 1981, *36*(7), 762–773.

Waterman, A. S. *The Psychology of Individualism.* New York: Praeger, 1984.

3

Developing Emotional Capacity and Organizational Health

Lee L. Holmer

*I*F THERE IS ONE FACT on which all psychologists and personality theorists might agree, it is that we human beings are much given to deceiving ourselves. We seem to be designed with an automatic and omniscient self-censoring function that is ready to kick in whenever reality threatens to be more than we can bear. We have tremendous capacities to edit and shape incoming information so that the outside world appears to conform better to our inner expectations, preferences, and comfort. And we have perhaps even greater capacities to edit and shape the content of messages sent out from our inner selves so that we ourselves appear to conform better to the expectations, preferences, and comfort of the outside world.

While it can be argued that our capacity to avoid and distort reality protects us from psychological harm, the contemporary costs of this emotional shield loom large in the face of rapid social change and complexification. The less we attend to "what is really going on," the further we are left behind when others correctly detect and act upon opportunities for change.

Nowhere are the costs of "bounded emotionality" (Mitroff and Pauchant, 1990) more acutely felt than in today's business, government and nonprofit organizations. While economic and social tumult magnify pressures on organizations to respond fully, squarely, and constructively to potentially threatening realities, this same tumult simultaneously magnifies people's tendencies to withdraw into blaming, avoidance, and denial. Although many recent writers have recognized the emotional roots of our flagging economic, technological, and sociopolitical effectiveness, we have yet to achieve a clear, comprehensive, and practical focus on the problem.

The beginnings of such a focus are offered here. This chapter presents an emotionally based model of organizational health that has its deepest roots in the self-esteem and self-awareness of an organization's members. The model integrates the work of a number of organization theorists who share, though from different perspectives, a common understanding of organizations as manifestations of the psychological and emotional habits of the people who comprise them. Where people's psychological and emotional habits are healthy or highly developed, reflecting higher capacities of human nature, organizations theoretically manifest greater success across a broad range of values. Where these habits are unhealthy or underdeveloped, organizations can be expected to manifest less success and to achieve it within a narrower range of values.

This model turns upon the idea that our individual and collective *orientation and response to emotional challenge* is the central dynamic of healthy organizational decision making and behavior. Orientation and response to emotional challenge (OREC) is a bipolar continuum of human possibilities: at one end is our capacity for self-deception and avoidance of reality; at the other is our capacity for full awareness and responsiveness. Our human proclivities to distort our perceptions, deny our true thoughts and feelings, ignore troublesome complexities, and shut out painful realities are positioned opposite our more highly developed (and potentially developable) capacities to respond effectively to psychological threats. As we develop access to our higher capacities, we achieve a state of "emotional readiness" that permits us to engage reality more fully, to know our true thoughts and feelings consciously, to communicate valid information effectively, to respond constructively and creatively to conflict, and to recognize and seize learning opportunities in the face of threat and anxiety.

The term *emotional capacity* refers to a person's ability to respond constructively to emotional challenge or psychological threat. *Ego energy* is assumed to mean any psychological energy that is used by the ego as it executes its function of dealing with external and internal reality. The contention here is that emotional capacity plays a controlling role with respect to how well people manage their ego energy: it determines the extent to which they can direct energy to rational and constructive—as opposed to irrationally defensive and destructive—patterns of behavior.

To exemplify my use of these terms, say I am reading a report that in some way conflicts with my own opinion. My ego becomes energized to deal with the discrepancy and may proceed along one of two general tracks. If my emotional capacity is low, I will be inclined to avoid the emotional challenge of facing up to this threat to my concept of myself as an expert. I will be likely to either dismiss the relevance of what I am reading or become mentally involved in justifying my own position and attacking the offending writer. Either way I will take in very little of what is actually on the page. If my emotional capacity is high, however, I will be more likely to be aware of feeling threatened by what I am reading and also more inclined to make a conscious effort to put some energy into understanding the material nonetheless. In the first case my (ego) energy will have been directed to obscuring what could have been an opportunity to learn something and actually enhance my expertise. In the second case I will have negotiated an emotional challenge and put my energy to constructive use.

This chapter focuses on orientation and response to emotional challenge as a fundamental aspect of an organization's success and is intended to stimulate interest in the development of emotional capacity as an essential organizational strategy for our times. The chapter addresses the following topics:

- The pervasiveness of concepts related to OREC in personality and organization theory, including the role of emotional capacity in definitions of psychological health

- A summary and integration of organizational literature addressing how OREC plays out in organizations as norms of interpersonal behavior, the effectiveness of organizational processes, and the quality of organizational success
- A discussion of what an OREC focus suggests for human and organizational development

With respect to the third topic—practical implications of the OREC model—there are two key points to consider. First, the evidence suggests that society accepts a relatively low standard of response to emotional challenge as "normal," so most of us probably function far below our true capacity most of the time. In light of this, it is unfortunate that much of the psychological and organizational literature addresses emotional capacity from the perspective of mental disease, deviance, and dysfunction, making the topic seem irrelevant or threatening to the average person. If we are to claim the rewards of our emotional potential, we must first frame the building of emotional capacity as a developmental rather than a pathological issue. Second, realizing that we are dealing with a culturally pervasive suboptimal standard, we must look for developmental strategies capable of cutting through accepted assumptions, habits, and embedded patterns of self-deception and denial. Because twelve-step recovery programs such as Alcoholics Anonymous demonstrate one system that has empowered many to break out of their personal unrealities and respond constructively to emotional challenge, I will comment on what these programs might suggest for effective development of emotional capacity in organizations.

Emotional Capacity and Response to Challenge in Theories of Personality

Psychological theory devotes considerable attention to human proclivities to avoid emotionally challenging realities. The following paragraphs review established psychological theory with regard to the pervasiveness of the topic of response to emotional challenge, the role of emotional capacity in definitions of psychological health, the relationship of emotional capacity to self-esteem and interpersonal competence, and the connection between these personal characteristics and organizational success.

Pervasiveness of the Concepts

Some examples of the different names that have been given to our self-censoring, reality-avoiding function are defense mechanisms (Freud, 1966), denial (Schaef, 1987), and distancing and disconnectedness (Argyris, 1982). While there are as many variations and interpretations of these terms as there have been psychologists and organization theorists, the essential aspects of reality avoidance are hardly controversial.

Personality theorists universally acknowledge the basic human tendency to avoid the anxiety that would be caused by facing discrepancies between our desired or expected reality and the reality we perceive. According to Freud (1966), we use unconscious psychological defense mechanisms such as repression, projection, and introjection to avoid the discomfort that would be caused by facing the conflict between our animal and social natures. Object relations theorists elaborate the defense of "splitting" in which the anxiety caused by perceptions of both good and bad in a single person (self or other) creates a tendency to split off either the good or the bad perception and project it onto someone or something else (Klein, 1975). For Rogers (1959), perceived discrepancies between our actual and ideal selves cause a state of "psychological incongruence" that can arouse defenses and distortions. From a cognitive position, Kelly (1955) acknowledges that the anxiety aroused by being caught with mental constructs (theories) that do not match reality can cause people to defend themselves by shutting off their mental reasoning processes. And according to cognitive dissonance theory (Festinger, 1957), people whose expectations do not match reality are much more likely to distort reality to suit their expectations than to change their expectations to match reality. In each of these examples, the operation of our rational mental processes is seen to be affected if not controlled by our capacity to cope with emotional discomfort. The quality of our response to emotional challenge clearly affects our perceptions and interpretation of "the facts" and hence our ability to take appropriate action.

As we will see in the following section, the organizational manifestations of emotional capacity have been explored by a number of writers who develop organizational extensions of various personality theories. Quite a few theorists adopt "psychodynamic" perspectives of Freudian and Jungian descent in which unconscious defense mechanisms serve as the organizational effectors of reality avoidance. Other social and organization theorists, however, depart from the psychodynamic perspective but base their work on theories of personality that are concerned with the same self-censoring dynamics.

One of these theorists is Chris Argyris (1982), for whom the concepts of disconnectedness and distancing reflect deceptive anxiety-avoiding processes. In a process similar to Freudian repression, people are disconnected from faulty reasoning processes by learned mental programs which not only hide the fact that reasoning processes are faulty but also hide the fact that the faultiness is being hidden. (People are unable to see that their actions produce undesirable results and they are unable to see that they cannot see this.) Distancing, which reflects the human tendency to avoid accepting personal responsibility for causing problems, corresponds to defense mechanisms such as splitting and projection. While Argyris prefers to look at these processes as learned and tacit as opposed to inherent and unconscious, from a practical perspective they serve the same function and produce the same results as their psychodynamic counterparts.

For Schaef and Fassel (Schaef, 1987; Schaef and Fassel, 1988), a broad concept of denial is central to understanding the operation of addictive versus healthy processes for both individuals and organizations. Addictive personalities function on a basis of denial—a refusal to see the self and the world as they actually are. Denial prevents the person (or organization) from accepting responsibility for dealing effectively with problems. In Schaef's scheme, denial is partly inherent and partly learned. It can be seen as an umbrella concept that covers the operation of diverse psychological defenses.

Emotional Capacity and Psychological Health

As suggested by the Schaef and Argyris examples, the self-censoring function often plays a central if not defining role in the dynamics of psychological (and organizational) health. Most personality and related organization theories embrace some form of the idea that psychological health reflects the ability to respond directly to challenging stimuli rather than uncontrollably or unwittingly using defense mechanisms to avoid, control, or suppress them. Responding directly to emotional challenges allows the person to face the truth, thereby creating an opportunity to learn and to resolve issues in a process of positive growth and development.

Carl Rogers conceived the healthy or fully functioning person as one who is able to perceive realistically, who is not defensive, who can accept responsibility for himself, and who is able to "live fully in and with each of his feelings and reactions" (1961, p. 191). Freudian and related theorists generally view the excessive substitution of defense mechanisms for reality to be the basis of neurosis in milder cases of psychological malfunction and psychosis in more severe cases. Jung (1966) conceived of health in terms of individuation, the process through which we develop in the direction of a true expression of self. Healthy people are able to recognize and consciously express all aspects of personality—including the "unacceptable" ones they might be inclined to repress as the dark side or "shadow" personality.

In these examples, the ability to stay open versus the impulse to shut down in the face of emotional challenge is a central, if not *the* central, dynamic of psychological health. Moreover, many personality theorists, most notably Rogers and Jung, think that developing the capacity to stay open in the face of emotional challenge is the central process of human development. Our natural growth toward achievement of higher human potentials is seen as a process of overcoming the limits of bounded emotionality. It is this emphasis that provides the most viable basis for building emotional capacity in organizations.

Self-Esteem as the Basis of Healthy Response to Emotional Challenge

Two factors are generally recognized as essential to the minimization of defenses and hence the ability to respond constructively to emotional challenge: self-awareness and self-esteem. For Rogers

(1959), the ability to face psychological incongruence constructively is a function of positive self-regard, meaning an ability to accept the self as it is without shame or apology. Positive self-regard, defined in terms of unconditional self-acceptance, reduces the tendency to respond with anxiety when stimuli suggest there is a gap between what we are and what we think we ought to be. If I believe that to be acceptable as a manager I must always be the first to know every bit of information that is relevant to my job, I am practicing what some would call perfectionism (Schaef, 1987) as opposed to unconditional self-acceptance. If my subordinate tries to call my attention to an issue I was not aware of, my lack of self-acceptance will often cause me to deny the validity of his claim. Because I am not acceptable to myself if I am not always perfectly informed, the suggestion that there is something I do not know produces anxiety and a defensive as opposed to a constructive response.

In the same vein, Argyris recognizes self-esteem as the basis of people's "ability to send and receive information to and from others with minimum distortion" (1964, p. 25). In discussing the relationship between personality and organization, Argyris builds his argument on a chain of factors related to self-esteem and self-awareness. People with greater self-esteem are better able to process comments about themselves, leading to more self-awareness. Self-awareness allows people to control defensive tendencies that would otherwise obstruct constructive responses to emotionally challenging messages.

Argyris's chain is not as linear as it may sound. As Branden (1990) has observed, the relationship of self-esteem to other personal characteristics and behavior appears to be one of reciprocal causation. No matter what the causal relationship, however, self-esteem (or self-regard or self-worth) consistently emerges as a critical factor in discussions involving emotional capacity and response to threat.

Interpersonal Competence

The ability to be open to emotional challenge permits the achievement of interpersonal competence, which in Argyris's view (1964) plays out as the key determinant of organizational success. One's interpersonal competence reflects the interaction of one's emotional capacity with other people's behavior. It can be defined as the extent to which a person is able to act and respond fully, validly, directly, and constructively in relation to emotional challenges in interpersonal relationships. For Argyris, interpersonal competence is part of the chain of factors related to defensiveness—or what is here interpreted as emotional capacity. Self-awareness is required for interpersonal competence; the ability to receive feedback without distortion enhances self-awareness; and self-esteem reduces the need to distort feedback. Argyris makes a point of distinguishing between interpersonal competence and intellectual cognitive competence: he maintains that the former controls the extent to which we are able to use the latter to produce organizational success. This observation echoes the point made earlier with respect to theories of personality—that people's emotional capacity often determines the effectiveness with which they are able to apply rational skills. I may have full intellectual command of the principles of total quality management, for example, but still be emotionally incapable of allowing a subordinate to do things his own way.

Emotional Challenge in Organizations

Much of applied organization theory and research has been concerned with overcoming the limitations of "bounded rationality" (Simon, 1957) through the design and application of technical and procedural systems, role structures, organizational structures, and behavioral training strategies—all mechanisms designed to constrain the role of emotion in organizational life. The foregoing discussion suggests that this exclusionary approach is both illusory and counterproductive—indeed, a contrasting theoretical perspective has been concerned with an *imbalance* of rational vis-à-vis emotional capacities in organizations.

Insufficient emotional capacity or "bounded emotionality" (Mitroff and Pauchant, 1990) has been implicitly if not explicitly associated by various writers with organizational crises such as the *Exxon Valdez* and *Challenger* incidents, with tendencies toward crisis management, with lack of innovation and resistance to change, with declining productivity, service quality, and economic competitiveness in the face of an increasingly complex and demanding environment, with increased levels of employee stress, health problems, and disaffection, with environmental damage and corporate social irresponsibility, and with increased corruption in both public and private sectors.

A number of these writers build models on various theories of personality to explain the patterns of connection between psychological health and organizational success. They may use different jargon and approach the topic from different angles, but they all say essentially the same thing with respect to how orientation and response to emotional challenge play out in organizations as individual behavior, cultural norms, organizational processes, and ultimately the quality of an organization's success.

Emotional Challenge in Models of Organization

From the perspective of object relations theory (Hirschhorn, 1988), people manage anxiety by using psychological defenses such as splitting, projection, and repression. These personal habits function as "social defenses" at interpersonal, group, and organization levels. Hirschhorn explains Bion's well-known (1959) fight/flight, dependency, and utopian typology of dysfunctional group dynamics as the operation of social defenses arising to manage anxiety in organizations. Other manifestations of emotional defensiveness are said to include organization rituals such as bureaucratic procedures and routines that help employees depersonalize their relationship to work.

Also from an object relations perspective, Schwartz (1990) explains organizational totalitarianism and failure to respond effectively to external challenges as a function of people's inability to respond directly to internal challenges. In order to avoid anxiety, people construct mental images of themselves as belonging to an "organization ideal" and then refuse to recognize organizational reality when it does not correspond to the constructed image.

Kets de Vries and Miller's "neurotic organizations" (1984) reflect an essentially Freudian approach to the analysis of organizational manifestations of psychological defense mechanisms. Neurotic personality styles of organization leaders, shared fantasies at the group level, and defective interpersonal relations arising from psychological transference and resistance become manifest as impulsive decision making, poor morale, inadequate leadership, and untenable strategies and structure.

Emotional avoidance of the psychological conflict between fear of life and fear of death (Rank, 1936) has been associated with paradoxical conflicts arising in group processes (Smith and Berg, 1988). Here the lack of capacity to respond constructively to emotionally challenging conflict is manifest in dysfunctional group phenomena such as double binds, polarization, and scapegoating. Organizational polarization (Smith, 1989) has been shown to occur when constructive responses to organizational conflict are thwarted by psychological defenses of splitting and triangulation. The tendency for corporations to be prepared for crisis rather than crisis-prone (Mitroff and Pauchant, 1990) has been associated with the psychological defenses of employees. Crisis results when managers, attempting to cope with anxiety related to self-esteem, refuse to acknowledge and respond rationally to impending difficulties and conflicts.

Mitroff and Pauchant devote considerable attention to the undesirable effects of preoccupation with rational versus emotional processes in organizations. In other treatments of this "imbalance" hypothesis, the unidimensional assumptions and ethics of the "machine view" (Bowles, 1990) or "rational model" (Denhardt, 1981) of organization have been associated with undesirable consequences for individuals, organizations, and society. As bureaucratic structures and norms of interpersonal behavior come to reflect and reinforce the repression of people's moral and psychological conflicts, increasing amounts of energy are diverted from productive work. Rather than producing outputs of value, people spend time and energy maintaining the various rituals and illusions that are needed to mask the real feelings and issues repressed by bureaucratic norms. Related to this point, Michael Diamond sees bureaucracy in modern culture as "the result of psychological defenses in operation. . . . Tendencies for bureaucratization of human relations in the workplace are the result of externalized interpersonal defense mechanisms" (1984, p. 195).

All of these models reflect more or less psychodynamic personality theories of Freudian descent. Two other models that depart from a psychodynamic framework yet describe similar patterns are those put forth by Argyris (Argyris, 1982; Argyris and Schon, 1978) and by Schaef and Fassel (1988). While Argyris's perspective is cognitive and Schaef and Fassel frame the concepts of organizational health in the language of addiction and recovery, the key concepts of these models are fundamentally the same.

The Model I/Model II dichotomy (Argyris and Schon, 1978; Argyris, 1982) links psychological variables with a learning-oriented concept of organizational health and performance. People's mental and emotional habits are expressed as norms of interpersonal behavior at the group and organizational levels. Where Argyris attributes the cause of individual and organizational dysfunction to faulty reasoning processes of distancing and disconnectedness, Schaef and Fassel dig deeper in ascribing faulty reasoning to the addictive process of denial. Regardless of origin, however, the pattern of symptoms and consequences is identical in many respects. Behavior in both Argyris's Model I and Schaef and Fassel's addictive organization is governed by intent to control, inhibition of feelings, and suppression of valid information. Both models pose theoretical structures in which psychological and interpersonal processes are embodied in organizational norms and systems that reciprocally reinforce individual behavior; unhealthy behavior is accepted as normal; patterns of dishonesty, secrecy, and contradiction prevail. Like defense mechanisms, distancing, disconnectedness, and denial all function as substitutes for constructive responses to emotionally threatening situations. All produce the familiar litany of faulty processes and outcomes: excessive bureaucratization, double binds, intergroup rivalry, failure to innovate, and inadequate response to changing environmental conditions.

An Integrated Model

Whether the root psychological functions are seen as conscious or unconscious, cognitive or psychodynamic, Freudian, Jungian, or Wilsonian (Bill Wilson was a founder of Alcoholics Anonymous), all of the above writers are concerned with problems caused when people's avoidance of emotional challenge gives rise to dysfunctional norms of interpersonal behavior—which in turn give rise to

faulty organizational processes that constrain organizational success. Figure 3.1 shows a four-level model of the basic dynamic that
runs through this body of work. In this generic OREC model, individual factors (Level I) including self-esteem, emotional capacity,
and interpersonal competence are manifest in the organization's
established norms of interpersonal behavior (Level II). Norms of

**Figure 3.1. Orientation and Response to Emotional Challenge:
Four Levels of Manifestation.**

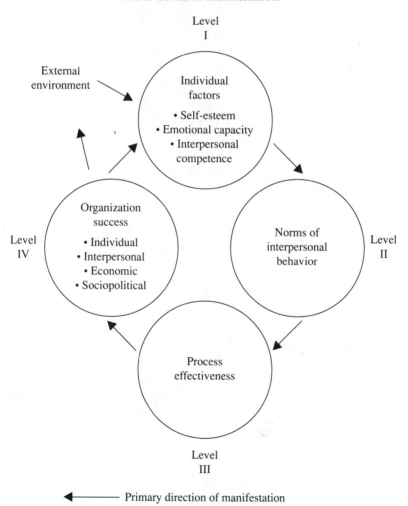

interpersonal behavior are manifest in human processes such as group dynamics, problem solving, and communications. The resulting process effectiveness (Level III), defined as how people use time, energy, and information, is in turn reflected at Level IV: quality of organizational success. Organizational success encompasses a holistic range of values including individual, interpersonal, economic, and sociopolitical concerns. These values are derived from Vaill's (1989) typology.

Elements of the external environment enter the model through people's perceptions and responses and are ultimately cycled back as the organization in turn affects its environment. What happens at each level can be seen as a manifestation of the response to emotional challenge as well as the source of emotional challenges that must be responded to at other levels. While Figure 3.1 shows the primary flow of manifestation and process going from the deepest level outward, the model recognizes that all levels mutually influence each other.

Table 3.1 examines the content of each level described by Figure 3.1. The characteristics listed in the table reflect an integrated summary of the theoretical and empirical work discussed earlier. These characteristics are normatively divided into a bipolar configuration reflecting more healthy/developed behavior on the left side and less healthy/undeveloped behavior on the right. The more healthy/developed characteristics at each level are manifest as the more healthy/developed characteristics at other levels. While empirical support for these assumptions is provided by the case material on which the various theories are based, systematic theory testing is under way (Holmer, 1992).

A special note on the relationship between process effectiveness and ego energy is in order. Processes are effective to the extent that minimal time, energy, and information are lost or diverted to nonconstructive purposes. The diversion of time, energy, and information from constructive organizational purposes can thus be seen as the larger manifestation of a misdirection of ego energy such as that exemplified at the beginning of this chapter.

Subdimensions of OREC

My efforts to index the content of Table 3.1 (Holmer, 1992) suggest that there are three dimensions of orientation and response to emotional challenge: interpretation, reception, and action.

Table 3.1. OREC Characteristics by Level of Manifestation.

More healthy/developed	Less healthy/undeveloped
Level I: Individual Factors	
High self-esteem and awareness; internal referencing. Defenses minimized; anxiety stimulates inquiry and openness to change.	Low self-esteem and awareness; external referencing. Anxiety stimulates defense mechanisms, distancing, disconnectedness, denial.
Interpersonal competence and interactions dominated by positive regard, inquiry, acceptance of feelings, commitment to process, authenticity, honesty, desire for feedback, flexibility, appropriate assertiveness, mutuality, trust.	Interpersonal competence and interactions dominated by self-interest, control motivation, suppression of feelings, impression management, manipulativeness, dishonesty, difficulty receiving criticism, rigid dualistic thinking, displaced aggression, competitiveness, fear.
Level II: Norms of Interpersonal Behavior	
Consistency or discussable discrepancies between espoused and actual theories.	Unacknowledged or undiscussable discrepancies between espoused and actual theories.
Recognition of inherent value of people and process as well as goal attainment.	Instrumentalism, people treated as objects, process devalued, emphasis on control and manipulation.
Recognized importance of self in role; secondary emphasis on hierarchy and rules.	Depersonalization of work, reliance on structure, rules, roles, rituals.
Practice and open acknowledgment of ethics, achievement of valued purposes, mutuality, cooperation.	Practice of competitiveness, self-interest, overriding pursuit of personal gain.
Consistency of formal and informal communication.	Discrepancies between formal and informal communication.
Communication characterized by valid information, candor, directness, free exchange, dialogue, multidirectionality.	Communication characterized by invalid information, secrets, confusion, indirectness, vagueness, unidimensionality.
Interactions demonstrate trust, appropriate responsibility, integrity, positive regard.	Interactions demonstrate manipulation and control, dishonesty, impression management, approval seeking.

Table 3.1. OREC Characteristics by Level of Manifestation, Cont'd.

More healthy/developed	Less healthy/undeveloped
Expression of feelings accepted as valid communication. Emotions remain connected to actions.	Communications must be strictly rational—feelings suppressed. Emotions disconnected from actions.
Direct engagement of problems, conflict, interpersonal difficulties. Interventions characterized by inquiry, appropriate assertiveness, multiple options, constructive criticism.	Problems, conflict, and interpersonal difficulties met with denial, avoidance, forcing, manipulation. Interventions characterized by non-inquiry, caretaking, punishment, blaming.

Level III: Process Effectiveness

Process gains and synergistic effects on constructive use of time, energy, and information result from:	Process losses and diversion of time, energy, and information from constructive purposes result from:
• Organizational due process and effective resolution of conflict	• Perpetration of and preoccupation with injustice and polarization of conflict
• Cooperative effort and sharing of information	• Power struggles, turf battles, intergroup rivalry
• Functional feedback and appropriate action regarding performance	• Dysfunctional feedback and inappropriate (or no) action regarding performance
• Learning orientation, effective detection and correction of errors, concern for substance, appropriate levels of risk	• Control orientation, covering up, double binds, concern for appearances, excessive or insufficient risk

Level IV: Quality of Organizational Success

Employees reinforced in development of autonomous self-esteem, accomplishment of valued purposes, expanded concept of self and personal potential.	Employees reinforced in defensive behavior, externalized self-worth, cynicism, limited view of self and personal potential.
Personal relationships characterized by trust, integrity, equity, justice. Good labor/management relations.	Personal relationships characterized by lack of trust, integrity, equity, justice. Labor/management hostility.

Table 3.1. OREC Characteristics by Level of Manifestation, Cont'd.

More healthy/developed	*Less healthy/undeveloped*
Enhanced efficiency and effectiveness of production, innovation, response to opportunities and threats.	Reduced efficiency and effectiveness of production, innovation, response to opportunities and threats.
Positive environmental and social impact; good public image and balanced stakeholder relations.	Negative environmental and social impact; poor public image and conflicted stakeholder relations.

Interpretation has to do with how we see our universe and others around us. Do we operate from a basic assumption of scarcity or from one of abundance? Do we see others as competitive threats or as potential partners? Is our universe a friendly or a hostile one— do we interpret reality from a place of love or a place of fear? How inclined are we to be threatened by whatever stimuli come our way? This dimension in some ways parallels Schein's (1985) concept of the "assumptions" level of organizational culture.

Reception is concerned with our capacity to accept stimuli we have consciously or unconsciously interpreted to be threatening. Do we deny threatening messages access to our conscious mind, or do we inquire into them? How willing are we to discover the truth about ourselves and our organizations?

Action has to do with what we do in response to threatening messages. Are we able to consider a full range of behavioral choices in response to a perceived threat, or do we react unthinkingly to suppress discomfort and conflict? Do we try to control ourselves and others in relation to a fixed set of goals, or do we encourage exploration of all values that may be relevant to the situation? Do we take the risk of providing truly valid information, or do we hide what we really think in order to maintain control? Do we take responsibility for ourselves?

The OREC model traces these dimensions through the various aspects and levels of organization and suggests that here lies the basis of sustainable organizational success. We now turn to the practical implications of this theoretical framework.

Implications

If so many people agree that lack of emotional capacity is the root of so many individual, organizational, and social problems, why are we not doing more about it? Why don't our organization and human resource development technologies focus more directly on building emotional capacity? And if we were to emphasize this focus, where could we look for a viable model of change?

With respect to the first question, I suspect that the Freudian orientation of much organization theory has delayed popular acceptance of these ideas. Freudian jargon itself is emotionally challenging—people resist thinking of themselves and their organizations as narcissistic, as neurotic, as unconsciously acting out transference. To speak in Freudian terms seems to imply that one is "sick," that one is outside the norm, and, worst of all, that one must give oneself up to countless hours of expensive interpretation by some inscrutable analyst.

Argyris and Schaef offer more palatable models. Both clearly specify a concern with changing behavioral norms. They focus on what we accept as normal, more than what is deviant, yet still the focus is negative. If we accept Argyris and Schon's (1978) model, we must think in terms of our incompetence; if we turn to Schaef and Fassel (1988), we must describe ourselves in terms of our addictive processes. Both frameworks have an advantage, however, in that they present a developmental as opposed to pathological orientation. Argyris fixes on learning as the central process of overcoming incompetence. And while Schaef's process of recovery is concerned with addiction as a disease, movement toward health is presented as self-generated and self-attainable if there is adequate social support.

Where do we look for a model? Here Schaef moves beyond Argyris in suggesting a new and possibly more practical strategy for human resource and organization development. Argyris's approach to developing Model II (healthy emotional capacity) in organizations is painstaking, consultant-intensive, and appears to have met with limited success at least in relation to the amount of effort involved. As an alternative approach, Schaef and Fassel (1988) suggest that twelve-step recovery programs such as Alcoholics Anonymous (AA) provide a model for achieving personal and cultural transformation of the OREC variety. This idea has been considered by other organization theorists including Pauchant and Mitroff (1992) and Schwartz (1990).

My own study of these programs leads me to agree that they demonstrate emotional capacity-building strategies for organizations. This chapter opened with a comment on the relationship between self-deception and emotional defensiveness—a relationship that is not lost on twelve-step practitioners. Indeed, if there is one thing that characterizes these programs, it is the imperative of self-honesty in all matters of life. The programs consist of a series of mental, emotional, and spiritual precautions against the ever-present threat that denial of reality will gain sway over rationality. AA's effective arsenal against the denial of alcoholism may not immediately suggest that its precepts apply to organizational malfunction. But the self-deception and denial that afflict addicts are the same psychological processes that lead managers and employees to practice outmoded worldviews, ineffective decision-making processes, and self-contradictory habits of interpersonal behavior. If twelve-step programs have found a way to use simple peer support and individual effort to help people build emotional capacity sufficient to break free from virtually any addiction or compulsive behavior, our organization development programs might be able to use similar principles to help us attain more self-mastery in organizational affairs.

While a complete discussion of the applications of twelve-step programs is beyond the scope of this chapter, three general parameters are readily deduced from their prominent features: self-selection, ongoing social support, and adherence to key developmental principles.

Regarding the parameter of self-selection, the people who use twelve-step programs to change deep-seated patterns of behavior come to the programs voluntarily. The implication for organizations is that an approach which concentrates exclusively on managers, receptive or not, may not be the most direct route to success. While most of these efforts have the ultimate goal of spreading change to every organizational nook and cranny, they frequently take a top-down approach to implementation. Twelve-step expe-

rience suggests that rather than targeting unwilling managers, intervention resources would be better used to stimulate emotional
potential wherever it may be found. Emotional development programs might therefore work best if made available to all employees
on a voluntary basis.

Ongoing social support refers to the fact that many of the
people who change themselves through twelve-step programs rely
extensively on the programs and their members for social support.
They attend meetings frequently, develop friendships with other
members, and establish mentoring relationships with each other.
Through these relationships, personal change is interwoven with
the fabric of their day-to-day lives. This practice suggests that organizational efforts to build emotional capacity should try to build
support networks *within* the organizational context. Regular group
meetings—perhaps the emotional capacity-building equivalent of
quality circles—could be offered at work. Interested employees
could be encouraged to network with each other across organizational levels and divisions. These strategies would therefore effect
a grass-roots approach to changing organizational culture.

Perhaps the critical factor in the success of twelve-step programs is their adherence to a clear and simply structured set of
recovery or developmental principles: the twelve steps. While the
specific language of the twelve steps (Alcoholics Anonymous, 1976)
has been the subject of skepticism and controversy, the material
lends itself to wider application. Other writers (Pauchant and Mitroff, 1992; Schwartz, 1990) have offered organizational versions of
AA's twelve steps, and such interpretations could provide a helpful
foundation for emotional development programs. With or without
the twelve steps, however, four principles seem to underlie successful change via AA's route:

- Reprieve from cynicism: The programs create a positive (safe)
  culture for the expression and pursuit of nonmaterialistic, altru-
  istic, and spiritual values—for example, personal integrity and
  organizational ethics.
- Reprieve from perfectionism: The programs create a positive

(safe) culture for accepting and recognizing one's limitations and their undesirable consequences.

- Norms of self-honesty and self-disclosure: Ideal participation exemplifies rigorous self-examination and genuine self-disclosure.
- Norms of self-mastery: Ideal participation exemplifies a focus on the self and taking responsibility for oneself rather than controlling, analyzing, or blaming other people, places, and things.

These four principles, combined with self-selection and social support, are offered here for consideration with respect to the design of emotional capacity-building programs for organizations. The success of twelve-step programs suggests that, given an appropriate foundation of philosophical and operating principles, an organizational approach based on support groups and networking might empower people to set higher standards of response to emotional challenge in the workplace.

I want to conclude by summarizing what the OREC model offers as a basis for the development of emotional capacity in organizations. There are two primary benefits. First, by eliminating the use of unfamiliar and threatening jargon while maintaining the solid underpinnings of a broad theoretical base, the OREC model provides a trustworthy and user-friendly developmental framework. Second, and more important, the OREC model focuses on building emotional capacity as a developmental rather than a pathological issue. Instead of framing the issue in terms of dysfunction and disease, it reflects the conviction that if we are going to make headway against our emotional limitations, we must stop presenting emotion as a deviant flaw exhibited by inferior people. Rather, we must start looking at emotional capacity as a source of untapped human potential—and start talking about encouraging emotional readiness in everyone as opposed to curing the defensive practices of a troublesome few.

If humanity had devoted even one-millionth of the resources we have used to develop rational technology to the development of our emotional capacity instead, we would not now be faced with such grievous conditions of social and economic distress. Yet if we can now accept that our technological and rational abilities far outstrip our emotional capacity to use them wisely, perhaps we will be more willing to invest in the realization of our emotional potential. This is a commitment we can no longer avoid.

References

Alcoholics Anonymous. *Alcoholics Anonymous.* (3rd ed.) New York: Alcoholics Anonymous World Services, 1976.

Argyris, C. *Integrating the Individual and the Organization.* New York: Wiley, 1964.

Argyris, C. *Reasoning, Learning, and Action: Individual and Organizational.* San Francisco: Jossey-Bass, 1982.

Argyris, C., and Schon, D. A. *Organizational Learning.* Reading, Mass.: Addison-Wesley, 1978.

Bion, W. *Experiences in Groups.* New York: Basic Books, 1959.

Bowles, M. L. "Recognizing Deep Structures in Organizations." *Organization Studies,* 1990, *11*(3), 395–412.

Branden, N. "What Is Self Esteem?" Address presented to the First International Conference on Self Esteem. Beverly Hills: Branden Institute for Self Esteem, 1990.

Denhardt, R. *In the Shadow of Organization.* Lawrence: University Press of Kansas, 1981.

Diamond, M. A. "Bureaucracy as Externalized Self Systems: A View from the Psychological Interior." *Administration and Society,* 1984, *16*(2), 195–214.

Festinger, L. *A Theory of Cognitive Dissonance.* Stanford, Calif.: Stanford University Press, 1957.

Freud, S. "New Introductory Letters on Psychoanalysis." In *The Complete Introductory Lectures on Psychoanalysis.* New York: Norton, 1966. (Originally published 1932.)

Hirschhorn, L. *The Workplace Within: Psychodynamics of Organizational Life.* Boston: MIT Press, 1988.

Holmer, L. "Interpersonal Norms and Processes Inventory for Organizations." Unpublished instrument, Worklife Consultation Services, 1992.

Jung, C. G. *Two Essays in Analytical Psychology.* Princeton, N.J.: Princeton University Press, 1966.

Kelly, G. A. *The Psychology of Personal Constructs.* Vol. 1: *A Theory of Personality.* New York: Norton, 1955.

Kets de Vries, M. F., and Miller, D. *The Neurotic Organization: Diagnosing and Changing Counterproductive Styles of Management.* San Francisco: Jossey-Bass, 1984.

Klein, M. "A Contribution to the Psychogenesis of Manic-Depressive States." In *Love, Guilt, Reparation, and Other Works, 1921–1945.* London: Hogarth Press, 1975.

Mitroff, I. I., and Pauchant, T. C. *We're So Big and Powerful Nothing Bad Can Happen to Us.* New York: Birch Lane Press, 1990.

Pauchant, T. C., and Mitroff, I. I. *Transforming the Crisis-Prone Organization: Preventing Individual, Organizational, and Environmental Tragedies.* San Francisco: Jossey-Bass, 1992.

Rank, O. *Will Therapy and Truth and Reality.* New York: Knopf, 1936.

Rogers, C. "A Theory of Therapy, Personality and Interpersonal Relationships, as Developed in the Client-Centered Framework." In S. Koch (ed.), *Psychology: A Study of a Science,* vol. 3. New York: McGraw-Hill, 1959.

Rogers, C. *On Becoming a Person.* Boston: Houghton Mifflin, 1961.

Schaef, A. *When Society Becomes an Addict.* San Francisco: Harper & Row, 1987.

Schaef, A. W., and Fassel, D. *The Addictive Organization.* San Francisco: Harper & Row, 1988.

Schein, E. H. *Organizational Culture and Leadership.* San Francisco: Jossey-Bass, 1985.

Schwartz, H. S. *Narcissistic Process and Corporate Decay: The Theory of the Organization Ideal.* New York: New York University Press, 1990.

Simon, H. A. *Administrative Behavior: A Study of Administrative Decision-Making Processes in Administrative Organization.* (2nd ed.) New York: Free Press, 1957.

Smith, K. K. "The Movement of Conflict in Organizations: The

Joint Dynamics of Splitting and Triangulation." *Administrative Science Quarterly*, 1989, *34*, 1-20.

Smith, K. K., and Berg, D. *Paradoxes of Group Life: Understanding Conflict, Paralysis, and Movement in Group Dynamics*. San Francisco: Jossey-Bass, 1988.

Vaill, P. B. *Managing as a Performing Art: New Ideas for a World of Chaotic Change*. San Francisco: Jossey-Bass, 1989.

4

Setting the Spirit Free:
Tapping Ego Energy

Terrence E. Deal, Pamela C. Hawkins

And whatever else high performance and excellence may be based on, they would seem to have something to do with the quality of Spirit . . . human Spirit, our Spirit, the Spirit of our organizations. [Owen, 1987, p. 1]

THE TERM *EGO* IS OFTEN EQUATED with the self, a person's internal center. The self, or ego, integrates counterforces of basic animal drives and society's conventions to form a conscious identity or character. The term ego has come to have several meanings, many misleading. Too often we think of ego as a rational state of mind rather than, as Webster defines it, "a spiritual substance on which experience is superimposed." In this chapter we will explore the spiritual side of ego: spirit as the peerless source of ego energy. Our view is that human spirit summons a vast reservoir of vitality that is seldom tapped. In fact, modern managers have often, consciously or otherwise, sought to sterilize today's organizations—to deaden spirit rather than to encourage it. In doing so, they deplete ego energy at its primary source and create organizational anemia. But the time is right to revitalize the spiritual side of organizations—to set the spirit free and unleash vast amounts of latent individual and collective ego energy. Such energy depends on spirit for its accumulation and release. Ego energy is an inner stockpile fed and replenished by its source: human spirit.

The chapter is organized around seven propositions:

- Spirit is the essence of human life.
- People are inherently spiritual beings.
- Organizations are spiritual enterprises.
- Leadership is a spiritual activity.
- Changing an organization involves spiritual metamorphosis.
- Expressive activity liberates spirit and thereby creates ego energy.
- Spirit can be a competitive advantage.

Spirit Is the Essence of Human Life

Explaining the purpose and essence of spirit is a formidable task. Spirit, as we have come to understand it, defies definition. The spirit of Christmas, for example, glows radiantly once each year. It inspires people to experience the magic of the season. It creates an abundant if temporary supply of ego energy. As the spirit rises, the world looks and feels different: more radiant and hopeful. As Parker Palmer (1990, p. 3) observes: "We create [the] world, in part, by projecting our spirit on it—for better or worse." When the holiday's reign ends, the spirit subsides and people return to their normal existence. The ego energy settles into an internal reservoir to be reclaimed a year later. Spirit is a template that guides and shapes human experience. Like a template, when spirit is removed only the basic form remains—the energy slips away. Spirit is most present in silence and most visible when we are alone. When we need the ego energy, we tap our vital internal storehouse of the spirit.

If asked to prove the existence of spirit, one will undoubtedly fail. Spirit, like culture, is a matter of faith and belief. In contemporary times people have attempted to capture the essence of spirit in terms such as soul, myth, devotion, and inspiration. Spirit and spirituality are most often a manifest part of organized religion. In secular organizations people seem to feel self-conscious about spirituality. While ego energy is an acceptable, desirable resource, spirit falls outside our rationally constricted vision.

Yet when faced with exhilarating success or sheer devastation we witness ourselves and others moved by an indescribably unearthly force that lies beyond reason. The resultant ego energy seems to emerge from an unknown source deep inside or beyond ourselves. It is in peak moments of happiness or despair, success or failure, that we "feel the spirit." We depend on it for ego energy, but also for comfort, courage, and hope. Victor Frankl's (1974) firsthand experience in a Nazi concentration camp led him to conclude: "Man *can* experience a vestige of spiritual freedom . . . even in such terrible conditions of psychic and physical stress" (p. 104). Frankl could sense the dissipation of ego energy once someone's spirit was crushed. Giving up often means having faith that the spirit will be resurrected in another world. But the crucial wellspring of ego energy is gone.

Spirit is transcendent, yet at the same moment it weaves itself throughout our intellect and emotion to direct us toward our ultimate destiny. Spirit is what compels us to search far beyond our feeble human bias, deceit, ignorance, jealousy, bigotry, and hatred. Generation after generation, spirit helps us to lift ourselves up, dust off, and find the energy to start over again. Spirit moves us beyond failure toward new goals, new attitudes, new accomplishments.

We live now in a society driven by efficiency, productivity, and materialism. It leaves little room outside of our religious institutions for spiritual enlightenment. In most organizations, achieving the goal is the main objective. Nourishing the soul is some other institution's business. We therefore look for our daily inspiration from other sources—human or otherwise. In a world where seeing is believing and corporate strategy has replaced vivid prophetic visions and dreams, spirit has developed a credibility problem: "Knowing in the cognitive sense cannot produce proof of nonphysical reality any more than it can produce proof of God" (Zukav, 1989, p. 92).

Yet, despite our rationally inspired doubts and our compensatory quests for ego energy, the term spirit frequently weaves itself into everyday discourse: "Keep the spirit," "the spirit is willing but the flesh is weak," "team spirit," "esprit de corps," "school spirit," "his spirits are up"—these are phrases we use all the time. Palmer sees this presence in everyday language as a sign that spirit is an essential part of life: "Spirituality is not about values and ethics, not about exhortations to do right and live well. The spiritual traditions are primarily about *reality*. The spiritual traditions are an effort to penetrate the illusions of the external world and to name its underlying truths" (1990, p. 4).

Our presidents seem to agree. As President Clinton so vividly pointed out on the day of his inauguration, "I believe with all my heart that a lot of the problems of America are the problems of the spirit as well as physical." He was not the first president to focus on spirit as the key problem. President Carter, for example, earlier called attention to America's "spiritual malaise." But we rarely stop to think about what these references mean and how they might be connected to an incorporeal source of ego energy we might take more seriously. In America, particularly, alcoholic spirits are often used to keep our human spirits up. But what is really letting us down is our failure to recognize one of life's most powerful sources of energy and hope.

Spirit, like culture, ultimately draws people closer together and propels them toward common purpose and meaning. It gives us zeal. If we can accept the premise that we are spiritual beings, if we can see spirit as the primary source of ego energy, it makes a difference in how we see ourselves and modern organizations. Archaeological evidence documents the role that spirit has played throughout the human experience. It manifests itself in all of our cultural forms. Drawings, myths, traditions, music, and artifacts all show traces of the struggle to understand the essence of spirit— because spirit is the essence of life. The sad thing is, we may be losing (or killing) the very heart of what we need most. A biological anthropologist comments: "We are losing the sense of wonder, the hallmark of our species and the central feature of the human spirit. . . . We must try once again to experience the human soul as soul, and not just a buzz of bioelectricity; the human will as will, and not just a surge of hormones; the heart not as a fibrous, sticky pump, but as the metaphoric organ of understanding" (Nichols, 1992, p. 12).

People Are Inherently Spiritual Beings

Although we spend most of our lives as members of human groups—families, tribes, associations, communities—we are ultimately individual spirits. There are points where our individuality and solitude are pronounced, sometimes painfully so. In these situations, we are struck by our finitude and insignificance. The struggle to understand our existence and purpose has resulted in some of our most profound intellectual breakthroughs. To name a few: Freud's theory of the unconscious, Frankl's commentary on the power of the "search for meaning," and Tillich's contributions about existence and the "question of being." But we should remind ourselves that the intent of these great works was not to reinforce our separateness but to enhance our spiritual corporateness. To arrive at an understanding of what lies at the core of ourselves is a step toward a better understanding of how we can form healthy, nurturing, culturally cohesive communities.

The common denominator within these cultures must be revealed before the latent human equation can be understood and solved, before the true source of collective ego energy can be discovered. Human spirit, we believe, may be the most binding cultural webbing that holds people together. Along these lines theologian John Wagner (1988) writes: "If spirituality is understood as having to do with fundamental matters, with our lives at their deepest, with what counts most for us, it cannot be segregated from any aspect of our existence. It has to do with our solitude and our corporate life. It has to do with the way we think and feel and act in every circumstance. It has to do with the whole of our lives, our public selves as well" (pp. 15-16).

If we accept this image of spirit as central, we can conclude that we are above all individuals of spirit. We then seek out kindred spirits to nourish our individual souls, to find the common wellspring of ego energy. We find these people in culturally cohesive organizations that acknowledge and nurture human spirit and create a corporate soul. In the words of Jan Van Eys: "We are a

mixture of many forces that determine our lifestyle. These onrush-
ing urges turn a waterwheel of spiritual power that can be put to
useful work or disengaged and used decoratively. There are many
of these driving forces, such as concern for our image in the eyes of
others and recognition of needs and patterns, that are otherwise left
unfinished. When these forces achieve their ends, that success per-
petuates the forces" (1981, p. 8).

Organizations Are Spiritual Enterprises

After an impressive come-from-behind victory over Miami University, a jubilant Notre Dame football team headed for the locker
room. Midfield, a television commentator put a microphone directly in front of Coach Lou Holtz and congratulated him on winning the game. Holtz shot back, "I didn't win this game, the spirit
of Notre Dame won it." He then turned his back on the camera and
walked away.

To many people, Holtz's remark may seem like a throwback
to times long past. Recruiting, fundamentals, coaching, game
plans, and individual talent are highly touted as the primary components of successful athletic teams. Many of the same features are
attributed to success in other team endeavors. Clear goals, prime
talent, financial incentives, and a solid competitive strategy are
widely promoted as the key elements of winning teams. But clearly
there is more to it. As the former head of VISA, Dee Hock, explains:
"In the field of group endeavor, you will see incredible events in
which the group performs far beyond the sum of its individual
talents. It happens in the symphony, in the ballet, in the theater,
in sports, and equally in business. It is easy to recognize and impossible to define. It is a mystique. It cannot be achieved without
immense effort, training and cooperation. But training and cooperation alone rarely create it" (Schlesinger, Eccles, and Gabarro,
1983, p. 486).

In our view, the mystical "it" that Hock credits for virtuoso
performance is the spiritual essence of culture. In fact, Peter Vaill
(1989) concluded after an extensive study of teams that spirit was at
the core of every successful group he studied. Group member "felt
the spirit" and the feeling of spirit was essential to the value and

meaning of the group's work. Culture, not command, propelled the group toward its successful destiny.

Spirit can also be evidenced in its absence. A recent *New York Times* article (Erlanger, 1992, p. 3) reporting on the condition of Russian troops in Latvia and Estonia observed: "The thousands of Russian troops remaining in the Baltic, on what is now foreign soil, are dispirited and somewhat angry." Their spirit had been crushed by their harsh treatment at the hands of local residents. But there was also a sense among them that they had lost their collective vigor. As one soldier remarked, "The ship is sinking and we're still mopping the decks." The sense of being dispirited is not uncommon in today's business world. Many modern companies are in financial trouble because of their spiritual bankruptcy. Cultural collapse soon leads to pecuniary trouble. General Motors and IBM are cases in point.

In all successful organizations, a powerful but elusive force galvanizes people and encourages the will, resolve, and ego energy to strive for seemingly unreachable levels of human performance. Burton Clark (1975, pp. 98–99) found this force in his study of distinctive colleges. He cites "saga" as the key ingredient that bonded the administration, faculty, students, alumni, and parents of these institutions together in a deeply held common quest:

> An organizational saga is a collective understanding of unique accomplishments in a formally established group. The group's definition of the accomplishment, intrinsically historical but embellished through retelling and rewriting, links stages of organizational development. The participants have added affect, an emotional loading which places their conception between the coolness of rational purpose and the warmth of sentiment found in religion and magic. An organizational saga presents some rational explanation of how certain means led to certain ends, but it also includes affect that turns a formal place into a beloved institution, to which participants may be passionately devoted. Encountering such devotion, the observer may become unsure of his own analytical de-

tachment as he tests overtones of the institutional
spirit or spirit of place.

Tracy Kidder (1981) uncovered a comparable example in the
business world when a group of Data General engineers built a new
computer from scratch in record time. The Eagle Group's impressive performance was not the product of laudable goals, efficient
management, or superior talent. The team had none of these advan-
tages. Kidder attributes the group's success to its culture—its soul:
"The initiative belonged entirely to West and the members of his
team. What's more, they did the work, both with uncommon spirit
and for reasons that, in a most frankly commercial setting, seem
remarkably pure. . . . Presumably the stonemasons who raised the
cathedrals worked only partly for their pay. They were building
temples to God. That's what West and his team of engineers were
looking for, I think" (pp. 272–273).

Another example comes from a corporation struggling to
refind its spiritual center. GM's new experimental automobile plant
was launched with principles far different from those of its parent
company. At Saturn, there is an observable team spirit—a shared
culture. It is not just felt among the plant's "team members." The
Saturn spirit extends to its "retail partners" and its union, the
UAW. The company is trying to create a new world of work as well
as a brand-new, high-quality product. Early successes show them to
be well under way. The ego energy created by its distinctive culture
is evident everywhere. It is customary for Saturn employees to stop
and offer help if they see one of their cars parked alongside a road-
way. They visit retail partners while on vacation in another city to
see how customers like the product. Recently the union placed new
demands on the bargaining table—not for higher pay, but for as-
surances that even higher quality standards would be set. The head
of the union shares an office suite with the company's president.
The Saturn plant is technically the most advanced in the world. But
its success is due primarily to the obvious fact that it is also spiritually radiant. Few companies have souls that can compete with
Saturn's doctrine, its core cultural commitments.

But other business leaders are beginning to recognize that
spirit matters as much to the province of business as that of the

church. Ben Cohen of Ben and Jerry's Ice Cream, for example, credits spirit as a major factor in the company's success: "I am certainly aware that there are a lot of business and economic theories that spiritual values, a concern for people, a concern for the general public welfare has no place in business. I strongly disagree." Cohen realizes that leadership has more to it than we typically realize. Symbols and spirit, rather than traits or decisions, form the essence of leadership.

Leadership Is a Spiritual Activity

In 1984, Admiral Carlisle A. H. Trost, the Navy's Chief of Naval Operations, raised some foreboding issues about our contemporary approach to leadership: "There is a trend in our society today to sterilize the leadership problem, to drain it of its content of flesh and blood. . . . Leadership is flesh and blood. It's people not systems that deter and win wars" (Trost, 1984). The admiral went on to comment on the absence of spirituality in our modern society and to highlight the importance of leadership that taps the deeper levels of the human spirit: "People will give all to the leader who stirs their blood."

Trost's observations have applications well beyond the military. In many aspects of organized life, we have sterilized the issue of leadership and thereby eliminated one of the prime sources of ego energy. In fact, American society itself is often viewed as experiencing a leadership crisis—a soulless vacuum linked to the waning of the American spirit. We have come to equate spirit and leadership with spiritual leadership as exercised by those powerful, often charismatic, figures who have shaped the history of religion. These same assumptions spill over into secular organizations. Here too we tend to define leadership in terms of personal qualities or the means by which a person's influence is exercised toward the achievement of certain goals. As a result, vast resources are spent grooming leadership skills, disseminating the latest theories and techniques, and searching for new definitions. Deep down we hope that someone will emerge who fits our ideal profile and will lead us to the success and happiness we seek. We just can't seem to find within ourselves or our organizations the energy to move ahead.

But we should be seeking leaders of spirit, rather than spiritual leaders. A leader of spirit recognizes and authorizes the talents of everyone. Such leaders find themselves in the humbling position of looking for the wholeness, gifts, and hearts of others in order to weave them into a unified cultural tapestry. When they succeed, organizational dimensions so often at odds become, instead, the warp and woof of a healthy culture. For a leader of spirit creativity, loyalty, and fairness would have equal merit to productivity, accountability, and diversity. More important, this commitment would be widely known throughout the culture. Leaders of spirit create a nourishing environment in which people can explore their unique spirit, connect with the souls of others, and weave individual stories into a powerfully moving and energizing collective story:

> We are people shaped by stories of who we are and who we are called to become. We are people of restless hearts, longing for direction and purpose in an uncertain world, for a story that will make sense of our existence, and for leaders who will help embody that story. Those who would lead us must ultimately appeal to our hearts, calling into being the deepest aspirations of our personal and communal existence and making stories of the good accessible to the hearts of ordinary people. They must make it possible to link "my story" and "your story" with "our story" and "their story" and to connect all the smaller stories with the larger ones that give the world meaning and purpose. [Bondi, 1989, p. 13]

Leadership of spirit is driven by mutual influence. Influence is different from power and authority, even though we often lump the three together. Influence is defined by Webster as "an ethereal fluid thought to flow from the stars and affect the character and actions of people; a spiritual and moral force." As a potent spiritual and moral force, mutual influence or leading the spirit can take us to heights previously unimagined, as noted by Henry Ford in 1926: "I know there are reservoirs of spiritual strength from which we human beings thoughtlessly cut ourselves off. . . . I believe we shall someday be able to know enough about the source of power and the realm of spirit to create something ourselves. . . . I firmly believe that mankind was once wiser about spiritual things than we are today. What we now only believe, they knew" (Senge, 1990, p. 141).

Changing an Organization Involves
Spiritual Metamorphosis

There should be little doubt in anyone's mind that we have a lot to learn about how to change organizations. Each year billions of dollars are wasted on ambitious efforts to alter patterns and practices in businesses, hospitals, and schools. Most of these initiatives start with a bang, quickly begin to sputter, and end with things very much the same as they were. Whatever energy is created in the beginning is lost or misplaced somewhere along the way. The cause of this bleak track record is clear: we approach change from a technical mindset—assuming that simply changing strategy or restructuring roles is going to do the trick. Everything we try is quickly absorbed by the very cultural patterns and practices we want to change.

If we think about changing as a spiritual undertaking, a different set of issues present themselves. We now use a different vocabulary and embrace different, less familiar, assumptions. We pose questions that are commonplace in other aspects of our lives but rarely pondered in business or other organizations. How can we transform our company's spirit? How can we become transformed by spirit? How can we convert our people to a new faith or affirm them in an old faith long since abandoned? How can we reclaim the spiritual underpinnings needed to create new sources of ego energy that will sustain the journey? The concepts of transformation or conversion are helpful because they recast the problem of changing in an organic, cultural, or spiritual mold.

There is a spiritual flow in every organization. In some cases it is necessary to slow down the flow of spirit before the organization blows up. In other cases it is important to speed up the flow before the organization bogs down (Owen, 1987). In either case it is essential to tap the flow of energy so that it can be fully utilized. When to do which—slow down or speed up—is an important judgment call by leaders of spirit. Sears, IBM, and General Motors may need a spiritual transfusion to refocus their vision and energy. Many newly launched start-ups need to constrict the flow of spirit in order to avoid cultural hyperactivity and individual burnout.

But what happens when an organization's spiritual commitments go sour? Spirit can be either constructive or destructive. Positive spirit creates hope, ego energy, and an existential buoyancy. Negative spirit is the root of despair. It saps energy, shatters hope, and creates an existential anchor that drags performance down. When an organization is plagued by bad spirit, what can be done? Northwest Airlines offers a case in point. In the wake of the airline industry's deregulation and Northwest's merger with Republic, Northwest's public image hit an all-time low. Frequent flyers typically referred to the company as "Northworst." Many passengers would choose double connections in another airline rather than fly a Northwest nonstop in order to avoid the poor attitudes and service they came to expect. The company's spirit was down. And it showed.

Recently, however, a new culture seems to be emerging. We have witnessed it firsthand. In two straight round-trip flights between Nashville and the Twin Cities, the flights were perfect. The planes were clean; the flight attendants were well groomed and courteous; the service was impeccable. The energy flow was contagious. On the fourth leg, the flight attendant was playfully queried: "What's wrong? The service is great!" She immediately beamed and responded, "Maybe you haven't seen our ads, 'You'll never see us like we were.' Now we have a new Northwest training program. It's called 'Northbest.' We were given a chance to exorcise our demons so that we wouldn't vent our spleen on passengers. Then we were encouraged to take pride in ourselves and our jobs. The program has made a big difference to me personally as well as professionally. I believe in myself and what I am doing. I now receive praise from passengers rather than hearing how pissed off they are." Northwest has evidently begun a remarkable journey toward transforming its spirit—transformed by a spiritual source of positive ego energy.

There is another kind of spiritual challenge. What happens when an organization's spirit is high, its cultural core is cohesive, and its business environment changes abruptly? That happened recently when AT&T was found to be in violation of antitrust legislation. The hundred-year-old culture was now pulling people in the wrong direction. Its sacred symbols were no longer a source of positive energy. No longer would Angus McDonald's struggle through the blizzard of 1891 to restore telephone service between New York and Boston occupy a pivotal place in the company's lore. The new faith was competition. But how could the company transform a cultural focus on universal service to a focus on competition and cost?

Owen (1987) contends that the process of transformation involves several stages:

1. Hitting the depths—reaching the point where things have literally bottomed out
2. Entering open space—leaving the past without an idea of what comes next
3. Entertaining novel possibilities, formulating a new vision, and letting go of the old while grasping the new
4. Celebrating the new vision

Metamorphosis is a scary journey, full of pitfalls, and there is a constant temptation to return to familiar ground. People withdraw into private cocoons to avoid the chaos and uncertainty, but in doing so they slow the process of moving forward into new territory. In this sense, change is akin to a trapeze act. First you must have the courage to climb the ladder and push off from the platform. While in midair, you need a sharp sense of timing and the courage to let go when it's time to grasp the next bar. If you let go too soon, you fall. If you hang on too long, you stall. AT&T's struggle has shown just how difficult it is to move from a culture that has been rendered legally obsolete to one equally strong but built on a new set of values. Spiritual metamorphosis is an uncertain undertaking. It is a process of energy conversion that people have always marveled at but never fully understood.

Conversion, like spirit, has often been restricted to a religious context, thereby limiting the exploration of its meaning and contribution to secular organizations. But novel explorations in organizations would not, as is often feared, result in the opening of Pandora's box. Rather, it might reveal a treasure chest of understanding about transforming relationships and cultural patterns. Although he was describing a personal conversion, theologian David K. O'Rourke's description of conversion seems extraordinarily applicable to any setting: "Conversion . . . involves a turning from a path we are on to another. The incongruities of our present state build up to the point where they become intolerable. Questions suppressed, decisions postponed too long, realities ignored, items of personal agenda tabled once too often, whatever it may be, they mount up and bring us face-to-face with the realization that things have got to change" (1985, p. 34).

This perspective helps us to consider novel approaches to change. We now can tackle the issues of faith and belief to help people move from one set of spiritual commitments to another. While the undertaking will not be easy, it may improve our ability to create new organizational forms. O'Rourke continues: "Conversion is not a magic moment. It is a human process. It is a process with moments and characteristics we can understand. The process may occur quickly or have the appearance of surprise. . . . It may occur over a long period of time" (p. 16).

We are now at the point where tinkering with the structural features of organizations is not getting us where we need to go. We need bold, risk-taking leaders who are willing to leave the safety of the status quo—to enter open space in the hope of finding new spirit. Otherwise our organizations will continue to lose faith and lose face in intense global competition.

Owen (1987) offers a vivid example of the inner workings of a successful transformation. An entrepreneur named Harry invented a product that created enough demand to support a company of 3,500 people eventually. But following a long period of success, Delta Corporation's performance went downhill. Soaring costs, flattened sales, and a decline in creativity and new products finally forced Harry to retire. Harry's replacement developed a metaphor to communicate a new vision for Delta. She saw a company of "engineers who could fly," rather than a company that was rapidly going downhill. But instead of a shared story that once held all the employees together, each function in the company now had its own version representing a different theme.

The finance division's stories, for example, praised the new breed of executives brought in after Harry's departure. "The Killing of '82" told about a young vice president who managed to sell so many of the tax losses incurred under Harry's management that he actually turned a profit. The "Cash Flow Kid" was a story about a new arrival in middle management who managed cash flow expertly enough to realize a solid return on short-term deposits. "In Praise of Wilbur" was a story about an in-house computer that circulated through the ranks in the finance group.

Stories in the research and development division were notably different. At the executive level, Old Harry stories carried on the creative accomplishments of the former CEO. Among middle managers, stories focused on the Golden Fleece award—a dubious distinction awarded monthly to the researcher who proposed an idea with the least bottom-line potential. Among rank and file researchers, two stories were commonly shared. The tale of Serendipity Sam was about a researcher who managed to accumulate the most Golden Fleece awards—his exploits continued the legend of excitement and innovation from Harry's regime. The Leper Colony was composed of Harry's contemporaries who had chosen, or been pushed into, a state of semiretirement.

The production side of Delta had its own stories. "Making the Quota" exemplified a value that put numbers ahead of quality. "Reuben" was a story about an ambitious superior whose ability to cover his errors and exaggerate his accomplishments led to a series of promotions. On the shop floor, most of the stories focused on the Zebra, a local bar where workers gathered after hours. Those who met there were a tight group constantly conspiring against their superiors.

In sum, then, Delta Corporation was a balkanized company pulled in many different directions. If there was any single theme, it centered on the tension between the management orientation of the new arrivals and the innovative traditions of the company's early history. These competing themes were doing more than pulling the company apart—they were pulling its performance downward. The new CEO envisioned a company where "engineers could fly." How could these opposite forces be redirected? The CEO recognized the potential energy, but she knew that it had to be channeled in one direction. When she invited thirty-five people from around the company to a management retreat, her opening strategy surprised everyone:

> She opened with some stories of the early days, describing the intensity of Old Harry and the Garage Gang (now known as the Leper Colony). She even had one of the early models of Harry's machine out on a table. Most people had never seen one. It looked rather primitive, but during the coffee break, members of the Leper Colony surrounded the ancient artifact and began swapping tales of the blind alleys, late nights, and exciting breakthroughs. That dusty old machine became a magnet. Young shop floor folks went up and touched it, sort of snickering as they compared this prototype with the sleek creations that they were manufacturing now. But even as they snickered, they stopped to listen as the Leper Colony recounted tales of accomplishment. It may have been just a "prototype," but that's where it all began. [Owen, 1987, p. 172]

After a coffee break, the CEO divided the group into several subgroups to express their hopes for the company. When the participants returned, their chairs had been rearranged into a circle with Old Harry's prototype in the center. With everyone now face-to-face, the CEO led a discussion linking the stories from the various subgroups. Serendipity Sam's report was a torrent of technical jargon. Members of the Leper Colony quickly jumped in to add details and elaborate on the theme. Before long, they and Sam were engaged in an animated conversation:

> The noise level was fierce, but the rest of the group was being left out. Taking Sam by the hand, the CEO led him to the center of the circle right next to the old prototype. There it was, the old and the new—the past, present, and potential. She whispered in Sam's ear that he ought to take a deep breath and start over in words of one syllable. He did so, and in ways less

than elegant, the concept emerged. He guessed about applications, competitors, market shares, and before long the old VP was drawn in. No longer was he thinking about selling [tax] losses, but rather thinking out loud about how he was going to develop the capital to support the new project. The group from the shop floor forgot about the Zebra and began to spin a likely tale as to how they might transform the assembly lines in order to make Sam's new machine. Even the Golden Fleece crowd became excited, telling each other how they always knew that Serendipity Sam could pull it off. They conveniently forgot that Sam had been the recipient of a record number of their awards, to say nothing of the fact that this new idea had emerged in spite of all their rules. [Owen, 1987, pp. 173-174]

The event knitted different stories into a new shared version that supported the CEO's vision. By recapturing and reinterpreting the company's roots, a disparate group of competing interests were united in a common spiritual quest.

Expressive Activity Liberates Spirit and Thereby Creates Ego Energy

The example of Delta Company's transformation illustrates how the liberation of spirit can tap and channel new reservoirs of zest and élan. The case relies on symbols, stories, drama, and other expressive, rather than technical, activities. It takes us back to approaches that modern people have essentially forgotten but primitive people knew: expressive actions cause the spirit to rise. In *Boiling Energy*, Richard Katz (1982, p. 34) describes the healing dance of the !Kung, a tribe in the Kalahari Desert on the northwestern edge of Botswana:

Four times a month on the average, night signals the start of a healing dance. The women sit around the fire rhythmically clapping. The men, sometimes

joined by the women, dance around the singers. As the
dance intensifies, *NUM,* or spiritual energy, is activated in the healers, but mostly among the dancing
men. As *NUM* is activated in them, they begin to *KIA,*
or experience enhancement of their consciousness.
While experiencing *KIA,* they heal all those at the
dance. Before the sun rises fully the next morning, the
dance usually ends. Those at the dance find it excit-
ing, joyful, powerful. "Being at a dance makes our
hearts happy," the !Kung say.

Dance does several things to the !Kung. It creates spiritual
energy, healing mind or body. It mends the social fabric by releasing
hostility or enhancing social solidarity. It protects the village from
misfortune. By enhancing consciousness it brings people into direct
contact with the spirits and gods. It makes their hearts happy. Is all
this true? Who can know for sure? The important thing is that the
!Kung share the belief that it is. Their primary source of spiritual
energy is created by their dance. Once created this ego energy has
important personal and social benefits.

How do modern people create spiritual energy? In church or
synagogue, spirit is summoned or released through scripture, lit-
urgy, music, and ritual. But how do we tap spiritual energy in
modern organizations? Gary Zukav, a physicist, suggests that the
first step is to recognize that ours is a spiritually, as well as a technically, driven world: "The conscious path to authentic power requires the recognition of the non-physical dimensions of the
human being, of the soul, and a growing knowledge of what the
soul is and what it wants" (1989, p. 200).

But where do we start? How do we find the soul of the modern organization and begin to liberate human spirit? Spirit is
created, released, or transformed by people engaged together in
meaningful expressive activity. Just as the !Kung find their spiritual
center in the healing dance, people in modern organizations will
find theirs in myth, ritual, ceremony, stories, metaphors, music, art,
theater, and other forms.

As Cox (1969) observes: "The spirit of festivity, like a muse,
has a mind of its own. It can fail to show up even when elaborate

preparations have been made, leaving us all feeling a little silly, It may pop up when no one is expecting it. . . . [But] if you ice a cake, light sparklers, and sing, something celebrative may happen" (p. 108). Cox is alluding to celebrative forms, such as the following, that can be keys to celebrative feelings and events.

• Metaphor is a form that helps us see one thing in terms of another. (See Brown, 1976; Manning, 1979; Morgan, 1980; Reddy, 1979.) It captures patterns that otherwise remain hidden or unformed. Thinking about an organization as a tree, an animal, or a book can help people clarify subtle issues that are observed in the jumble of human complexity (Gordon, 1961; Schon, 1979). In the case of Delta Company, the CEO employed a metaphor—"engineers who can fly"—to capture and communicate her vision of what the company needed to become.

• Poetry is another linguistic form that allows people to communicate on a level beyond ordinary language. A poem invites interpretation and allows people to express and enjoy the richness of human experience. Through poetry people can express what they could not otherwise say. Thinking about policies as poetry, memos as meter, or routine as rhythm can often illuminate what is hidden behind the curtain of rationality. The poem Maya Angelou delivered at President Clinton's inauguration provides an example:

> Come rest here by my side.
> Each of you a bordered country,
> Delicate and strangely made proud,
> Yet thrusting perpetually under siege.
> Your armed struggles for profit
> Have left collars of waste upon
> My shore, currents of debris upon my breast.
> Yet today, I call you to my riverside,
> If you will study war no more. Come,
> Clad in peace, and I will sing the songs
> The Creator gave to me when I and the
> Tree and the stone were one.

• Stories offer a way of communicating important lessons and building strong bonds among people. (See Martin, 1980; Mitroff and Kilmann, 1975; Enderud, 1976; Wilkins, 1976.) By grounding intangible issues in personalized examples, cultural lessons can be passed from one generation to another. Telling stories provides a medium through which the rich spiritual texture of life in organizations can be shared. Hearing stories is the primary way that people learn the ropes and the organization's way of doing things. Stories provide still another avenue for imparting its vital essence. As an example, Harry Quadracci of Quad Graphics believes that "we're dead serious about what we're doing, but that doesn't mean we can't have fun doing it" (Kehrer, 1989, p. 307). Stories about Harry's behavior reinforce his pronouncements—like the time he arrived at the Christmas party riding an elephant or, another time, when he rode in on a tractor trailer.

• Theater has traditionally provided an important stage on which the human drama can unfold to be applauded or panned. (See Turner, 1982; Mangham and Overington, 1987; Manning, 1979; Brissett and Edgley, 1990.) In the theater, deep dilemmas and paradoxes are shared, appreciated, and sometimes resolved. The living tension between empirical fact and noble lie is what makes drama what it is. In theater, people see themselves; they laugh, cry, and experience an emotional catharsis. Bringing the everyday drama in organizations on stage provides a medium through which both players and audience can communicate intangible themes in depth. The theater creates an opportunity for people to express spiritual values and emotional issues.

As an example, Virginia Mason Hospital and Clinic sets up a stage each year at its management retreat. Any person or group can sign up to present a skit or dramatic episode of their choice. The event lasts for over two hours. During that time many of the group's most sensitive issues are publicly portrayed in ways that they are acknowledged, appreciated, and applauded. The intense ego energy created during the occasion spills over well after the event has ended.

• Ritual and ceremony enable people to act out their values and beliefs. (See Manning, 1979; Moore and Meyerhoff, 1977.) Unlike theater, however, ritual has no audience. The people are players and the repetitious, stylized sequence of moves helps them to experience and share key meanings and emotions (Blum, 1961). In ritual, one experiences a culture's spirit (Geertz, 1973; Trice, Belasco, and Alutto, 1969).

Ben and Jerry's, for example, created in 1988 its "Joy Gang," a roving band of merrymakers who at any given moment may be seen celebrating lesser-known holidays like national clash dressing day: "This holiday provides the *un*-fashion-conscious workers with a chance to show off their stuff—exaggerated to the limit, of course." On another occasion the Joy Gang catered an Italian dinner for a shift of workers, featuring a DJ who played tunes on request. Its human resource department has organized a winter solstice party and a gift week. Ben and Jerry's uses ritual to summon spirit, thereby reinforcing the company's spiritual commitments.

• Music is another expressive form that allows people to communicate feelings and ideals well below the level of ordinary consciousness. Melodies create meaning and mental images. Lyrics add another dimension by putting poetry into rhythm and harmony. "Music has the paradox of both bringing order and allowing chaos, often simultaneously. As a disciplinary art form, it can bring organization of emotions and channel strong feelings" (Guardian News Service, 1993, p. 7A).

At a meeting of federal agency heads, the participants were asked to return from lunch prepared to sing a song that would capture each agency's essential character. After a period of intense grumbling the agency heads had lunch and in turn sang their songs for each other. The IRS chose "I've Got You Body and Soul." The FAA picked "Leaving on a Jet Plane." The Bureau of Mines head sang "Dark as a Dungeon." After everyone had finished, a participant in the group remarked, "I think we've all been reminded of what our agencies really stand for." Through music, the agencies had rediscovered their corporate souls. And there is another dimension to music. Adding music to ritual creates the dance—an uplifting surge of human spirit.

• Visual images and pictures provide yet another expressive form. (See Langer, 1951; Siegel, 1978; Arnheim, 1969.) Through art, people are able to see, share, and interpret experience (Edwards, 1986; Schaverien, 1987). For finding meaning in modern organizations, a picture can indeed be worth a thousand words.

Modern managers have recently been barraged with the "vision thing." What once would have put someone away in an institution is now being touted as a necessary part of management. The dilemma is that having a vision is often seen as a technical design problem. Managers wait hopelessly for a blinding revelation that can be written into a mission statement. If the revelation ever comes, it manifests itself in a rational form and is captured in technical prose that no one reads or, if they do, fully understands. But having a vision means searching deep within the resonant chambers of a culture to discover a visual image of the collective soul, the corporate spirit, at its most fundamental. Modern prophets paint on a chaotic canvas a poignant portrait that touches and inspires vision in others even though their interpretations may be somewhat different than what the artist tried to capture. "Without a vision, people perish." And if they do, their decline can be traced to an absence of artful visual images that tie people together and connect them to their collective soul.

How do these expressive forms liberate spirit? Think of a time when you were particularly swayed or uplifted. Almost always the exhilaration of spirit comes in response to an expressive form: a work of art, a song, a poem, a moving ceremony, a meaningful ritual, a well-told story. Every Saturday, for example, Garrison Keillor draws his listeners into the magic of Lake Wobegon. It is a spiritual journey which draws us into a mystical world that touches deep internal needs. Through his stories, Keillor brings us back into touch with America's core spiritual values.

Others have noted that the modern corporation should pay more attention to the expressive side of human experience (Owen, 1987; Cox, 1969). Through several case studies, besides the Delta Company's experience described earlier, Owen (1987) has documented the interplay of expressive forms and activity in transforming organizations that had lost their spirit. Kidder shows us, in *The Soul of a New Machine,* how spirit created by expressive forms propelled a group of engineers to produce a new computer in record time. Renewing and reforming spirit may be one of the most promising avenues for attaining the energy, results, and competitive edge all organizations are striving for.

Spirit Can Be a Competitive Advantage

Tapping human spirit gives an organization a competitive edge. Internally, as we have seen, spirit infuses cohesion, purpose, and focus. It encourages ego energy, zest, liveliness, courage, backbone, and commitment. It makes an organization a cultural way of life rather than just a bureaucratic place of work. But there are also external reasons why spirit provides a competitive advantage.

There was a time when corporate logos and trademarks meant something. Interestingly, the Greek term *logos* is linked to spirit (Frankl, 1974), and the logo used to represent the spirit behind a corporate name. A respected name was once synonymous with a guarantee of quality for a product or service. A purchase was a matter of trust. Customers had faith and confidence in what stood behind a familiar logo. Much of this trust has vanished in recent memory. A business transaction is now often purely an economic exchange. The lowest price is the best buy. Generic products, without a label, are cornering a share of the market. If buying a name brand confers no real advantage, why not pay less for its anonymous counterpart? If beer is beer, why pay more for Budweiser?

Modern marketing strategies try to convince the consumer that there is something safer, sexier, or superior in a particular product. And they are often successful in persuading the consumer to pay more for a brand name. But little attention is paid to the human organization that produced the goods or services. Faith Popcorn (1991) predicts that all this is about to change. Popcorn is the futurist who accurately predicted such modern trends as cocooning, the Decency Decade, and cashing out (young people leaving the corporate rat race for a more leisurely life). Her recent *Popcorn Report* predicts that the 1990s will witness a revolution in consumer attitudes and behavior. One of her more intriguing forecasts is that consumers in the nineties will buy goods and services from companies with a soul (that is, spirit). This is what she predicts:

> It used to be enough just to make a fairly decent product and market it. Not anymore. In the 90s you've got to have a corporate soul. The consumer will want to

know who you are before buying what you sell
[p. 159]. . . . You can't fake a corporate soul; either
you have one or you'd better create one, fast. Depending on your industry, the Decency Decade demands
that you send out a loud-and-clear message (a Corporate Promise) [p. 162]. . . . The status that an M.B.A.
held for marketers in the 1980s will be replaced by the
status of a new M.B.S. (Master of Business Souls) [p.
163].

Essentially, Popcorn is predicting that the financially based consumer choices of the 1980s are going to give way to more spiritually
guided decisions. If this is true, organizations infused with spirit
will do much better than those without.

Capturing the Spirit

Most advocates for a new emphasis on the expressive, spiritual side
of organizations base their arguments on historical precedent and
philosophical precepts rather than empirical evidence. One of the
most interesting of these thinkers, Harvey Cox in *The Feast of Fools*
(1969), argues that modern people have lost their sense of fantasy
and festival. As a result our spirits and ego energy sag, unmotivated
by the rational, technical, results-oriented context of many contemporary organizations. Cox advocates "a world for which a fiesta or
even a love-in is a better symbol than a computer or a rocket. Technology need not be the enemy of man's spirit in the modern world.
But it should be a means to a man's human fulfillment, not the
symbol or goal of that fulfillment itself" (p. 162).

We have come to a juncture in our knowledge about organizations and what makes them tick. On the one hand, we know
that most of our rational, technical efforts to improve organizations
have not worked. But on the other, we seem unduly reluctant to
experiment with other possibilities that might work better. This
may be a good time to see if more attention to the spiritual side of
organizations might create the human ego energy we need to get the
results we so desperately want.

References

Angelou, M. "Only a Little Lower Than the Angels." Poem delivered at President Clinton's inauguration, Washington, D.C., Jan. 17, 1993.

Arnheim, R. *Visual Thinking*. Berkeley: University of California Press, 1969.

Blum, A. "Collective Bargaining: Ritual or Reality." *Harvard Business Review*, Nov./Dec. 1961, *39*, 63–69.

Bondi, R. *Leading God's People: Ethics for the Practice of Ministry*. Nashville, Tenn.: Abingdon Press, 1989.

Brissett, D., and Edgley, C. (eds.). *Life as Theatre: A Dramaturgical Sourcebook*. New York: Aldine, 1990.

Brown, R. "Social Theory as Metaphor: On the Logic of Discovery for the Sciences of Conduct." *Theory and Society*, 1976, *3*, 169–197.

Clark, B. R. "The Organizational Saga in Higher Education." In J. V. Baldridge and T. E. Deal (eds.), *Managing Change in Educational Organizations*. Berkeley, Calif.: McCutchan, 1975.

Cox, H. *The Feast of Fools*. Cambridge, Mass.: Harvard University Press, 1969.

Edwards, B. *Drawing on the Artist Within*. New York: Simon & Schuster, 1986.

Enderud, H. G. "The Perception of Power." In J. G. March and J. Olsen (eds.), *Ambiguity and Choice in Organizations*. Bergen, Norway: Universitetsforlaget, 1976.

Erlanger, S. "Russian Troops in Baltic Tell of Harassment." *New York Times*, Dec. 22, 1992, p. 3.

Frankl, V. E. *Man's Search for Meaning*. New York: Pocket Books, 1974.

Geertz, C. *The Interpretation of Cultures*. New York: Basic Books, 1973.

Gordon, W. J. "Play and Irrelevance." *Synectics*. New York: Harper, 1961.

Guardian News Service. "Music Can Tame the Hyperactive Child." Feb. 14, 1993, p. 7a.

Katz, R. *Boiling Energy: Community Healing Among the Kalahari !Kung*. Cambridge, Mass.: Harvard University Press, 1982.

Kehrer, D. *Doing Business Boldly: The Art of Taking Intelligent Risks.* New York: Time Books, 1989.

Kidder, T. *The Soul of a New Machine.* Boston: Little, Brown, 1981.

Langer, S. *Philosophy in a New Key: A Study in the Symbolism of Reason, Rite and Art.* Cambridge, Mass.: Harvard University Press, 1951.

Mangham, I. L., and Overington, M. A. *Organizations as Theatre: A Social Psychology of Dramatic Appearances.* New York: Wiley, 1987.

Manning, P. *Police Work: The Social Organization of Policing.* Cambridge, Mass.: MIT Press, 1979.

Martin, J. A. "Stories and Scripts in Organizational Settings." Research Report 543. Stanford University School of Business, July 1980.

Mitroff, I. I., and Kilmann, R. H. "Stories Managers Tell: A New Tool for Organizational Problem Solving." *Management Review,* 1975, *64*(7), 18–28.

Moore, S. F., and Meyerhoff, B. G. *Secular Ritual.* Assen, Netherlands: Van Goerum, 1977.

Morgan, G. "Paradigms, Metaphors, and Puzzle Solving in Organization Theory." *Administrative Science Quarterly,* 1980, *25*, 605–622.

Nichols, J. T. "What Is a Naturalist Anyway?" *Natural History,* 1992, *101*(11), 12.

O'Rourke, D. K. *A Process Called Conversion.* New York: Doubleday, 1985.

Ortony, A. *Metaphor and Thought.* Cambridge: Cambridge University Press, 1979.

Owen, H. *Spirit: Transformation and Development in Organizations.* Potomac, Md.: Abbott, 1987.

Palmer, P. "Leading from Within: Reflections on Spirituality and Leadership." Address given to the Meridian Street United Methodist Church, Indianapolis, Mar. 23, 1990.

Popcorn, F. *The Popcorn Report.* New York: Doubleday, 1991.

Reddy, M. "The Conduit Metaphor." In A. Ortony (ed.), *Metaphor and Thought.* Cambridge: Cambridge University Press, 1979.

Schaverien, J. "The Scapegoat and the Talisman: Transference in

Art Therapy." *Images of Art Therapy*. New York: Tavistock, 1987.

Schlesinger, L., Eccles, R., and Gabarro, J. *Managerial Behavior in Organizations*. New York: McGraw-Hill, 1983.

Schon, D. A. "Generative Metaphor and Social Policy." In A. Ortony (ed.), *Metaphor and Thought*. Cambridge: Cambridge University Press, 1979.

Senge, P. M. *The Fifth Discipline: The Art and Practice of the Learning Organization*. New York: Doubleday/Currency, 1990.

Siegel, I. E. "The Development of Pictorial Comprehension." In B. S. Randhawa and W. E. Coffman (eds.), *Visual Learning, Thinking, and Communication*. New York: Academic Press, 1978.

Trice, H. M., Belasco, J., and Alutto, J. A. "The Role of Ceremonials in Organizational Behavior." *Industrial and Labor Relations Review*, 1969, *23*, 40–51.

Trost, C.A.H. "Leadership Is Flesh and Blood." Speech given at Annapolis, Md., 1984. Videotape.

Turner, V. "Social Dramas and Stories About Them." *From Ritual to Theatre: The Seriousness of Play*. New York: Performing Arts Journal, 1982.

Vaill, P. B. *Managing as a Performing Art: New Ideas for a World of Chaotic Change*. San Francisco: Jossey-Bass, 1989.

Van Eys, J. *Humanity and Personhood*. Springfield, Ill.: Thomas, 1981.

Wagner, J. "Spirituality and Administration: The Sign of Integrity." *Weavings: A Journal of the Christian Spiritual Life*, 1988, *3*(4), 15–16.

Wilkins, A. "Organizational Stories as an Expression of Management Philosophy." Unpublished thesis, Stanford University Business School, 1976.

Zukav, G. *The Seat of the Soul*. New York: Simon & Schuster, 1989.

Part Two

Basic Theory
and
Action Implications

5

Self-Efficacy, Self-Esteem, and Behavior in Organizations

Mark A. Mone, Dawn Kelly

As COGNITIVE PROCESSES IN GENERAL, and personality processes in particular, become more popular explanations for human activity in organizations, self-efficacy and self-esteem have received increasing research and managerial attention. Campbell (1990) notes that studies on self-esteem number in the thousands, and recent reviews (Bandura, 1986; Gist, 1987; Gist and Mitchell, 1992; Lent, Brown, and Larkin, 1987) indicate similar growth in self-efficacy studies. Much of this attention can be traced to the significant influence that these two personality constructs have on individual behavior, cognition, affective states, and, consequently, important organizational outcomes. For example, both self-efficacy and self-esteem have been shown to affect occupational choice, work performance, satisfaction, commitment, absenteeism, turnover, and substance abuse. (See Brockner, 1988; Pierce, Gardner, Cummings, and Dunham, 1989; Tharenou, 1979; Wood and Bandura, 1989.)

Although self-efficacy and self-esteem have been related independently to organizational behavior in past research, they are in fact overlapping constructs—for example, both have been demonstrated to affect choice and level of work behavior. (See Bandura and Cervone, 1983; Brockner, 1988; Gist, 1987; Locke, Frederick, Lee, and Bobko, 1984; Rosenberg, 1979; Tharenou, 1979.) Due to the overlap in these constructs, there is a lack of clarity concerning the variables that are affected by self-efficacy and self-esteem as well as the antecedents underlying self-efficacy and self-esteem. This lack of clarity is dysfunctional for both theoretical and practical reasons. If self-efficacy and self-esteem are not conceptually clarified as the two research streams grow, their distinctions become less clear. Without conceptual clarity as to their consequences and their determinants, researchers may employ inappropriate research designs and measures and managers may devote resources to ineffective human resource programs.

In this chapter, self-efficacy and self-esteem are integrated into a concept that may be described as ego energy. We begin by defining these two constructs and reviewing their theoretical underpinnings. We then relate self-efficacy and types of self-esteem to ego energy. Next we examine the individual and organizational antecedents, consequences, and correlates of these personality constructs. Finally, we consider the implications for managers and researchers.

Self-efficacy is a person's belief regarding his or her ability to perform specific tasks at a particular level (Bandura, 1977, 1982, 1986; Gist, 1987). Sources of self-efficacy include past performance levels on the same or similar tasks, vicarious learning (such as modeling), and enactive mastery (success, training, education); see Bandura (1986) and Farr and Ford (1988). As task experience increases and tasks are mastered, increasing levels of self-efficacy are attained that result in higher aspirations. If task mastery is not developed over successive experiences, self-efficacy beliefs may remain low or decline, resulting in reduced goals, and, subsequently, lower performance.

Self-esteem is a general sense of self-worth that incorporates such dimensions as self-competence, self-respect, and self-integrity (Rosenberg, 1965, 1979). Two common but conflicting explanations of sources of self-esteem are self-consistency (Korman, 1977) and self-enhancement (Jones, 1973). According to the self-consistency argument, people are thought to develop attitudes about certain situations and behave accordingly (Korman, 1976). In an organizational work situation, for example, Hollenbeck and Brief (1987) found that people with high self-esteem favored high goal attainment and performed at higher levels than those with low self-esteem. According to the self-enhancement or "looking-glass self" argument, people behave in ways that will be viewed favorably by others (Cooley, 1964; Gecas and Schwalbe, 1983). Thus high self-esteem is realized when a person perceives that others view his or her behavior with acceptance, respect, and admiration. Similar to self-efficacy, self-esteem has also been shown to influence goals and performance, along with an array of other individual and organizational outcomes. These outcomes include career choice, mental health, general satisfaction, work attendance, and organizational commitment. (For representative reviews see Brockner, 1988, and Tharenou, 1979.)

There are several types of self-esteem, which may be ordered hierarchically in terms of increasing specificity. Simpson and Boyle (1975) discussed a three-tier approach to self-esteem: *global* self-esteem, an overall evaluation of self-worth; *role-specific* self-esteem, the self-evaluation emanating from various life roles (parent, employee, spouse); and *task-* or *situation-specific* (competence-based) self-esteem, the self-evaluation resulting from behavior in a specific situation. We argue, as have others, that self-efficacy is conceptually similar to situation-specific self-esteem (Gecas and Schwalbe, 1986). Pierce and others (1989) have developed and validated an additional level of self-esteem, *organization-based* self-esteem, which would probably occupy a position on the hierarchy between role-specific and global self-esteem.

Although research suggests that the relationship between self-efficacy and self-esteem is generally positive, the two constructs may also be independent of one another. Someone could lack confidence (have low self-efficacy) for conducting performance appraisals, for example, but possess a positive sense of global self-esteem. The strength and direction of the relationship between self-efficacy and self-esteem are affected by the consistency (repetition over time) and the centrality (salience) of the task outcomes (Brockner, 1988). If the person in the previous example is a manager whose ability to evaluate employees' performance is central to his life's pursuits but he consistently experiences problems delivering these appraisals, his global self-esteem may well decline—or different tasks will be chosen for which he has higher self-efficacy.

   In this chapter we view ego energy as a composite representing some of the cognitive energies that people exert toward affective reactions, choices, and behavior. In particular, we view ego energy as including self-efficacy and types of self-esteem as depicted in Figure 5.1. Viewing these personality constructs as part of a larger concept—ego energy—represents an extension of past research. For example, the identification allows one to integrate several self-regulatory constructs with distinct antecedents, consequences, and correlates. Through an integration and comparison of diverse antecedents, consequences, and correlates of each dimension, we may attain greater understanding of the complexities underlying individual and organizational behavior.

   In the following sections we review the behavioral, cognitive, affective, and organizational antecedents and consequences of self-efficacy and types of self-esteem. The discussion is organized by hierarchical levels and by type of antecedent, consequence, or correlate (see Figure 5.1). The hierarchical levels begin with the more situation-specific constructs (self-efficacy, task- or competence-based self-esteem), become more generalized with role-specific or organization-based self-esteem, and conclude with global self-esteem.

Behavioral Antecedents, Consequences, and Correlates

We first consider individual and organizational behaviors that constitute antecedents, consequences, and correlates of self-efficacy and self-esteem. Such behaviors include task persistence and performance, employee attendance, absenteeism, turnover, and organizational productivity and performance.

Behavioral Antecedents

One antecedent shared by self-efficacy and self-esteem is a person's evaluation of past performance. There is a considerable amount of literature supporting Bandura's contention (1977, 1986) that self-efficacy is partly determined by past performance (Bandura and Cervone, 1983, 1986; Cervone and Peake, 1986; Mone and Baker,

Figure 5.1. Antecedents, Consequences, and Correlates of Ego Energy.

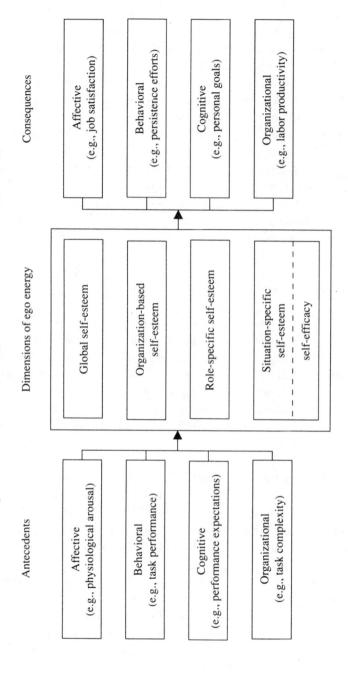

1992; Wood and Locke, 1990). These studies indicate that successive task mastery builds confidence, whereas successive task failures lead to decrements in confidence.

Hall (1971) formulated a psychological success model in which there is an upward spiral of global self-esteem, goal setting, task performance, and subsequent self-esteem. In examinations of components of this model (Hall and Nougaim, 1968; Hall and Foster, 1977), successful task performance has been found to engender subsequent global self-esteem. This finding is consistent with an argument presented by Gecas and Schwalbe (1983) that people focus on efficacious action as a source of their self-esteem. Later (1986) they developed and factor-analyzed a self-esteem instrument in which three independent factors emerged, including a self-efficacy factor.

Behavioral Consequences

Historically there has been some controversy over the effects of personality variables on workplace behavior. (Compare Mitchell, 1979, with Weiss and Adler, 1984.) Mitchell (1982) and others (Frayne and Latham, 1987; Gist, 1989) have recently argued that one of the most effective methods of affecting an employee's behavior may be by influencing the cognitions that mediate work performance. Recent research indicates that self-efficacy positively affects coping efforts and persistence toward tasks (Lent, Brown, and Larkin, 1987; Stumpf, Brief, and Hartman, 1987). Bandura (1989) contends that people with high self-efficacy beliefs persist longer in the face of failure, redoubling their efforts to reach performance levels they believe they are capable of attaining. Conversely, people low in self-efficacy perceive failure as an affirmation of their ineptitude and are more inclined to abandon their goals without exerting a great deal of effort.

Global self-esteem has also been shown to affect behavior. People with low self-esteem were demonstrated to perform less effectively under stress and failure than their high–self-esteem counterparts (Schalon, 1968; Schrauger and Rosenberg, 1970). In reviewing the literature, Tharenou (1979) found that those with low self-esteem were more likely to exhibit poor social skills and less sociability (Berger, 1955; Fitts, 1972a; Rosenberg, 1965). Brockner (1988) has also presented an argument, similar to Bandura's (1989) position, that people with high global self-esteem persist at challenging tasks whereas those with low global self-esteem are more likely to withdraw.

Behavioral Correlates

Reviews by Tharenou (1979) and Brockner (1988) suggest that there is little evidence supporting a positive relationship between global self-esteem and quality or quantity of performance—and the evidence that does support this relationship reveals only weak (.10 to .20) correlations (Ghiselli, 1963; Jacobs and Solomon, 1977). There is, however, a fair amount of evidence supporting the idea that task-specific self-esteem is associated with performance levels (Brockner, 1988; Tharenou, 1979; Simpson and Boyle, 1975), though a study by Tharenou and Harker (1982) found that supervisor-rated job performance was not related to task-specific self-esteem.

Although the association between self-esteem and performance is weak, there are stronger relationships between self-esteem and absences, stress, and stress-related physiological factors. In Tharenou's (1979) review, for example, number of employee absences and global self-esteem were unrelated (Lefkowitz, 1967; Vroom, 1962), but work-role self-esteem was related to number of absences (Hackman and Lawler, 1971; Quinn and Shepard, 1974). Propensity to leave was found to be negatively related to both role-specific self-esteem (Quinn and Shepard, 1974) and task-specific self-esteem (Gardell, 1973). Moreover, task-specific self-esteem was a weak but significant predictor of actual turnover six months later (Ekpo-ufot, 1976). Tharenou (1979) also reviewed evidence suggesting that global and work-role self-esteem are negatively associated with coronary heart disease risk, company dispensary visits, and job stress.

Cognitive Antecedents, Consequences, and Correlates

In this section, we consider individuals' cognitions, which have been examined as antecedents, consequences, and correlates of self-efficacy and self-esteem. Such cognitions include self-evaluation of past performance, vicarious learning processes, personal goals and aspirations, task strategies, and occupational choice.

Cognitive Antecedents

Cognitions are thought to play a prominent role in the development of self-efficacy beliefs. While the behavioral and affective antecedents influence self-efficacy, it is the cognitive evaluation of these factors—as well as vicarious learning and feedback from others—that ultimately determines self-efficacy (Bandura, 1982). Bandura (1988) has suggested that it is precisely because task-specific capability judgments are involved that self-efficacy is distinct from global self-esteem. From the perspective of Bandura and others (Gist and Mitchell, 1992; Hollenbeck and Brief, 1987), self-efficacy is more domain-specific and more easily influenced through task mastery, vicarious learning, feedback, and modeling. According to these theorists, global self-esteem is a more stable (traitlike), generalized, affective evaluation of the self.

Despite the contention that global self-esteem is more stable than self-efficacy or task-specific self-esteem, the malleability of global self-esteem has been the subject of a fair amount of research. Brockner (1983, 1988; Brockner and Guare, 1983) has developed a model of global self-esteem plasticity in which those low in self-esteem are much more easily influenced than those high in self-esteem. The rationale behind this model includes the propositions that people low in self-esteem may be more attentive to social cues, may extract more meaning from the cues, and may be more yielding. Brockner and others (such as Campbell, 1990) have found that those low in self-esteem react much more negatively to pessimistic feedback and positively to optimistic feedback; they are also much more easily influenced by experimental intervention. These findings have significant implications for research that has found people low in global self-esteem to be more likely to lack initiative and assertiveness (Crandall, 1973), to be more persuadable and conforming (Wells and Marwell, 1976), and to have lower aspirations and expectations of success (Rosenberg, 1965).

There have been divergent perspectives on the elements that

constitute global self-esteem. For example, global self-esteem, also known as self-worth, is thought to be the result of a complex cognitive process in which discrete judgments about oneself and life activities are combined into one evaluative construct (Rosenberg, 1979) or the weighted function of esteem in more specific areas (Simpson and Boyle, 1975). Somewhat differently, both James (1963) and Cooley (1964) consider global self-esteem to be a summary of attitudes concerning the many dimensions of one's life. Recent research suggests that these dimensions can be ranked from most to least important in the following order: (1) physical appearance; (2) intimate relationships; (3) (tied) intelligence, sociability, and adequacy as a provider; and (4) (tied) job competence, morality, sense of humor, and nurturance. (For a review see Harter, 1990; for a divergent perspective see Bandura, 1990.) From a more integrative perspective, Pelham and Swann (1989) found three factors that contribute uniquely to global self-esteem: people's positive and negative feelings about themselves, their specific beliefs about themselves, and the way these beliefs are framed (framing factors).

These framing factors, which influence how self-evaluations are considered, include such items as attribute centrality (salience), attribute certainty (confidence in possessing the attribute), and self-ideal discrepancy (comparison between the actual and ideal self). These factors translate the evaluation from one that asks "How good or bad am I?" into "What does it mean to be good or bad at different life dimensions?" This integrative perspective underscores the idea that people not only recognize their own self-evaluations but also consider the approval of others to be important. (See, for example, Cooley's [1902] 1964 and Mead's 1934 self-concept and Festinger's 1954 social comparison theory.) Gecas and Schwalbe (1986, p. 79) have noted: "Human beings derive a sense of self not only from the reflected appraisal of others, but also from the consequences and products of behavior that are attributed to the self as an agent in the environment."

Cognitive Consequences

Perhaps the most prominent consequence of self-efficacy is its positive effect on subsequent personal goals—and the correlates of goals. In a large number of empirical studies (Locke, Frederick, Lee, and Bobko, 1984; Mone and Baker, 1992; Schunk, 1984; Taylor, Locke, Lee, and Gist, 1984), self-efficacy has had a significant, positive effect on the difficulty level of chosen goals and commitment to them. The importance of this effect becomes clear when one considers the robust positive effect of goals on performance. (For reviews see Locke and Latham, 1990.) Self-efficacy also affects the cognitive interpretation of feedback (Silver, Mitchell, and Gist, 1990) and the affective reactions mentioned earlier, both of which affect subsequent self-regulatory processes and performance (Gist and Mitchell, 1992). Self-efficacy has been shown to influence choice of tasks and activities and strategies for pursuing them (Earley, Wojnaroski, and Prest, 1987; Lent, Brown, and Larkin, 1987; Stumpf, Brief, and Hartman, 1987). Finally, self-efficacy positively affects the degree of persistence toward completing tasks and, ultimately, how successfully tasks are performed (Lee, 1984).

A comparison between the consequences of task-specific self-esteem and global self-esteem was conducted by Hollenbeck and Brief (1987). They found that under personal goal conditions, task-specific self-esteem had a significantly greater positive influence on goal choice difficulty than did global self-esteem. Under assigned goal conditions, there was a stronger expectation of goal attainment for those high in task-specific self-esteem than for those low in this dimension. For those who had high global self-esteem, there was both higher valence and higher goal difficulty chosen, compared to those who were low in this trait. This research is corroborated by an examination of Hall's (1971) psychological success model (Hall and Foster, 1977) that reported a significant, positive correlation (.40) between generalized self-esteem and global difficulty chosen. In personal goal conditions, individual differences apparently affect the goal level chosen; in assigned goal conditions, individual differences apparently affect the reaction to the goal. In the latter cases, it appears that assigned goals should not diverge widely from the goal levels that people would otherwise set for themselves.

Cognitive Correlates

Global self-esteem has often been related to occupational choice. For example, both Dipboye (1977) and Korman (1977) review findings that college students high in self-esteem chose or preferred occupations that were consistent with their personalities and self-perceived traits. Yet, for the most part, this evidence does not provide any proof that these occupations determine the subsequent self-esteem levels of their incumbents.

Affective Antecedents, Consequences, and Correlates

In this section, we review affective dimensions and emotions that have been considered antecedents, consequences, and correlates of self-efficacy and self-esteem. Such affective dimensions include arousal, anxiety, fear of failure, and task and job satisfaction.

Affective Antecedents

Bandura (1982) has suggested that self-efficacy perceptions are based, in part, on levels of physiological arousal and associated affective states. How anxious one feels about performing a particular task, for example, may mediate one's level of confidence for that task: "Because high arousal usually debilitates performance, people are more inclined to expect success when they are not beset by aversive arousal than if they are tense and viscerally agitated" (Bandura, 1986, p. 401). Similarly, fear of failure can result in self-fulfilling prophecies as people become distressed and, consequently, dysfunctional in the tasks they fear. As a different type of affective antecedent, Tharenou and Harker (1982) found general job satisfaction to be a predictor of task-specific self-esteem.

Global levels of self-esteem are also influenced by the reactions of others. Pelham and Swann (1989) note that even very young infants seem aware that they are usually accepted or usually rejected by others. Adolescents may be more affected than adults by these reactions since they occur at an earlier, more formative stage. Nonetheless, the affective reactions to people's behavior is thought to influence self-esteem even in adulthood. People judge how good or bad they feel about themselves, and these affective judgments become an important part of their global self-esteem (Pelham and Swann, 1989; Rosenberg, 1979).

Affective Consequences

Self-efficacy has been shown to influence affective reactions (such as emotional reactions) to a task (Kanfer and Ackerman, 1989; Gist, Schwoerer, and Rosen, 1989). People who are high in self-efficacy will generally experience greater satisfaction from their performance attainments than those low in self-efficacy. One explanation for this phenomenon is that high self-efficacy has been found to lead to more internal attributions for successful outcomes, which subsequently result in more favorable affective reactions (Silver, Mitchell, and Gist, 1990).

Organization-based self-esteem also has been related to organizational and general satisfaction (Pierce and others, 1989). From her review, Tharenou (1979) found that both global and work-specific self-esteem were positively associated with job satisfaction, the organization, and work role. Conversely, global self-esteem is also related to propensities for anxiety, depression, and neurotic behavior (Fitts, 1972a, 1972b, 1972c; Wylie, 1961).

Global self-esteem has been shown to affect interpretations of feedback, which, in turn, influence affective responses (Campbell, 1990; Jones, 1973). For instance, Adler (1980) found that those high in self-esteem were significantly more internal in their attributions for satisfaction than those low in self-esteem; the level of self-esteem did not affect attributions for dissatisfaction. Different reactions to feedback also have been explained from an enhancement argument: people lower in self-esteem are thought to have greater enhancement needs and are therefore more pleasurably or painfully affected by positive or negative feedback, respectively (Campbell, 1990).

Affective Correlates

Research on affective correlates of both self-efficacy and self-esteem is sparse—indeed, we found no research on the affective correlates of self-efficacy. In studies in which there is an association, but no causal direction implied from the study design, Tharenou (1979) found positive correlations ranging from .10 to .50 between global and task-specific self-esteem and general job satisfaction.

Organizational Antecedents, Consequences, and Correlates

Finally, in this section, we consider the organizational antecedents, consequences, and correlates of self-efficacy and self-esteem. Some of these factors include organizational position, job complexity, worker autonomy, compensation and promotion policies, and organizational productivity and performance.

Organizational Antecedents

Although no research on organizational antecedents to self-efficacy is presently available, there is evidence suggesting that the fit between a person and the organizational position affects subsequent task-specific self-esteem. (For a review see Tharenou, 1979.) For example, Morse (1975) found that when job characteristics such as complexity were aligned with personality predispositions for new employees, their sense of task competence increased significantly over a control group when assessed eight months later. Morse (1970) also found a high sense of task competence resulting from managers who operated under organizational characteristics (such as structure and climate) and task characteristics (such as complex versus routine) that were compatible with personality predispositions. Other job and organizational characteristics found to affect the worker's sense of competence (defined and operationalized in a manner highly similar to self-efficacy and task-specific self-esteem) were reported by Sekaran and Wagner (1980). Their findings indicate that, in both the United States and India, the amount of autonomy and meaningfulness experienced significantly affected the employee's sense of competence.

In Hall and Nougaim's (1968) longitudinal study of AT&T managers, it was found that high performers who were rewarded with greater pay developed higher global self-esteem and achievement satisfaction relative to lower-performing, unrewarded managers. Of course, there are many potential conundrums in this study— not the least of which is that these managers were also likely to be promoted and have much more promising futures than their lesser-performing counterparts. Tharenou also found that Leavitt's (1973) training program that included promotion, pay increases, better uniforms, and more job skills for nurses' aides increased global self-esteem. Again, there was no attempt to separate the effects of the different components of the training program.

Organizational Consequences

Many of the affective, behavioral, and cognitive consequences of self-efficacy and self-esteem (satisfaction, individual attendance, health and performance, occupational choice) have significant organizational consequences. People low in self-efficacy often have lower expectations of success (Bandura, 1986), for example, and may consequently exert less effort on personal and organizational goals, withdraw from socialization activities, and ultimately perform at lower levels on the job and experience higher turnover rates. Research examining organizational performance as a consequence of global self-esteem has generally not found significant relationships, whereas measures of specific types of self-esteem and self-efficacy have been much more predictive.

Tharenou's (1979) review suggests that global self-esteem has some influence over choice of occupation and the choice of intrinsic and extrinsic factors within those jobs. It appears that the intrinsic characteristics of the job (skill variety, challenge, interest, autonomy) and, to a lesser extent, extrinsic factors (such as job status and level) affect global self-esteem. Further, such characteristics as autonomy, challenge, skill variety, job complexity, role clarity, and lack of overload are positively associated with task-specific, work-specific, and global self-esteem.

Organizational Correlates

Tharenou (1979) also documents an association between levels of self-esteem and organizational outcomes, but without specifying the direction of these relationships. For example, task-specific self-esteem (Argyris, 1960; Gardell, 1971, 1973), work-role self-esteem (Beehr, 1976; French and Caplan, 1972; Hackman and Lawler, 1971; Hite, 1975), and global self-esteem (Kohn and Schooler, 1973; Kornhauser, 1965; Vroom, 1962) have been positively correlated (.15 to

.30) with job content that is varied, skilled, and involves learning and participation in decision making. Worker autonomy has been correlated (.30) with global self-esteem (Levitan, 1970) and work-role self-esteem (French and Caplan, 1972; Gardell, 1971). Low work-role self-esteem has been associated with role ambiguity (Beehr, 1976) and with qualitative role overload (French and Caplan, 1972). In contrast, work-role self-esteem has been found to be positively correlated with the amount of co-worker interaction and supervisory support (Beehr, 1976; Gardell, 1971; Hackman and Lawler, 1971). Finally, Tharenou (1979) reviews literature suggesting that low pay, piece rate payments, and dissatisfaction with pay have been negatively correlated with a sense of task-specific and work-role self-esteem.

Implications

In this chapter we have tried to clarify the relationships between self-efficacy, self-esteem, and organizational behavior. Viewing these personality constructs as dimensions of ego energy has revealed diverse antecedents and consequences. For example, we have seen that a number of diverse antecedents contribute to the development of self-efficacy compared with types of self-esteem. If one is concerned with influencing these personality variables, it seems necessary to recognize the disparate effects that may occur as a result of altering the different antecedents. Similarly, a number of different consequences emanate from self-efficacy and different types of self-esteem. If one is interested in affecting these consequences through the personality variables, it seems important to understand not only the antecedents that affect self-efficacy and types of self-esteem but also the diverse outcomes these constructs affect. With a clear understanding of these relationships, those interested in influencing these personality constructs may allocate resources more effectively.

From the discussion of the antecedents, consequences, and correlates of self-efficacy and self-esteem, several implications emerge for managers and researchers. In this section we discuss three managerial implications. First, the evidence supports the idea that task-specific and organizational behavior may be affected most

directly by *self-efficacy* and *specific levels of self-esteem.* For increased predictive power, the more specific the behavior in question,
the more specific the targeted self-efficacy or self-esteem should be.
Thus self-efficacy or self-esteem for specific tasks and behavior can
be used to enhance selection, training and development, performance appraisal, employee attendance and productivity, assessment
centers, and other human resource applications. Apart from the
higher predictive utility of task-specific measures, self-efficacy and
task-specific self-esteem are also more malleable. This means that
specific programs can be developed to increase desired behavior and
reduce undesired behavior associated with self-efficacy and task-
specific self-esteem. (See, for example, Frayne and Latham, 1987;
Gist, Schwoerer, and Rosen, 1989.)

Second, the findings presented in this chapter indicate that
managers can indeed improve the self-efficacy and self-esteem of
their workers to positively affect individual and organizational outcomes. We have noted a number of antecedents to self-efficacy and
self-esteem over which managers exert direct or indirect influence.
Primary among these are sharing their positive evaluations of employees, providing opportunities for employees to experience positive mastery experiences, and matching the challenge of the job to
the skills, knowledge, and abilities of the employee. This means
that organizational training programs should assess worker self-
efficacy or task self-esteem at different stages of learning and modify
the training content and context accordingly. It also suggests a need
for increased coordination between the measurement of self-efficacy
and training and development, performance goals and appraisals,
and career management (Mone and Baker, 1989). Collectively, these
efforts can lead to improvements in employees' self-esteem, satisfaction, and organizational productivity (Tharenou and Harker, 1984).

Third, managers and society can benefit from the knowledge
that self-efficacy and self-esteem are not just antecedents to personal
and organizational outcomes; they are consequences as well. This
implies an opportunity and a responsibility: management must
monitor these personality variables to ensure they are providing an
environment that maximizes the efficacy and esteem potentials of
their employees. Such an environment could afford opportunities
for economically disadvantaged people or those with low self-

esteem, develop programs to train people who are chronically unemployed, and create openings and resources for those with disabilities. Through such programs, organizations may benefit by drawing from a culturally diverse workforce, improving the social acceptance of the organization, and increasing legal compliance with federal law (such as the Americans with Disabilities Act of 1990).

There are also three implications for future research. First, there exist conceptual, definitional, and methodological similarities between self-efficacy and the situation-specific types of self-esteem. Accordingly, the antecedents, consequences, and correlates of these constructs appear to be highly similar, although they have not been directly compared in research. From the research we have reviewed, clearly there is considerable divergence in the measurement of this specific type of self-esteem, which precludes further comparison. This leaves unanswered the question of how different these constructs really are from each other. Potentially fruitful research could be conducted in this area to further investigate the similarities and differences between self-efficacy and task-based self-esteem.

The second research implication concerns the difference between specific and global conceptualizations and measures of self-esteem. The evidence strongly suggests that different factors lead to and follow from each of the different types of self-esteem. This research indicates the need for a close match between level of organizational or individual variables and the type of self-esteem that is proposed as an antecedent or consequence. If task performance predictions are relevant, then task-based self-efficacy should be assessed; if occupational choice is relevant, then global self-esteem should be measured. Although this point has been argued elsewhere (Tharenou, 1979), it seems to bear repeating here as organizational scholars and managers still tend to discuss self-esteem without specifying type or level.

The third research implication involves the paucity of longitudinal, comparative, and integrative research in this area. As indicated by the articles cited here, there has been little attempt to conduct longitudinal research on these dynamic phenomena or to employ rigorous experimental designs to firmly establish the directional nature of the relationships. One gap concerns the organizational antecedents to self-efficacy—an important area for future research since organizations provide opportunities for task mastery. Moreover, little multivariate research has examined behavioral, cognitive, affective, and organizational factors simultaneously as antecedents or consequences (or both antecedents *and* consequences) of self-efficacy and types of self-esteem. The classification scheme developed in this chapter brings order to a body of diverse literature. Further theoretical development and research designs merging several or all of these factors may well contribute to an even greater understanding of the complex dynamics underlying these personality processes.

References

Adler, S. "Self-Esteem and Causal Attributions for Job Satisfaction." *Journal of Applied Psychology*, 1980, *65*, 327–332.

Argyris, C. "Individual Actualization in Complex Organizations." *Mental Hygiene*, 1960, *44*, 226–237.

Bandura, A. "Self-Efficacy: Toward a Unifying Theory of Behavioral Change." *Psychological Review*, 1977, *84*, 191–215.

Bandura, A. "Self-Efficacy Mechanism in Human Agency." *American Psychologist*, 1982, *37*, 122–147.

Bandura, A. *Social Foundations of Thought and Action: A Social Cognitive Theory.* Englewood Cliffs, N.J.: Prentice-Hall, 1986.

Bandura, A. "Self-Regulation of Motivation and Action Through Goal Systems." In V. Hamilton, G. Bower, and N. Frijda (eds.), *Cognitive Perspective on Emotion and Motivation.* Dordrecht, Netherlands: Kluwer, 1988.

Bandura, A. "Self-Regulation of Motivation and Action Through Internal Standards and Goal Systems." In L. A. Pervin (ed.), *Goal Concepts in Personality and Social Psychology.* Hillsdale, N.J.: Erlbaum, 1989.

Bandura, A. "Conclusion: Reflections on Nonability Determinants of Competence." In R. J. Sternberg and J. Kolligian, Jr. (eds.), *Competence Considered.* New Haven, Conn.: Yale University Press, 1990.

Bandura, A., and Cervone, D. "Self-Evaluative and Self-Efficacy Mechanisms Governing the Motivational Effects of Goal Systems." *Journal of Personality and Social Psychology*, 1983, *45*, 1017–1028.

Bandura, A., and Cervone, D. "Differential Engagement of Self-Reactive Influences in Cognitive Motivation." *Organizational Behavior and Human Decision Processes*, 1986, *38*, 92–113.

Beehr, T. A. "Perceived Situational Moderators of the Relationship Between Subjective Role Ambiguity and Role Strain." *Journal of Applied Psychology*, 1976, *61*, 35–40.

Berger, E. M. "Relationships Among Acceptance of Self, Acceptance of Others, and MMPI Scores." *Journal of Counseling Psychology*, 1955, *3*, 279–283.

Brockner, J. "Low Self-Esteem and Behavioral Plasticity: Some Implications." In L. Wheeler and P. R. Shaver (eds.), *Review of Personality and Social Psychology*, vol. 4. Newbury Park, Calif.: Sage, 1983.

Brockner, J. *Self-Esteem at Work: Research, Theory, and Practice*. Lexington, Mass.: Lexington Books, 1988.

Brockner, J., and Guare, J. "Improving the Performance of Low Self-Esteem Individuals: An Attributional Approach." *Academy of Management Journal*, 1983, *26*, 642–656.

Campbell, J. D. "Self-Esteem and Clarity of the Self-Concept." *Journal of Personality and Social Psychology*, 1990, *59*, 538–549.

Cervone, D., and Peake, P. K. "Anchoring, Efficacy, and Action: The Influence of Judgmental Heuristics on Self-Efficacy Judgement and Behavior." *Journal of Personality and Social Psychology*, 1986, *50*, 492–501.

Cooley, C. H. *Human Nature and the Social Order*. New York: Schocken Books, 1964. (Originally published 1902.)

Crandall, R. "The Measurement of Self-Esteem and Related Constructs." In J. P. Robinson and P. R. Shaver (eds.), *Measures of Social Psychological Attitudes*. Ann Arbor: University of Michigan Press, 1973.

Dipboye, R. L. "A Critical Review of Korman's Self-Consistency Theory of Work Motivation and Occupational Choice." *Organizational Behavior and Human Performance*, 1977, *18*, 108–126.

Earley, P. C., Wojnaroski, P., and Prest, W. "Task Planning and Energy Expended: Exploration of How Goals Influence Performance." *Journal of Applied Psychology*, 1987, *72*, 107–114.

Ekpo-ufot, A. "Self-Perceived Abilities Relevant to the Task (SPARTS): A Potential Predictor of Labor Turnover in an Industrial Work Setting." *Personnel Psychology*, 1976, *29*, 405–416.

Farr, J. L., and Ford, C. M. "Individual Innovation." In M. A. West and J. L. Farr (eds.), *Innovation and Creativity at Work: Psychological and Organizational Strategies*. Chichester, England: Wiley, 1988.

Festinger, L. "A Theory of Social Comparison Processes." *Human Relations*, 1954, *7*, 117–140.

Fitts, W. H. *The Self-Concept and Psychopathology*. Nashville, Tenn.: Counselor Recordings and Tests, 1972a.

Fitts, W. H. *The Self-Concept and Performance*. Nashville, Tenn.: Counselor Recordings and Tests, 1972b.

Fitts, W. H. *The Self-Concept and Behavior: Overview and Supplement*. Nashville, Tenn.: Counselor Recordings and Tests, 1972c.

Frayne, C. A., and Latham, G. P. "Application of Social Learning Theory to Employee Self-Management of Attendance." *Journal of Applied Psychology*, 1987, *72*, 387–392.

French, J.R.P., and Caplan, R. D. "Organization Stress and Strain." In A. J. Marrow (ed.), *The Failure of Success*. New York: AMACOM, 1972.

Gardell, B. "Alienation and Mental Health in the Modern Industrial Environment." In L. Levi (ed.), *Society, Stress and Disease*. Oxford: Oxford University Press, 1971.

Gardell, B. "Job Satisfaction Among Forest Workers." *Reports from the Psychological Laboratories*. Stockholm: University of Stockholm, 1973.

Gecas, V., and Schwalbe, M. L. "Beyond the Looking-Glass Self: Social Structure and Efficacy-Based Self-Esteem." *Social Psychology Quarterly*, 1983, *46*, 77–88.

Gecas, V., and Schwalbe, M. L. "Parental Behavior and Adolescent Self-Esteem." *Journal of Marriage and the Family*, 1986, *48*, 37–46.

Ghiselli, E. E. "The Validity of Management Traits in Relation to Occupational Level." *Personnel Psychology*, 1963, *16*, 109–112.

Gist, M. E. "Self-Efficacy: Implications for Organizational Behavior and Human Resource Management." *Academy of Management Review*, 1987, *12*, 472–485.

Gist, M. E. "The Influence of Training Method on Self-Efficacy and Idea Generation Among Managers." *Personnel Psychology,* 1989, *42,* 787-805.

Gist, M. E., and Mitchell, T. R. "Self-Efficacy: A Theoretical Analysis of Its Determinants and Malleability." *Academy of Management Review,* 1992, *17,* 183-211.

Gist, M. E., Schwoerer, C. E., and Rosen, B. "Effects of Alternative Training Methods on Self-Efficacy and Performance in Computer Software Training." *Journal of Applied Psychology,* 1989, *74,* 884-891.

Hackman, J. R., and Lawler, E. E. "Employee Reactions to Job Characteristics." *Journal of Applied Psychology,* 1971, *55,* 259-286.

Hall, D. T. "A Theoretical Model of Career Subidentity Development in Organizational Settings." *Organizational Behavior and Human Performance,* 1971, *6,* 50-76.

Hall, D. T., and Foster, L. W. "A Psychological Success Cycle and Goal Setting: Goals, Performance and Attitudes." *Academy of Management Journal,* 1977, *20,* 282-290.

Hall, D. T., and Nougaim, K. E. "An Examination of Maslow's Need Hierarchy in an Organizational Setting." *Organizational Behavior and Performance,* 1968, *3,* 12-35.

Harter, S. "Causes, Correlates, and the Functional Roles of Global Self-Worth: A Life-Span Perspective." In R. J. Sternberg and J. Kolligian, Jr. (eds.), *Competence Considered.* New Haven, Conn.: Yale University Press, 1990.

Hite, A. L. "Some Characteristics of Work Roles and Their Relationships to Self-Esteem and Depression." Unpublished doctoral dissertation, University of Michigan, 1975.

Hollenbeck, J. R., and Brief, A. P. "The Effects of Individual Differences and Goal Origin on Goal Setting and Performance." *Organizational Behavior and Human Decision Processes,* 1987, *40,* 392-414.

Jacobs, R., and Solomon, J. "Strategies for Enhancing the Prediction of Job Performance from Job Satisfaction." *Journal of Applied Psychology,* 1977, *62,* 417-427.

James, W. *The Principles of Psychology.* New York: Holt, Rinehart & Winston, 1963. (Originally published 1890.)

Jones, S. C. "Self and Interpersonal Evaluations: Esteem Theories vs. Consistency Theories." *Psychological Bulletin*, 1973, *79*, 185–199.

Kanfer, R., and Ackerman, P. L. "Motivation and Cognitive Abilities: An Integrative/Aptitude-Treatment Interaction Approach to Skill Acquisition." *Journal of Applied Psychology*, 1989, *74*, 657–690.

Kohn, M. L., and Schooler, C. "Occupational Experience and Psychological Functioning: An Assessment of Reciprocal Effects." *American Sociological Review*, 1973, *38*, 97–118.

Korman, A. K. "Hypothesis of Work Behavior Revisited and an Extension." *Academy of Management Review*, 1976, *1*, 50–63.

Korman, A. K. "An Examination of Dipboye's 'A Critical Review of Korman's Self-Consistency Theory of Work Motivation and Occupational Choice.' " *Organizational Behavior and Human Performance*, 1977, *18*, 127–128.

Kornhauser, A. *Mental Health of the Industrial Worker*. New York: Wiley, 1965.

Leavitt, A. "Alienation and Self-Esteem: Effects of a Work-Related Training Program." Unpublished doctoral dissertation, New York University, 1973.

Lee, C. "Efficacy Expectations and Outcome Expectations as Predictors of Performance in a Snake-Handling Task." *Cognitive Therapy and Research*, 1984, *8*, 509–516.

Lefkowitz, J. "Self-Esteem of Industrial Workers." *Journal of Applied Psychology*, 1967, *51*, 521–528.

Lent, R. W., Brown, S. D., and Larkin, K. C. "Comparison of Three Theoretically Derived Variables in Predicting Career and Academic Behavior: Self-Efficacy, Interest Congruence, and Consequence Thinking." *Journal of Counseling Psychology*, 1987, *34*, 293–298.

Levitan, V. "Status in Human Organization as a Determinant of Mental Health and Performance." Unpublished doctoral dissertation, University of Michigan, 1970.

Locke, E. A., and Latham, G. P. *A Theory of Goal Setting and Task Performance*. Englewood Cliffs, N.J.: Prentice-Hall, 1990.

Locke, E. A., Frederick, E., Lee, C., and Bobko, P. "The Effect of

Self-Efficacy, Goals, and Task-Strategies on Task Performance."
Journal of Applied Psychology, 1984, *69*, 241–251.

Mead, G. H. *Mind, Self, and Society.* Chicago: University of Chicago Press, 1934.

Mitchell, T. R. "Organizational Behavior." In *Annual Review of Psychology*, vol. 4. Palo Alto, Calif.: Annual Reviews, 1979.

Mitchell, T. R. "Expectancy-Value Models in Organizational Psychology." In N. T. Feather (ed.), *Expectations and Actions: Expectancy-Value Models in Psychology*. Hillsdale, N.J.: Erlbaum, 1982.

Mone, M. A., and Baker, D. D. "Stage of Task Learning as a Moderator of the Goal-Performance Relationship." *Human Performance*, 1989, *2*, 85–99.

Mone, M. A., and Baker, D. D. "Antecedents and Consequences of Personal Goals: An Empirical Examination." *Motivation and Emotion*, 1992, *16*, 297–321.

Morse, J. J. "Organizational Characteristics and Individual Motivation." In J. W. Lorsch and P. R. Lawrence (eds.), *Studies in Organizational Design*. Homewood, Ill.: Dorsey Press, 1970.

Morse, J. J. "Person-Job Congruence and Individual Adjustment and Development." *Human Relations*, 1975, *28*, 841–861.

Pelham, B. W., and Swann, W. B., Jr. "From Self-Conceptions to Self-Worth: On the Sources and Structure of Global Self-Esteem." *Journal of Personality and Social Psychology*, 1989, *57*, 672–680.

Pervin, L. A. "Goal Concepts in Personality and Social Psychology: A Historical Introduction." In L. A. Pervin (ed.), *Goal Concepts in Personality and Social Psychology*. Hillsdale, N.J.: Erlbaum, 1989.

Pierce, J. L., Gardner, D. G., Cummings, L. L., and Dunham, R. B. "Organization-Based Self-Esteem: Construct Definition, Measurement, and Validation." *Academy of Management Journal*, 1989, *32*, 622–648.

Quinn, R. P., and Shepard, L. J. *The 1972-1973 Quality of Employment Survey: Descriptive Statistics with Comparison Data from the 1969-1970 Survey of Working Conditions*. Ann Arbor, Mich.: Institute for Social Research, 1974.

Rosenberg, M. *Society and the Adolescent Self-Image.* Princeton, N.J.: Princeton University Press, 1965.

Rosenberg, M. *Conceiving the Self.* New York: Basic Books, 1979.

Schalon, C. "Effect of Self-Esteem upon Performance Following Failure Stress." *Journal of Consulting and Clinical Psychology,* 1968, *32,* 497.

Schrauger, J., and Rosenberg, S. "Self-Esteem and the Effects of Success and Failure Feedback on Performance." *Journal of Personality,* 1970, *33,* 404–414.

Schunk, D. H. "Enhancing Self-Efficacy and Achievement Through Rewards and Goals: Motivational and Educational Effects." *Journal of Educational Research,* 1984, *78,* 29–34.

Sekaran, U., and Wagner, F. R. "Sense of Competence: A Cross-Cultural Analysis for Managerial Application." *Group and Organization Studies,* 1980, *5,* 340–352.

Silver, W. S., Mitchell, T. R., and Gist, M. E. "Interpreting Performance Information: The Influence of Self-Efficacy on Causal Attributions for Successful and Unsuccessful Performance." Unpublished manuscript, University of Washington, Seattle, 1990.

Simpson, C. K., and Boyle, D. "Esteem Construct Generality and Academic Performance." *Educational and Psychological Measurement,* 1975, *35,* 897–904.

Stumpf, S. A., Brief, A. P., and Hartman, K. "Self-Efficacy Expectations and Coping with Career-Related Events." *Journal of Vocational Behavior,* 1987, *31,* 91–108.

Taylor, M. S., Locke, E. A., Lee, C., and Gist, M. E. "Type A Behavior and Faculty Research Productivity: What Are the Mechanisms?" *Organizational Behavior and Human Decision Processes,* 1984, *34,* 402–418.

Tharenou, P. "Employee Self-Esteem: A Review of the Literature." *Journal of Vocational Behavior,* 1979, *15,* 1–29.

Tharenou, P., and Harker, P. "Organizational Correlates of Employee Self-Esteem." *Journal of Applied Psychology,* 1982, *67,* 797–805.

Tharenou, P., and Harker, P. "Moderating Influence of Self-Esteem on Relationships Between Job Complexity, Performance, and Satisfaction." *Journal of Applied Psychology,* 1984, *69,* 623–632.

Vroom, V. H. "Ego Involvement, Job Satisfaction, and Job Performance." *Personnel Psychology*, 1962, *15*, 159–177.

Weiss, H. M., and Adler, S. "Personality and Organizational Behavior." In B. M. Staw and L. L. Cummings (eds.), *Research in Organizational Behavior*, vol. 6. Greenwich, Conn.: JAI Press, 1984.

Wells, L. E., and Marwell, G. *Self-Esteem*. London: Sage, 1976.

Wood, R., and Bandura, A. "Social Cognitive Theory of Organizational Management." *Academy of Management Review*, 1989, *14*, 361–384.

Wood, R. E., and Locke, E. A. "Goal Setting and Strategy Effects on Complex Tasks: A Theoretical Analysis." In B. M. Staw and L. L. Cummings (eds.), *Research in Organizational Behavior*, vol. 12. Greenwich, Conn.: JAI Press, 1990.

Wylie, R. C. *The Self-Concept: A Critical Review of Pertinent Research Literature*. Lincoln: University of Nebraska Press, 1961.

6

Proactive Self-Appraisal in Organizations

James R. Bailey, Michael J. Strube,
John H. Yost, Michael Merbaum

PHILOSOPHERS AND HISTORIANS agree that much human striving can be portrayed as an attempt to render the unknown known. Whether through science or religion, the alleviation of uncertainty, actual or imaginary, prepares humans to interact effectively with a complex and threatening environment. Indeed, this general principle explains organizational efforts to survey business environments so that they may predict and even control those environments. The desire to reduce uncertainty, however, is not limited to the physical, spiritual, or commercial realms but is with equal ambition trained upon the self.

It is the central premise of this chapter that people are critically motivated to seek knowledge about themselves in order to reduce uncertainty regarding their abilities in relation to the environmental demands. Such self-knowledge allows them to act more

The writing of this chapter was supported in part by a Henry E. Rutgers Fellowship awarded to James R. Bailey and by National Institute of Mental Health Grant T32 MH19728 awarded to John H. Yost. The authors thank three anonymous reviewers for their insightful comments.

deftly and safely. Equally as important as self-knowledge, however, is self-esteem: the desire to hold one's self in positive regard. These two motives, self-knowledge and self-esteem, do not always act in concert. One major purpose of this chapter, then, is to explicate when and how both motives operate in an organizational domain.

In this context, ego energy is defined as the process by which people discover and display key features of the self-concept and yet maintain self-regard. Ego energy is what we expend to learn about, promote, and protect the self. In this way ego energy provides what we term a self-appraisal function. We will review research that demonstrates how ego-energized self-appraisal influences task choice, task construction, persistence, and even performance in the absence of external incentives. In this discussion, special attention will be paid to the role of feedback and individual differences and to how seemingly self-defeating behavior can be seen as adaptive, at least from the individual's standpoint. We then propose a model that resolves the conflicting motives of self-knowledge and self-esteem by focusing on the construction of performance arenas where abilities and situational demands are well matched. Finally, we will argue that organizations can capitalize on self-appraisal behavior through selection practices that are sensitive to the self-concept, as well as through job-design strategies and job-choice policies that allow employees to explore, exercise, and maintain their self-concepts.

Theories of Self-Evaluation

Several prominent social-psychological theories hold that people must understand their abilities before they can negotiate the environment. (See, for example, social comparison theory, Festinger, 1954; attribution theory, Heider, 1958; Jones and Davis, 1965; Kelley, 1967; competence motivation, White, 1959.) Further, to the extent that people doubt their abilities, they will engage in various forms of self-evaluation to assuage those doubts. Although these assumptions appear to be widely accepted, the specific manner of self-evaluation has been a source of debate from which have emerged two major contrasting viewpoints: the self-assessment view and the self-enhancement view.

Accurate Self-Assessment

Underlying the self-assessment view is the assumption that people are driven to assess both strengths and weaknesses accurately as a means of managing the environment (Trope, 1975; Trope and Brickman, 1975). Specifically, people seek information that is maximally diagnostic of abilities—that is, information that enables them to clearly distinguish their levels of ability.

Considerable empirical evidence supports the hypotheses derived from the self-assessment view. Chief among these is the hypothesis that when given a choice, people prefer diagnostic tasks over less informative tasks (Trope, 1975, 1979, 1980; Trope and Brickman, 1975). Further, this preference occurs regardless of task difficulty (Trope, 1975) and in accordance with the likelihood of reducing uncertainty about ability (Trope, 1979). Trope and Ben-Yair (1982, Experiment 1) have also found that when given an opportunity, people *construct* tasks that incorporate ability-related diagnostic properties.

The self-assessment model also predicts that a person's persistence and performance is a function of uncertainty reduction. Trope and Ben-Yair (1982, Experiment 2) have demonstrated that as task feedback increases in diagnosticity, the number of task attempts required to reduce uncertainty about abilities decreases. Hence diagnosticity and persistence are inversely related. Similarly, Trope (1982) found that performance improved for people who were highly uncertain (versus highly certain) about their abilities and, moreover, that performance was better (though less persistent) when a task was highly diagnostic.

Biased Self-Enhancement

There is, then, convincing evidence that people exercise initiative in choosing and constructing tasks that provide them with useful information about their competencies and, further, that achievement on these tasks is related to the extent that they reduce uncertainty about these competencies. Yet accurate self-assessment appears incompatible with evidence that people harbor many illusions about the self. For example, most normal, healthy people have an illusion of control or competence that argues against truly accurate self-assessment. (See research by Langer, 1983; Taylor and Brown, 1988.) Indeed, when people are accurate in their beliefs about ability/outcome contingencies their well-being suffers (Alloy and Abramson, 1979; Alloy, Abramson, and Viscusi, 1981). Accordingly, people should select tasks and behave in a fashion that highlights strengths and downplays weaknesses. This view—referred to as self-enhancement—argues that a positive sense of self-esteem is required to engage the environment and, therefore, that self-appraisal will be tempered to maintain a favorable image of the self.

The notion that self-appraisal is biased toward protecting self-esteem has also received support. One well-documented example is the self-serving bias: a tendency for people to take credit for success and deny blame for failure (Bradley, 1978; Snyder, Stephan, and Rosenfield, 1978). Despite its post hoc nature, the self-serving bias reflects a tendency to evaluate oneself in a positive manner. A more dramatic example of this tendency is people who strategically undermine their likelihood of success (Jones and Berglas, 1978)— that is, they construct impediments to performance in order to discount failures and, conversely, to augment successes. The implication of such self-handicapping strategies is that failure can be attributed to the impediment, whereas success allows the claim of extraordinary ability in surmounting the impediment. Preference for performance-inhibiting drugs (Berglas and Jones, 1978), hypochondriacal complaints (Smith, Snyder, and Perkins, 1983), test anxiety, and reduced effort (Smith, Snyder, and Handelsman, 1982) have all been identified as potential self-handicapping strategies. This research suggests that concern for self-esteem moderates the self-evaluation process.

It is clear from the preceding review that people are keenly aware of the diagnostic implications of their task-related behavior. It is equally clear, however, that the self-assessment and self-enhancement literatures stand in marked contrast to one another. Recently there have been efforts to reconcile these disparate perspectives by recognizing that individuals may differ in their approach to self-appraisal and delineating the complementary relation of accuracy and bias in maintaining adaptive responses to the environment.

Proactive Self-Appraisal

Strube and his colleagues have attempted to discover the conditions under which each view provides an adequate description of ego-energized self-evaluative behavior. (For a review see Strube, 1987; Strube and Yost, 1992.) Using the task-choice paradigm, Strube and Roemmele (1985) found that people with high self-esteem as well as people with low self-esteem but no tendency to use self-protective strategies (that is, to self-handicap) preferred test forms high in diagnosticity of both success and failure, whereas people with low self-esteem who also had a proclivity to use self-handicapping strategies preferred test forms that were high in diagnosticity of success but low in diagnosticity of failure. Thus self-assessment and self-enhancement were both supported, though for different types of people. Other research (Strube and others, 1986) indicates that task choice is governed by people's perceptions of diagnosticity in a way that supports both accurate and biased self-appraisal.

Because of the operation of individual differences, Strube, White, Shimabukaro, and Bailey (1988) developed and validated a measure of desire for self-appraisal (DSA); see Strube and Yost (1992) for a review of validation studies. Of special interest is research that examines the performance consequences of a varying emphasis on accurate self-appraisal. In particular, uncertainty about abilities that often accompanies performance feedback should affect subsequent performance differently for people high versus low in desire for appraisal. In a field study (Strube and Yost, 1992), high self-appraisers were found to perform more poorly than low self-appraisers on a second exam if performance on the first exam was above average. Presumably, when high self-appraisers were uncertain about ability (a likely occurrence on a first exam), they employed behavioral strategies designed to disentangle the role of ability and other contributing factors (for example, effort). So a high self-appraiser might actually withhold effort, thereby risking a performance decline, in order to extract meaningful ability-related feedback—essentially exploring whether success can be achieved by ability alone. A more definitive test of these findings was offered by Strube, Smith, and Bailey (1989) in a laboratory study that manipulated (as opposed to observed) certainty about ability. Once again, the results strongly indicate that reducing uncertainty is a particularly powerful concern for high self-appraisers—so much so that they will forgo future success in order to isolate the cause of a previous success. By contrast, when high self-appraisers were quite certain of their ability and its role in an initial success, subsequent performances were quite high.

This pattern of results implies that different performance conditions may be optimal for people with differing desire for self-appraisal. In particular, high self-appraisers may thrive under conditions of relative certainty, a situation that matches their desire for accurate appraisal of abilities and allows them to focus entirely on success as a goal. A situation that contains considerable uncertainty, however, appears to motivate in high self-appraisers behavior that may undermine success. Under conditions of uncertainty, then, the goals of success and accurate appraisal may not be compatible, and, at least for high self-appraisers, the desire for accuracy appears to win out. Simply stated, the energy supplied by the ego to evaluate and protect the self is not uniform but varies from person to person as a function of the desire for self-appraisal. Further, this desire interacts with circumstances (that is, task conditions) to determine performance.

This program of research suggests a dynamic interplay between self-assessment and self-enhancement. Therefore, this team of researchers (Strube, Yost, and Bailey, 1992; Yost, Strube, and Bailey, 1992) has proposed a framework for understanding how people cope with their changing environment while maintaining a positive (though biased) self-image. We argue that self-evaluation is a manifestation of a basic hedonistic drive and that the successful indulgence of pleasure and avoidance of pain serve as subjective markers that uncertainty about the relation between self and environment has been satisfactorily resolved. In other words, one must first know where and how to realize one's hedonism—a result best served by self-assessment—before one can do so—a result best served by self-enhancement.

All of this leads to a reasonable conclusion about the nature of ego energy as it is directed toward self-appraisal. The acquisition of accurate information about one's abilities and limitations allows one to select, or construct, performance arenas where abilities and situational demands are well matched. As people become more adept at judging the self/situation fit, they can avoid those settings where failure is certain or where success is achieved without challenge. Thus they can select, or construct, performance settings that maximize demonstration of their abilities and minimize display of their liabilities. Effective selection or construction of performance arenas, therefore, depends on a realistic and accurate view of abilities in relation to environmental demands. Ultimately, these two components act in concert: information about the person/environment fit can be used to tailor self-enhancement attempts, and the relative success of self-enhancement reflects the validity of the guiding information. Figure 6.1 summarizes this model. With the rudiments of self-appraisal in mind, we now turn our attention to the development of this process—especially the relationship between ego energy and the environment.

Development of Self-Appraisal

We contend that the development of self-appraisal is part of a general process called evolutionary self-construction (see Yost, Strube, and Bailey, 1992). Drawing from a pragmatic interpretation of natural selection (for instance, William James's essay "Great Men and Their Environment"), as well as revisionist, contemporary views of natural selection (for example, Gould, 1989), we view self-construction as a dialectic between organismic and environmental factors. The focus of self-construction is self-variation, or "possible selves" (Markus and Nurius, 1986), and the presentation of these variations to the environment. One advantage of adopting this evolutionary perspective is that it explicitly provides a mechanism for the proactivity of the ego in the construction process.

According to evolutionary self-construction, the processes of producing a variation and selecting for a variation are interdependent. People may produce a self-variation in response to their own idiosyncratic experiences with the environment. Once that variation is produced and introduced to the environment, the selection process will determine its fitness. For instance, a normally jovial line supervisor may observe that seriousness is valued in his organization. This supervisor may respond by adopting a more se-

Figure 6.1. A General Model of Proactive Self-Appraisal.

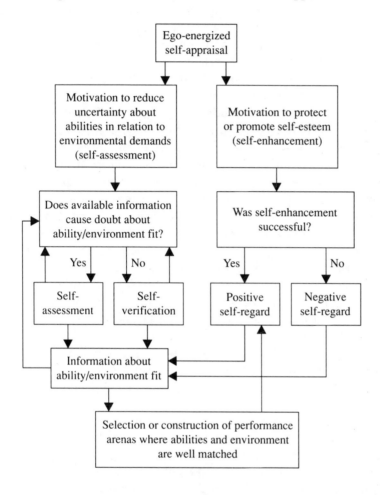

rious attitude in his work. If this variation proves fruitful—that is, if his new self allows for better work-related interaction—then it can be said that this variation was selected for.

It should be evident that people do not merely react to the environment; they also change, shape, and create the environment. At the most basic level, people are proactive both in their idiosyncratic interpretations of the environment and in their presentation of self-variations to the environment. Presenting self-variations can alter the environment, especially when those variations are accepted. Just as the advent of a new species changes the faunal and floral equilibrium of a region, the selection of self-variation changes the environment and prepares the way for future self-variations that might otherwise not have been selected. Thus the environment may select for self-variation, but it is fundamentally altered because of that selection.

Why does the ego produce self-variation? According to William James (1981), self-seeking is a fundamental instinct because it provides for the future as opposed to maintaining the present. James's self-seeking can be thought of as an empirical validation of proposed selves—a form of hypothesis testing—where proposed selves will most certainly be presented to the environment because the banishment of uncertainty from the future is a central principle of all animal behavior (1956, p. 78). Self-appraisal, then, is an evolving process for two reasons. First, people will continue to seek out or construct environments where their abilities can be exhibited in order to promote self-esteem and prepare for the future. Second, changes in the environment (a new job or a novel assignment) or dramatic personal events (a disturbing failure or social rejection) will instigate periodic reappraisal of abilities.

Within this integrative framework, it makes sense that people possess an inflated self-image: successful self-appraisal will produce more successes than failures, and this biased pool of outcomes will imply relatively greater competence than may actually be warranted. Nevertheless, this framework paints a picture of the self-appraiser as a proactive agent who analyzes talents against a backdrop of situations and consciously coordinates the two. When effectively and efficiently executed, the self-appraisal process results in both self-knowledge and, in most cases, high self-esteem. We qualify this for a reason, as there are instances where people persist in self-defeating behavior in order to confirm their negative self-evaluations.

Self-Verification

When self-appraisal leads to certainty about skills, processes engage that have as their goal the confirmation of existing abilities and beliefs (Swann, 1983, 1990). These confirmatory strategies maintain the integrity of self-knowledge against periodic challenge, essentially resisting unwarranted changes in self-views and reasserting the validity of ability beliefs. Self-verification is thus a conservative process that promotes the stability of the self and thereby fosters a perception of control that may provide comfort in the face of an ostensibly chaotic environment.

Self-verification theory assumes that people confirm their existing self-views to provide scripts for future behavior and expectations about future outcomes—in other words, to predict and control the environment. Swann (see Swann, 1990, for a review) has demonstrated self-verification processes in several ways. For example, people attend to self-confirmatory information and are better able to retrieve it. Similarly, people gravitate toward those who provide confirmation of known personal attributes. More important for our purposes, this research shows that self-verification is equally compelling for people with low self-regard. Hence the tendency to sustain firm beliefs of low ability translates into a behavioral pattern of poor performance and a negative intrapersonal evaluation. Swann (Swann, Griffin, Predmore, and Gaines, 1987) acknowledges that most people desire positive self-views, but when the evidence is to the contrary they prefer the control and security afforded by the existing negative self-view.

The proposition that people seek knowledge about their abilities but also long to feel good about themselves (in most cases) seems beyond reproach. Here we have surveyed the literature and proposed a model that describes how the ego operates through task-related behavior that is instrumental to both purposes. In the following section we explore how these processes are manifested in organizational pursuits and consider how management can strategically harness the ego energy that is directed toward self-evaluation.

Organizationally Relevant Self-Appraisal

Organizational and occupational affiliations provide role identities that are central to most people's self-concept. Not only do these affiliations offer meaningful self-descriptors ("I am a management professor at Rutgers University"), but they are also powerful deter-

minants of self-worth, status, and the security of group identification. To publicly reveal a valued organizational attachment conveys
an implicit or explicit sense of pride that reinforces a positive evaluation of the self. In contrast, undesirable organizational relationships usually go unmentioned or are offered in diffident whispers.

Work organizations are also the most pervasive arena in
which people can explore, evaluate, and subsequently display their
abilities. In the context of the workplace, the motivation to appraise
one's abilities accurately is absorbing for a number of reasons. From
the individual perspective, executing satisfactory work can confirm
specific competencies and general self-esteem. Furthermore, in
Western society, effective individual rather than group performance
is more highly regarded and scrutinized as a criterion for praise,
promotion, and financial reward. Thus self-appraisals that are
aligned with organizational objectives are instrumental in providing self-enhancing feedback that can lead to both internal gratifi-
cation and external payoffs. Distorted self-appraisals that
misapprehend organizational objectives may be met with social rejection and denial of opportunities. Processing performance in a
complex organizational framework is, however, fraught with political dynamics that are capriciously unstable. Schein (1990) illuminates the ambiguities inherent in organizational cultures, as well
as the dilemma that participants experience in deciphering the most
personally relevant ingredients of these complex environments.
Functionally accurate self-appraisal in organizations is therefore,
almost by definition, a tangled undertaking that blends technical
work skills with evaluations of personal worth that are embedded
in a web of social and emotional relations.

Perhaps the most compelling issue that working managers
and organizational scholars are challenged to resolve is the manner
in which the quality of work experience and people's productivity in
contemporary organizations converge. The most prominent approach to understanding work-related attitudes (satisfaction, commitment) and performance is the need-satisfaction mode. (See the work
by Alderfer, 1972; Hackman and Oldham, 1976; Hackman and Suttle,
1977.) In its most rudimentary form, the need-satisfaction model pro-
poses that people have enduring needs and the extent to which these
needs are met by equally enduring job characteristics determines sa-

tisfaction and motivation to perform. This model has come under criticism, however, for treating employees as passive beneficiaries or, conversely, victims of the compatibility of needs and job characteristics (Salancik and Pfeffer, 1977). These same critics have advanced a model of social information processing in which people actively construct their work experiences through perceptual and judgmental mechanisms (Salancik and Pfeffer, 1978). We are generally sympathetic with this approach and view it as complementary to our self-appraisal approach. As the previously detailed research attests, however, we hold that people construct mental realities (a positive job attitude, for example, or a flattering self-image) by selecting or constructing physical realities (applying for specific positions, for example, or accepting certain assignments).

An important issue that arises from the self-appraisal approach is that persistence and performance need not be purchased by organizational incentives. Rather, the ego energy expended on self-appraisal is a natural motive to reduce uncertainty about abilities and, in most cases, to promote self-esteem. Cognitive self-appraisal is translated into corrective action when individual and organizational standards require a better match. As an internal motivating system, self-appraisal can be construed as a type of intrinsic motive (Deci, 1975). Because intrinsic motivation has been applied to attitudes and performance in the workplace through the literature of self-reinforcement (Brief and Aldag, 1981), self-efficacy (Bandura, 1986; Gist and Mitchell, 1992), and goal setting (Locke and Latham, 1990), we will not belabor its value here, except to note that it operates in self-appraisal.

Personnel Selection

Management can build on the self-appraisal process through selection practices that are sensitive to the employee's desire for self-appraisal and the qualities of the job. For example, Hunter and Hunter (1984) conducted a meta-analysis comparing a broad range of tools frequently used for job selection. They concluded that cognitive ability was most highly correlated with job performance as measured by a variety of organizational criteria. Integrating these data with self-appraisal theory, it is possible that employees with better-articulated cognitive skills have acquired more accurate self-knowledge, which may also increase their motivation to achieve job success. Furthermore, with careful personnel assessment organizations can effectively match employees with relevant job qualities to ensure their proficiency in an assigned work setting. The likely payoff for the employee under these circumstances is the reinforcement of accurate self-appraisals and a concomitant lift in self-esteem. For an organization, the by-products of sensitive job selection are increased loyalty, commitment, and the employee's clear identification with the organization's objectives.

The selection of high-performing employees has been a long-standing priority of human resource departments, and organizational psychologists have introduced various combinations of assessment tools to improve talent selection. Research on self-appraisal has yielded some encouraging possibilities for strengthening these programs. For example, the Desire for Self-Appraisal scale is a potentially useful measure for identifying those who are especially oriented toward acquiring accurate knowledge of abilities. For these employees, the reduction of ability-related uncertainty and the perception of improved environmental control are major objectives. Recall that research on self-appraisal found that optimal performance was a function of both the desire for appraisal (as measured by the DSA scale) and performance feedback conditions (see Strube and Yost, 1992). Specifically, high self-appraisers performed best when conditions offered focused feedback regarding abilities, whereas low self-appraisers performed poorly in these conditions. This finding suggests that one way to improve employee performance is to match high self-appraisers with jobs that provide the diagnostic feedback they crave. Because low self-appraisers find diagnostic feedback unnerving, they should be assigned jobs that provide less performance feedback.

In general, research on self-appraisal finds that people are differentially receptive to feedback information, and this receptivity facilitates or debilitates their performance accordingly. In the quest for finding the right person for the right job, adding the desire for self-appraisal variable may represent an intriguing attitudinal dimension to complement standard assessment profiles.

Performance Appraisal

In a similar vein, the self-appraisal model helps explain how poor performance can be the result of a rational attempt to separate the contribution of ability from other factors. For employees who desire appraisal, the apparently paradoxical withholding of effort may not be the result of indolence or dissatisfaction but, rather, an attempt to gauge ability. Conversely, low self-appraisers may perform poorly on diagnostic tasks because the accompanying information is unwanted and psychologically disillusioning. In both situations the employee may possess the requisite skills to perform well and may even want to succeed. But for different reasons the feedback runs counter to the desire for appraisal. Although neither situation excuses poor performance, the desire for appraisal gives management an alternative means for understanding poor performance and, more important, taking steps to rectify it (by reassignment, for example, or changing the nature of job feedback).

What about people who lack the skills necessary to execute a job? Because of circumstances beyond their control or a temporary lack of insight, employees can find themselves in situations where their abilities are inadequate relative to environmental demands. For example, the mathematical whiz may be placed in a position—like staff counselor—where his or her analytic skills are not only dysfunctional but insufficient to achieve results. A poor person/ environment fit is undoubtedly aversive and will likely prompt defensive maneuvers to protect self-esteem. Self-handicapping represents one such self-protective strategy (Jones and Berglas, 1978); making excuses may represent another (Snyder and Higgins, 1988). Although such strategies guard against threats to the self-concept, they are most certainly not conducive to accomplishing organizational objectives. An organization would do well to avoid situations where employees are forced to choose between protecting their self-concept and executing their responsibilities.

Research on self-appraisal also sheds light on an especially vexing thorn in management's side: the chronically poor performer. The account manager who repeatedly confuses orders, fails to return calls, and neglects product innovations is but one example. Swann (1983, 1990) contends that employees perform poorly not because they want to see themselves as poor performers, but because they do see themselves as poor performers. By verifying a poor self-image, they justify their self-concept and, in an odd way, promote security, predictability, and control over their worldview. Hence, from an individual perspective, persistent failure may be the most internally adaptive strategy to manage environmental contingencies. De La Ronde and Swann (1993) have suggested that the only way to break the self-verification cycle for those with low self-regard is therapeutic intervention coupled with a change toward a more nurturing social environment.

Job Design and Job Choice

Enormous effort has been devoted to highlighting facets of job qualities. (See, for example, Hackman and Oldham, 1975, 1976.) In most of these schemes, feedback—defined as information about the effectiveness of performance—has played an important role in accentuating the performance features of various job functions. But performance feedback does not necessarily reduce uncertainty about abilities. A young advertising executive who recently secured a prestigious client for her firm may wonder if her success was due to luck, timing, advertising flair, or just plain hard work. This same executive may feel compelled to sabotage future success (perhaps by submitting a slipshod campaign) in order to determine the cause of previous success. When ability-related feedback is lacking or unclear, some employees (for example, high self-appraisers) may feel like impostors until they can resolve the reasons for their success. With self-appraisal theory and research in mind, we suggest that clearly articulated ability-related information be joined with descriptive performance data in generating job definition criteria.

Finally, if an organizaiton makes job characteristics available to the workforce, it follows from our model that employees would gravitate toward the jobs that allowed them to satisfy their desire for appraisal and best suited their abilities. Employees ambivalent about their logistical prowess, for instance, may seek administrative positions where that uncertainty could be reduced. Similarly, those confident of their diplomatic skills may enlist in boundary-spanning positions where those skills could be realized. We believe that people are well aware of their aptitudes, and when given an opportunity they will naturally occupy positions that accord with their desires and skills. Such job-choice policies may also instill a sense of agency or personal causation (Decharms, 1968) that in turn may increase satisfaction and commitment and reduce turnover.

Self-Appraisal in Retrospect

We have presented a model in which people vary in their desire for self-knowledge and consequently vary in their achievement-oriented behavior. Proactive self-appraisal posits that the ego marshals energy to reduce uncertainty—a key element in the realization of pleasures and the avoidance of pains and equally instrumental in maintaining the self-concept. At the heart of our theory is the ego, through which people come to understand and act upon their environment. Both purposes—understanding and action—are prefaced, however, by functional knowledge of the self/environment interface. Once self-knowledge is secured, people act as agents in selecting and constructing environments that are receptive to their abilities. In this way, they seek to occupy opportunity niches that are ideally suited to their unique competencies. We have also noted numerous implications of self-appraisal for human resource management. Although many of these implications are speculative, we believe they are well reasoned and hold potential value for organizations.

In closing we note that organizations have attempted to inculcate motivation through strutural innovations (for example, job design), socialization practices (for example, job training), and atmosphere control (for example, culture). Each of these strategies has its place, but each tries in its own way to *change* the employee so that he or she identifies with an organizational role. We propose that an artificially induced role identity can never compete with a self-identity arrived at naturally, and that the wisest way to encourage the former is to respect the latter.

References

Alderfer, C. P. *Existence, Relatedness, and Growth: Human Needs in Organizational Settings.* New York: Free Press, 1972.

Alloy, L. B., and Abramson, L. Y. "Judgment of Contingency in

Depressed and Nondepressed Students: Sadder But Wiser?" *Journal of Experimental Psychology: General*, 1979, *108*, 441–485.

Alloy, L. B., Abramson, L. Y., and Viscusi, D. "Induced Mood and the Illusion of Control." *Journal of Personality and Social Psychology*, 1981, *41*, 1129–1140.

Bandura, A. *Social Foundations of Thought and Action: A Social-Cognitive View*. Englewood Cliffs, N.J.: Prentice-Hall, 1986.

Berglas, S., and Jones, E. E. "Drug Choice as a Self-Handicapping Strategy in Response to Noncontingent Success." *Journal of Personality and Social Psychology*, 1978, *36*, 405–417.

Bradley, G. W. "Self-Serving Biases in the Attribution Process: A Reexamination of the Fact or Fiction Question." *Journal of Personality and Social Psychology*, 1978, *36*, 56–71.

Brief, A. P., and Aldag, R. J. "The 'Self' in Work Organizations: A Conceptual Review." *Academy of Management Review*, 1981, *6*, 75–88.

Decharms, R. *Personal Causation: The Internal Affective Determinants of Behavior*. New York: Academic Press, 1968.

Deci, E. L. *Intrinsic Motivation*. New York: Plenum, 1975.

De La Ronde, C., and Swann, W. B., Jr. "Caught in the Crossfire: Positivity and Self-Verification Strivings Among People with Low Self-Esteem." In R. Baumeister (ed.), *Self-Esteem: The Puzzle of Low Self-Regard*. New York: Plenum, 1993.

Festinger, L. "A Theory of Social Comparison Processes." *Human Relations*, 1954, *7*, 117–140.

Gist, M. E., and Mitchell, T. R. "Self-Efficacy: A Theoretical Analysis of Its Determinants and Malleability." *Academy of Management Review*, 1992, *17*, 183–211.

Gould, S. J. *Wonderful Life*. New York: Norton, 1989.

Hackman, J. R., and Oldham, G. R. "Development of a Job Diagnostic Survey." *Journal of Applied Psychology*, 1975, *60*, 159–170.

Hackman, J. R., and Oldham, G. R. "Motivation Through the Design of Work: Test of a Theory." *Organizational Behavior and Human Performance*, 1976, *16*, 250–279.

Hackman, J. R., and Suttle, J. L. *Improving Life at Work: Behavioral Science Approaches to Organizational Change*. Santa Monica, Calif.: Goodyear, 1977.

Heider, F. *The Psychology of Interpersonal Relations.* New York: Wiley, 1958.

Hunter, J. E., and Hunter, R. F. "Validity and Utility of Alternative Predictors of Job Performance." *Psychological Bulletin,* 1984, *91,* 72-98.

James, W. "Great Men and Their Environment: The Sentiment of Rationality." In *The Will to Believe and Other Essays in Popular Philosophy.* New York: Dover, 1956. (Originally published 1897.)

James, W. *The Principles of Psychology.* Cambridge, Mass.: Harvard University Press, 1981. (Originally published 1890.)

Jones, E. E., and Berglas, S. "Control of Attributions About the Self Through Self-Handicapping Strategies: The Appeal of Alcohol and the Role of Underachievement." *Personality and Social Psychology Bulletin,* 1978, *4,* 200-206.

Jones, E. E., and Davis, K. E. "From Acts to Dispositions: The Attribution Process in Person Perception." In L. Berkowitz (ed.), *Advances in Experimental Social Psychology,* vol. 2. New York: Academic Press, 1965.

Kelley, H. H. "Attribution Theory in Social Psychology." In D. Levine (ed.), *Nebraska Symposium on Motivation.* Lincoln: University of Nebraska Press, 1967.

Langer, E. J. *The Psychology of Control.* Newbury Park, Calif.: Sage, 1983.

Locke, E. A., and Latham, G. P. *A Theory of Goal Setting and Task Performance.* Englewood Cliffs, N.J.: Prentice-Hall, 1990.

Markus, H., and Nurius, P. "Possible Selves." *American Psychologist,* 1986, *41,* 954-969.

Salancik, G. R., and Pfeffer, J. "An Examination of Need-Satisfaction Models of Job Attitudes." *Administrative Science Quarterly,* 1977, *22,* 427-456.

Salancik, G. R., and Pfeffer, J. "A Social Information Processing Approach to Job Attitudes and Task Design." *Administrative Science Quarterly,* 1978, *23,* 224-253.

Schein, E. H. "Organizational Culture." *American Psychologist,* 1990, *45,* 109-119.

Smith, T. W., Snyder, C. R., and Handelsman, M. M. "On the Self-Serving Function of an Academic Wooden Leg: Test Anxiety as a Self-Handicapping Strategy." *Journal of Personality and Social Psychology*, 1982, *42*, 314–321.

Smith, T. W., Snyder, C. R., and Perkins, S. C. "The Self-Serving Function of Hypochondriacal Complaints: Physical Symptoms as Self-Handicapping Strategies." *Journal of Personality and Social Psychology*, 1983, *44*, 787–797.

Snyder, C. R., and Higgins, R. L. "Excuses: Their Effective Role in the Negotiation of Reality." *Psychological Bulletin*, 1988, *104*, 23–35.

Snyder, M. L., Stephan, W. G., and Rosenfield, D. "Attributional Egotism." In J. H. Harvey, W. J. Ickes, and R. F. Kidd (eds.), *New Directions in Attribution Research*, vol. 2. Hillsdale, N.J.: Erlbaum, 1978.

Strube, M. J. "A Self-Appraisal Model of the Type A Behavior Pattern." In R. Hogan and W. Jones (eds.), *Perspectives in Personality*, vol. 2. Greenwich, Conn.: JAI Press, 1987.

Strube, M. J. "In Search of Self: Balancing the Good and the True." *Personality and Social Psychology Bulletin*, 1990, *16*, 699–704.

Strube, M. J., and Roemmele, L. A. "Self-Enhancement, Self-Assessment, and Self-Evaluative Task Choice." *Journal of Personality and Social Psychology*, 1985, *49*, 981–993.

Strube, M. J., Smith, D. S., and Bailey, J. R. "Performance Effects of Certainty, Success, and Self-Appraisal Motivation." Paper presented at the annual meeting of the American Psychological Association, New Orleans, Aug. 1989.

Strube, M. J., and Yost, J. H. "Control Motivation and Self-Appraisal." In G. Weary, F. Gleicher, and K. Marsh (eds.), *Control Motivation and Social Cognition*. New York: Springer-Verlag, 1992.

Strube, M. J., Yost, J. H., and Bailey, J. R. "William James and Contemporary Research on the Self: The Influence of Pragmatism, Reality, and Truth." In M. E. Donnelly (ed.), *Reinterpreting the Legacy of William James*. Washington: American Psychological Association Press, 1992.

Strube, M. J., White, A., Shimabukaro, J., and Bailey, J. R. "Development of a Questionnaire for Assessing Self-Appraisal Motivation." Paper presented at the annual meeting of the American Psychological Association, Atlanta, Aug. 1988.

Strube, M. J., and others. "Self-Evaluation of Abilities: Accurate Self-Assessment Versus Biased Self-Enhancement." *Journal of Personality and Social Psychology,* 1986, *51,* 16–25.

Swann, W. B., Jr. "Self-Verification: Bringing Social Reality into Harmony with the Self." In J. Suls and A. Greenwald (eds.), *Psychological Perspectives on the Self,* vol. 2. Hillsdale, N.J.: Erlbaum, 1983.

Swann, W. B., Jr. "To Be Adored or to Be Known? The Interplay of Self-Enhancement and Self-Verification." In E. T. Higgins and R. M. Sorrentino (eds.), *Handbook of Motivation and Cognition: Foundations of Social Behavior,* vol. 2. New York: Guilford, 1990.

Swann, W. B., Jr., Griffin, J. J., Predmore, S. C., and Gaines, B. "The Cognitive-Affective Crossfire: When Self-Consistency Confronts Self-Enhancement." *Journal of Personality and Social Psychology,* 1987, *52,* 881–889.

Taylor, S. E., and Brown, J. D. "Illusion and Well-Being: A Social Psychological Perspective on Mental Health." *Psychological Bulletin,* 1988, *103,* 193–210.

Trope, Y. "Seeking Information About One's Own Ability as a Determinant of Choice Among Tasks." *Journal of Personality and Social Psychology,* 1975, *32,* 1004–1013.

Trope, Y. "Uncertainty-Reducing Properties of Achievement Tasks." *Journal of Personality and Social Psychology,* 1979, *37,* 1505–1518.

Trope, Y. "Self-Assessment, Self-Enhancement, and Task Preference." *Journal of Experimental Social Psychology,* 1980, *16,* 116–129.

Trope, Y. "Self-Assessment and Task Performance." *Journal of Experimental Social Psychology,* 1982, *18,* 201–215.

Trope, Y., and Ben-Yair, E. "Task Construction and Persistence as Means for Self-Assessment of Abilities." *Journal of Personality and Social Psychology,* 1982, *42,* 637–645.

Trope, Y., and Brickman, P. "Difficulty and Diagnosticity as Determinants of Choice Among Tasks." *Journal of Personality and Social Psychology*, 1975, *31*, 918–925.

White, R. W. "Motivation Reconsidered: The Concept of Competence." *Psychological Review*, 1959, *66*, 297–333.

Yost, J. H., Strube, M. J., and Bailey, J. R. "The Construction of the Self: An Evolutionary View." *Current Psychology: Research and Reviews*, 1992, *11*, 110–121.

7

Ego Psychology
and Organizations

Seth Allcorn

EMPLOYEES WITH LOW SELF-ESTEEM create more problems than might at first be appreciated. Supervisors all too often encounter angry, arrogant, bitter, moody, aggressive, depressed, tearful, withdrawn employees who are hard to manage and work with. At the same time these employees may feel compelled to outperform everyone else, and indeed they often produce outstanding work. Supervisors are therefore faced with the challenge of gaining the benefits of their productivity while minimizing their negative effects. And to do so they must know more about self-esteem. This chapter describes the self-esteem continuum, explains self-esteem in terms of ego psychology and its protection by psychological defenses, discusses its origins in family pathology and society, and illuminates its effects on men and women in the workplace. The chapter concludes with guidelines on working more effectively with employees who have low self-esteem.

The Self-Esteem Continuum

Self-esteem can be defined as how favorable a person's characteristic self-evaluations are (Brockner, 1988, p. 11). (For my purposes here, self-esteem is considered to subsume the notion of global self-esteem.) Self-esteem may therefore be viewed as existing along a continuum from excessive to low. Understanding low and excessive self-esteem begins with understanding adequate self-esteem. Adequate self-esteem permits one to function relative to others and events in a way that is noncompulsive and relatively free of anxiety. The employee feels that he or she is competent, likable, worthy, and admired. Those who have adequate self-esteem are described as self-confident, self-assured, self-aware, capable of autonomous behavior, responsible, and willing to try new things and take personal risks (Neilsen and Gypen, 1979; Schwalbe, 1985). They are able to deal with most people's behavior—however threatening or idiosyncratic it may be—without feeling unduly threatened, competitive, frustrated, or crushed by criticism. People with adequate self-esteem are spontaneous, energetic, independent, open-minded, flexible, and vital (Dyer, 1976, pp. 231-244). Not only are they fun to be around, but friends and colleagues do not feel they must be unduly careful about the person's feelings.

Low self-esteem, in contrast, results in employees who both know and feel that they are not powerful, likable, or worthy of admiration and respect (Basch, 1988; May, 1977; Sanford and Donovan, 1984). These employees consistently lack self-confidence with others (Brockner, 1988). Their unshakable but distorted self-knowledge (pathological certainty) leads to a hypervigilant state in which these feelings are constantly revalidated by the actions of others who, despite the best of intentions, are often found to be threatening, insensitive, disrespectful, and uncaring (Brockner, 1988, p. 225; Cermak, 1986, pp. 26-27; Korman, 1976). The result is a person who is extremely anxious about self and others and experiences a profound sense of anxiety that must be defended against (Horney, 1950). This likelihood is further exaggerated by two interpersonal dynamics.

First, the person holds uncommunicated and often unacknowledged expectations about how others should think, feel, and act toward him—expectations that, if honored, compensate for feelings of low self-esteem (Allcorn, 1992; Horney, 1950, pp. 197, 228). The fact that the employee may have a vast array of these expectations means that many of them will be disappointed—which ironically reinforces the person's feeling of worthlessness. Holding these concealed expectations is a self-defeating interpersonal strategy. Others learn about them only after the person's feelings are hurt.

Second, the employee becomes easily upset by unexpected turns of events and changes in hard-won relationships. A morbid sense of fear, rage, conspiracy, loss, depression, and despair may pervade this person's worldview (Basch, 1988, pp. 109–128; May 1977). Others do not appreciate that this person's network of relationships has an important role in maintaining his feelings of self-worth. Thus the loss of supporting bonds is usually greeted with anger, pain, and sadness. The employee might be described as a "raw nerve ending," a person who picks up on everything that happens.

In sum, the origins of low self-esteem lie in conscious and unconscious learning (Bowlby, 1969, pp. 11–18).

People are not born with low self-esteem. It is learned from relating to unnurturing people and in particular one's parents (Sanford and Donovan, 1984, pp. 83–94). It is also acquired from the world of unconscious object relations where the child learns to magically manipulate parental objects, perhaps to make them less threatening. When one considers how many employees grow up in families where one or both parents had drug or alcohol problems, fought interminably, were physically and emotionally abusive, demanding, punitive, or unavailable for consistent nurturing, it is easy to understand the frequent presence of low self-esteem in the workplace.

Much like low self-esteem, excessive self-esteem has its origins in inadequate childhood nurturing and unconscious responses to the world. In this case, however, the child, rather than accepting himself as deficient and worthless, compensates for these feelings by overvaluing himself. Fear of feeling deficient feeds compensatory thoughts, feelings, and actions where every effort is made to resist feeling worthless and not respected. The result is a person who may be a perfectionist, arrogant, competitive, vindictive when his pride is hurt, and hungry for power and admiration. In sum, excessive self-esteem may be understood as a flight from feelings of worthlessness associated with low self-esteem and, therefore, is a product of low self-esteem. We will return to this paradox when we consider lifestyle solutions to anxiety, but first we must examine ego psychology's contribution to self-esteem.

The Ego, the Self, and Self-Esteem

Ego psychology as originally formulated by Freud and elaborated by Rappaport, Hartmann, and countless others has become a theoretical perspective that is rich in its many and sometimes conflicting points of view. Theorists continue to strive to conceptualize a system that explains the complex and often paradoxical nature of the human psyche. This richness is captured by Levinson (1976) when he explains five aspects of ego psychology: the dynamic, economic, topographical, developmental, and adaptive perspectives. Figure 7.1 illustrates many of the guiding principles of ego psychology as they relate to the development of self and the quality of self-esteem. The figure also illuminates a central point of this chapter: we all use psychological defenses and overarching lifestyle solutions to minimize the experience of basic and neurotic anxiety arising from stressful events (Greenspan, 1989; Horney, 1950).

The Origins of Ego

The big bang theory regarding the creation of the universe may apply equally well to the explosive development of the human psyche. The id, ego, and superego exist in a fused undifferentiated state at birth and gradually become more differentiated with maturation (Brody and Axelrad, 1970; Greenspan, 1989). In this regard energy for the system is equally undifferentiated at birth as the infant strives for its first breath and subsequently uses its innate cognitive and affective organizers to address its new reality. Given time and nurturing, the infant begins to evolve a meaningfully differentiated awareness of self and others. This evolution gradually leaves the infant with three differentiated and autonomous but interactive conceptual networks that govern conscious and unconscious functioning. These three networks are the id, superego, and ego.

To the id is attributed innate feelings (aggression, sexual urges), processes, desires, and needs. It may be regarded as the foun-

Figure 7.1. Ego Psychology Model of Self-Esteem.

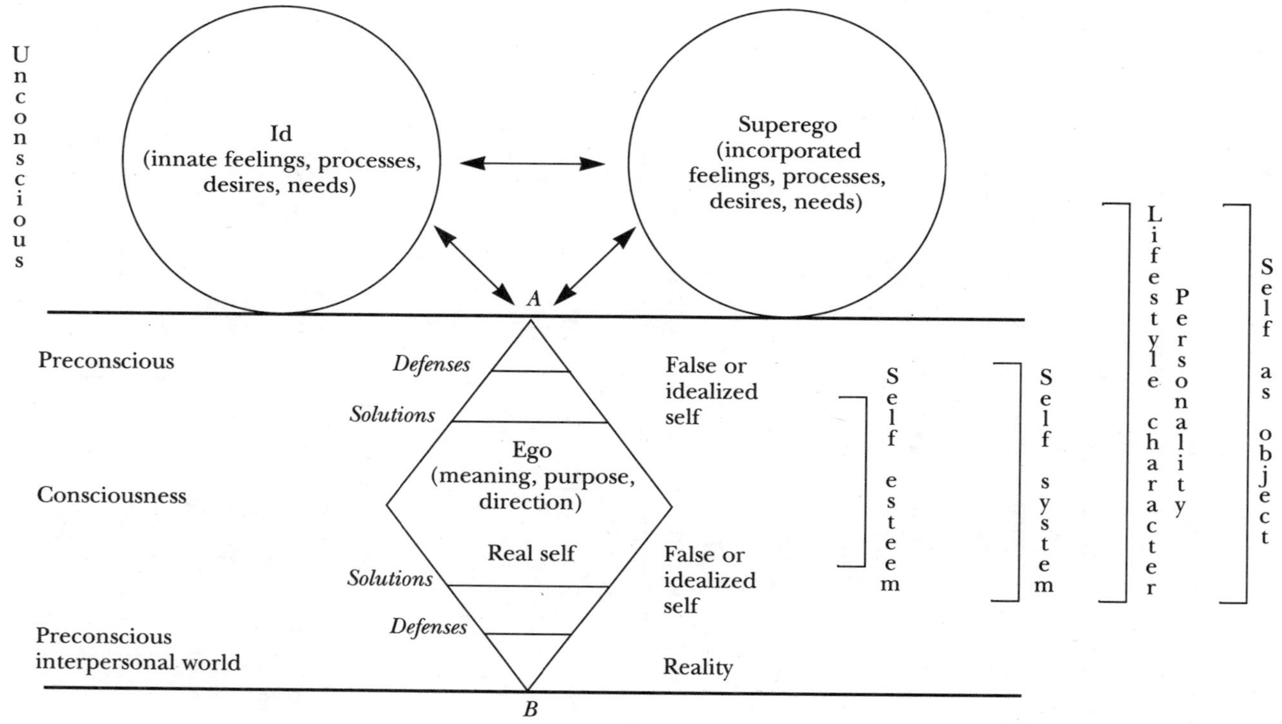

dation of the pristine or natural self. The energy for the id arises
from internal sources of tension and conflict. The superego contains internalized feelings and idealized expectations (the ego ideal)
that may well be a false or idealized self. The energy for the superego
arises from others. The ego is composed of memories, organized
thinking, and purpose that give meaning to the world and result in
self-direction that implicitly includes autonomy and reality testing
(Freud, 1960). Ego energy has its origins in the need to mediate
conflict between the id and superego and reality in order to achieve
anxiety reduction and ultimately survival (Brody and Axelrad, 1970;
Greenspan, 1989; Levinson, 1976).

Model Dynamics

The model depicts a situation where two conceptual entities, the id
and superego, interact in terms of exchanging content and energy.
(See the bidirectional arrows in Figure 7.1.) These exchanges may
be complementary or conflictual. Conflict and resulting anxiety are
mediated by innate primitive defenses such as repression and splitting. The content of the two networks interacts with the third conceptual entity, the ego, which balances the parts of the resulting
internal system with reality. In this regard the balancing process is
made more or less easy by the relative contributions of the id and
superego (size of the entities) to the intrapsychic milieu. For example, the massive incorporation of threatening, unpredictable, unnurturing, and punitive superego objects during infancy can
permanently tilt the balance toward the superego—thereby requiring the ego to shift its center (tilt in the opposite direction) and
redistribute defensive systems to rebalance the system at the cost of
less than optimal adaptation.

　　　Another aspect of the model is the development of two different but interactive sets of defenses that are gradually elaborated
with maturation (Hartmann, 1964). One system relies on time-tested
psychological defenses that are employed sequentially or in combination to relieve anxiety. The second system relies on lifestyle solutions aimed at controlling the origins of anxiety in the
interpersonal world (see Figure 7.1).

　　　At this point we should note that the ability to experience

anxiety is thought to be innate and serves to warn of threats originating from inner or outer phenomena. These two defensive systems operate at the points where the ego interacts with the internal and primarily unconscious world (point A in Figure 7.1) and the interpersonal world and reality (point B in Figure 7.1). (See: Brody and Axelrad, 1970; Horney, 1950; Sullivan, 1953.) The functioning of these defenses leads to the development of conflict between the true and false self (Horney, 1950). Although the two defensive systems function out of conscious awareness, they can be made explicit.

Here we must pause to consider the nature of basic and neurotic anxiety. Basic anxiety represents a baseline of anxiety (not unlike background radiation) that is omnipresent and predisposes one to be universally anxious about self, others, events, and the world (Horney, 1950). Neurotic anxiety, in contrast, involves the experience of internal conflicts between two or more defenses or conflict between a defense and an external stressor. Both forms of anxiety arise from learning, and a high baseline of basic anxiety predisposes a person to experience more neurotic anxiety, thereby provoking the disproportionate use of defenses.

Returning to Figure 7.1, the combination of the two types of defenses at points A and B may be regarded as an organized, internally consistent self-system that can be relied upon to minimize anxiety; it resembles armor plating and defines the self as a separate object. (See Freud, 1966; Klein, 1976; Reich, 1972; Rosen, 1977; Sandler and Freud, 1985; Shapiro, 1965, 1981; Sullivan, 1953.) The area between the defenses is a sphere of relatively conflict-free functioning that is consistent with the notion of real authentic self and self-esteem (Hartmann, 1958; Horney, 1950). This area of conflict-free functioning may be impinged upon by the development of ever greater and more massive defenses against anxiety. A person who possesses an out-of-balance internal system and consistently experiences self, others, and reality as threatening will respond by greater defensiveness—which, in Figure 7.1, increases their size and diminishes the ego's area of conflict-free functioning and, therefore, may be understood to increase self-alienation and diminish self and self-esteem.

The interaction of the two defensive systems raises several

additional considerations. Psychological defenses such as projection, denial, rationalization, regression, and repression are positioned as the first line of defense. There may be exceptions, however. It may not always be more economical to manipulate reality in one's mind as opposed to expending the energy to change one's self and the interpersonal world to relieve anxiety. The lifestyle solutions to anxiety, as we will see, may be active as an initial defense if they are highly developed and their use has consistently relieved anxiety.

There is also an interaction between the two defensive systems that may contain synergy (or conflict). When a person chooses lifestyle solutions to anxiety, the accompanying use of psychological defenses improves their anxiety-minimizing outcomes. Conversely, the more holistic notion of the solutions informs the use of psychological defenses that should be employed in a manner consistent with a person's unique lifestyle solutions. In this regard the two approaches to defenses can be complementary or conflicting. The use of psychological defenses serves similar outcomes when dealing with (or perhaps contributing to) either type of anxiety. The solutions, however, will be qualitatively different in dealing with basic anxiety, as their aim is controlling the interpersonal world. In this regard the solutions address the content and energy of the superego and its internalized objects. Yet another aspect of Figure 7.1 is that self-esteem is both a dependent and an independent variable. Although it may vary over time according to one's internal world and reality, it also exists as a quality of the moment that makes it an independent variable relative to stress. Parenthetically, much academic debate focuses on whether the ego is a dependent or independent variable. (The interaction of life events and self-esteem is illustrated later in Figure 7.2.)

The model in Figure 7.1, taken as a whole, represents a conception of human nature where such global attributes as lifestyle, character, and personality reside and where one's experience of self as an idealized, despised, or acceptable object exists. Within this representation of self as object lies the basis of self-hate and self-alienation. The self as object may be felt to be deplorable relative to one's idealized self-image (a feedback loop)—a feeling that may lead to renewed and willful behavior implying that the person does not acknowledge limitation to self. The person may feel that anything may be accomplished with enough effort and self-transformation. Realization of the idealized false self may take precedence. The idealized false self may take many forms, some of which lead to self-diminishing behavior.

In sum, then, the model in Figure 7.1 synthesizes many of the different viewpoints that constitute ego metapsychology and links to character structure. The figure also provides a foundation for the rest of the chapter, for the early development of one's sense of self, accompanying self-esteem, and persistent systems of psychological defensive tendencies come to dominate behavior in the workplace.

Traditional Psychological Defense Mechanisms

Employees with feelings of low self-worth control their anxiety by employing psychological defenses and changing themselves to control others. The compulsive and persistent nature of this control sets it apart from the norm. These employees *must* gain control and they *must* not have their motives and actions questioned (Masterson, 1988, pp. 1–19). Unquestioned control is seldom available to anyone at work, however, which leads to the perpetuation of anxiety and continued efforts to control uncontrollable workplace realities that do not always bolster self-esteem. Moreover, these defensive solutions create an important paradox: because they are intended to defend the employee from painful anxiety and from the knowledge of self-defeating behavior, they perpetuate the necessity for their use as the person avoids maturation and better adaptation (Diamond, 1986; Masterson, 1988). The defensive systems share one characteristic in common: the avoidance of self-knowledge which leads to the recognition that change is needed. This outcome, it may be noted, is not consistent with those who advocate a more rational approach to learning in the workplace (Argyris and Schon, 1978).

In sum, employees who rely on their irrational defensive systems experience conflicting feelings and hold conflicting and unrealistic views of themselves, others, and events. It is these unacknowledgeable and usually undiscussable conflicts that make it so hard to work with employees who consistently rely on such defenses. This point may be appreciated by exploring the traditional psychological defenses.

Denial

Denial is a simple defense. Denied are certain aspects of reality and the employee's feelings. In order to feel better about past and present injuries to a fragile self-esteem and disagreeable aspects of work or oneself, they are not acknowledged to have occurred or to have affected one's feelings. Poor decisions, criticism of poor performance, or unacceptable impulses (such as getting even) are denied to have occurred or to have hurt. The employee may calmly accept an adverse event that would bother others—reporting, for example, that it is acceptable that he is not liked and that his feelings are not really hurt. Denial is facilitated by the employee's becoming engrossed in his work. Aspects of reality, thoughts, and feelings are shut out by focusing exclusively on the work at hand. Selective inattention facilitates denial by controlling knowledge of painful feelings, self-defeating behavior, and contradictory information that does not support one's feelings of inferiority and worthlessness (Sullivan, 1953, pp. 170, 233). An employee may, for example, consistently ignore criticism—or he may nurture criticism in memory while ignoring positive expressions of approval. This process permits the employee to claim, "All you ever do is criticize me." Others learn that they have to be careful in dealing with the person as they come to appreciate that their communications are being rigorously filtered to allow only the acceptable—the approval or criticism. Similarly, comments about controlling behavior are filtered to avoid acknowledging the hidden agenda of interpersonal control. Denial is also involved in projection, as we will see, and may be inferred as a motive for the other defenses as some aspect of reality is being disposed of. In sum, denial and selective attention are strategies to avoid self-knowledge and awareness that change may be in order.

Emotional Insulation

Emotional insulation is an adaptive defense unless it is taken too far and becomes isolation, intellectualization, and dissociation.

This defense takes separation of feeling from thinking to extremes. When one would expect an employee to have feelings, there are none. Isolation permits employees to separate criticism from the here and now. No pain is felt. The pain of the criticism will be dealt with later. Intellectualization permits one to crowd out feelings and awareness. A threatening situation may be addressed by a great deal of thinking about alternatives, the pros and cons, and the introduction of abstract ideas—all of which are aimed at thinking and talking about the event rather than dealing with the feelings it generates. Moreover, dissociation permits employees to hold two conflicting attitudes or feelings. A precipitous loss of one's job is seen as a new opportunity. A dishonest executive is active in his church. An employee who should be angry after being abused is friendly to her aggressor.

Identification

A better sense of self may come from many things—the house an employee owns, his car, his colleagues, and his position with its associated prestige and power. To the extent that employees do not possess adequate self-esteem, they may compulsively associate with powerful others and acquire things, titles, and status in an effort to feel good about themselves. If they feel good about how they appear to others, they do not feel obliged to understand their true feelings of low self-esteem.

Introjection

One may also develop a sense of identity by adopting the values and images of others: "I want to be just like her." For those with low self-esteem, adopting admirable attributes of others is a means of feeling good about oneself. The employee becomes the ideal employee and deserves to be valued. Lost in this chameleon-like process, however, is the employee's true sense of self.

Projection

Projection involves denying an unacceptable aspect of self and then locating it in another person who usually possesses the attribute at least to some extent. An employee with a compelling but unacceptable need for control over others may deny the need and then locate it in a supervisor who may have unwittingly frustrated the employee's pursuit of control. The supervisor becomes "bad" and controlling—thereby permitting the employee to feel uncontrolling and victimized or perhaps justified in his renewed pursuit of control over the supervisor. A related defense is to attribute to others unacceptable feelings. An employee who is angry about a meager pay raise may deny her anger and then attribute it to her supervisor—who, it is then felt, is angry and getting even by giving a low raise.

Rationalization

Rationalization justifies past and present actions and softens painful disappointments by invoking self-deception. No learning occurs. Inconsistencies and contradictory evidence are explained away. The employee may, when treated poorly, think that it was inadvertent, or that everyone else got the same treatment, or that the supervisor was having a bad day—or, paradoxically, that he does not deserve better treatment. In contrast, good treatment may be taken for granted or paradoxically thought of as insincere, temporary, manipulative, or otherwise inspired by reasons unrelated to the employee's true worth. Discounting disposes of a compliment from a supervisor by denying its validity or the supervisor's sincerity. A compliment such as "Your work is very good" may be greeted with disbelief: "You can't possibly mean it." This statement may be followed by self-denigration: "It could have been done quicker and better." In extreme cases, the employee may proceed to complete self-discounting: "I doubt I will ever get it right." Any additional praise by the supervisor ("I really do think it's good") may go unheard as the employee flees from the subject by changing the topic or terminating the discussion. Discounting may also be used to dispose of information that the employee is too controlling or seems to feel that he deserves better treatment.

Regression

Regression means an adult acts like a child. An employee may have a temper tantrum, cry, sulk, and withdraw—actions that used to encourage his parents to respond to his needs. Implicit here is a lack of accountability. Supervisors and colleagues are expected to tolerate the behavior without taking offense with the "child." Regression often stops what is happening at the moment, but it seldom changes what others think and feel about the employee. The employee is once again able to avoid self-knowledge, further injury to his self-esteem, and recognition of his self-serving pursuit of control and self-aggrandizing efforts.

Repression

Repression is the most extreme effort to dispose of reality. Thoughts, feelings, and events are, without awareness, excluded from consciousness. Repression results in no recollection of a painful event, for example. The repressed material continues to unconsciously influence feelings and behavior, however, and may be recovered only under special conditions or during psychotherapy. Closely related to repression is suppression, an intentional effort to remove thoughts and feelings from consciousness. The material is not lost but rather not thought of.

Transference

Transference is not a defense but rather another important element of the interpersonal world that deserves mention. When an employee is confronted by a familiar cue such as a condescending or humiliating remark or being ordered about, he may respond with rage and animosity associated with past humiliations that fuel a here-and-now response that is disproportionate to the cue. An employee who is criticized as a part of routine work may respond with outrage and a torrent of verbal abuse or with hurt feelings, tears, and comments about quitting.

In sum, employees who compulsively rely on these psychological defenses are in flight from self-knowledge and an accurate understanding of others and events. They wish to rid themselves of anxiety in favor of feeling good about themselves and, therefore, sustaining an idealized self-image and self-esteem. They are to some degree out of touch with themselves and reality. Their actions, as well as their underlying feelings of powerlessness and worthlessness, are not open to inspection or discussion. But psychological defenses may not dispose of the anxiety and indeed, if not adaptive, may accentuate it. It is at this point that one's lifestyle solutions play a more active role in attempting to dispose of the anxiety.

Lifestyle Solutions to Anxiety

Karen Horney (1937, 1950) proposed a comprehensive and internally consistent theory of how people deal with basic and neurotic anxiety. Each solution that promises to control one's feelings involves changing oneself to gain control of the interpersonal context (Masterson, 1988). Each solution results in the appearance of behavior that may be relied on consistently. Each solution leads to a personality type and results in certain work-related behavior (Allcorn, 1988; Diamond and Allcorn, 1984, 1985b). The three basic solutions may be described as expansive, self-effacing, and resigned.

The *expansive* solution is proactive and mastery oriented. It represents a form of idealized self that strikes at feelings of powerlessness and worthlessness. The solution has three major components that may be relied on at different times: perfectionist, arrogant-vindictive, and narcissistic. The perfectionist response involves imposing performance standards so high that they cannot be consistently met, although the perfectionist strives to meet them. As a result, anxiety about self and others is disposed of by the knowledge that others are not as good as the person with the high standards. The arrogant-vindictive response involves an injury to excessive self-pride and a corresponding attack to get even. If the injury is great enough, considerable personal risk may be assumed to remedy the situation. The injury is compensated for by treating the defeated person as unworthy or, at the minimum, feeling good about having punished the offender. The narcissistic response is an unending search for approval and admiration. The person will do whatever is necessary to get attention, including performing attention-getting work or using organizational resources to grant favors. The ensuing approval and admiration compensate for feelings of not being likable or worthy of admiration.

The *self-effacing* solution is the opposite of the expansive solution and involves assuming a passive role of dependency. Others are expected to provide love and caretaking and deal with workplace problems. This employee, who voluntarily assumes a role of self-impoverishment, tolerates humiliation and abuse at the hands of others so long as they take charge and take care of him and love him in return for his devotion. Perfectionism is an important aspect of this solution, as well, as the person imposes rigid standards on himself that cannot be met and thus lead to feelings of helplessness, inadequacy, and worthlessness. This deficient person must look to others for help.

The *resigned* solution avoids the implications of the first two solutions through resignation and withdrawal. Rather than deal with the situation, the employee retreats. He wants only to be left alone. Authority may be resisted. Mental and social life are minimized. There is little hope of ever achieving anything. The employee becomes remote and unambitious, a person who just wants to be left alone to do his work.

These lifestyle solutions, as noted earlier, are comprehensive in nature, consistently relied on to relieve anxiety, and result in personality types. They are also found in the workplace. Each solution tries to reduce the experience of anxiety via actions taken to promote security. At the same time, these actions imply that the person has realized a false self in that his behavior is more a function of minimizing interpersonal anxiety and less a function of an autonomous individual exercising free will (Masterson, 1988). The reader is again reminded that these defensive lifestyle solutions are further supported by psychological defenses in which, for example, painful self-impoverishment is denied to be painful and rationalized as serving a greater good. These solutions create an overarching strategy for dealing with the interpersonal world, one that encourages coordination in the use of psychological defenses and is in turn supported by their use.

These lifestyle solutions may also be further understood to contain several important psychodynamics. The expansive solutions may be understood as a flight from a reaction to feelings of powerlessness and worthlessness and, therefore, constitute the basis of claims to extreme pride, self-glorification, and what was earlier called excessive self-esteem. A person realizing the expansive solutions abhors personal weakness that constitutes the despised self-image. This person's idealized self-image is one of being powerful, perfect, in control, admired. Any evidence to the contrary must be disposed of.

The self-effacing solution results in an idealized self that is compliant, selfless, supporting, dependent, and not assertive or aggressive. These are personal attributes that may be developed to the point of creating a morbid dependency that tolerates any type of abuse and humiliation. A person realizing the self-effacing solution despises a self-image that acts powerfully and aggressively to dominate others, actions that lack caring and nurturing. Implicit within these solutions is the transformation of the real or true self into the idealized or false self that contains one set of attributes and not the other (male versus female). The individual is split apart. His energy is spent trying to fulfill the idealized self-image that simultaneously minimizes the real or true self, an outcome that may also be explained as a loss of constructive ego energy.

The resigned solution may be thought of as a compromise that is invoked when the first two solutions fail to mediate basic and neurotic anxiety. When an employee who consistently adopts the expansive solution is confronted by a superior who is equally powerful and dominating, for example, the outcome may well lead to the necessity of "eating crow" and "swallowing one's (false) pride" in favor of retaining one's job. The employee may find this outcome intolerable, however, and the fantasy of getting even with the superior may not suffice either. As result, the employee may retreat from this superior so that he is not reminded of being dominated and unable to strike back. The retreat, therefore, actualizes the resigned solution.

The Complexity of Maintaining Self-Esteem

Figure 7.2 illustrates the complexity of maintaining self-esteem. The model elaborates the concept of self-esteem developed in Figure 7.1 by starting with the notion of self-esteem that is subjected to workplace reality where stress exists and basic and neurotic anxiety are provoked. Self-esteem (as an independent variable) is portrayed as having a core (global self-esteem) surrounded by situation-

Figure 7.2. Model of Psychodynamic Organizational Behavior.

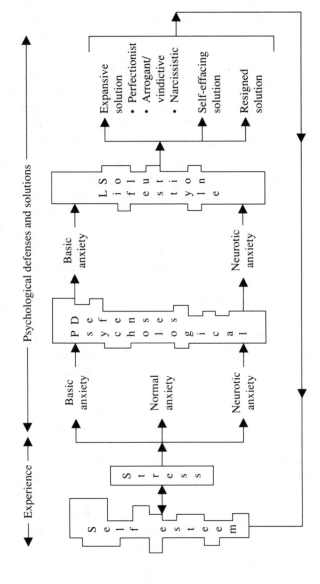

specific elements of self-esteem that are irregular in nature—which highlights the fact that some stress is experienced as threatening to self-esteem and some is not (Brockner, 1988, p. 11). The bidirectional arrow in Figure 7.2 underscores the interactive nature of self-esteem and stress.

The repertoire of psychological defenses is also portrayed as possessing an irregular shape relative to basic and neurotic anxiety. The repertoire may be adequate for some sources of anxiety, such as making a difficult business decision, and inadequate relative to others such as an unplanned visit by a mother-in-law or a yelling superior. The repertoire, therefore, allays anxiety more or less successfully. In the event of adequate mediation, normal levels of anxiety are experienced and intentionality is maintained. (Intentionality is an area of functioning where internal conflicts, anxiety, and the use of psychological defenses are at a minimum and reality testing and rational decision making are optimized.) In the event of unsuccessful mediation, the remaining basic and neurotic anxiety must be coped with by resorting to lifestyle solutions to anxiety that, as mentioned, are also supported by the repertoire of psychological defenses.

A lifestyle is most often thought of as chosen. When feelings of powerlessness and low self-worth become a dominant influence in one's life, however, coping with them is not intentionally chosen. These employees end up spending much of their lives monitoring the actions of others in search of threat. They also work hard to rid themselves of anxiety by either changing the interpersonal world in their minds or getting others to take care of them, admire them, or leave them alone (Horney, 1950). These efforts may grow so pervasive that they become a compulsive preoccupation, an agenda that must be fulfilled at any personal cost. The systematic effort to minimize anxiety, in effect, becomes a way of being. Compulsive repetition forms a personality type or lifestyle that dominates behavior not only at work but outside as well (Beattie, 1989; Cermak, 1986).

We will return to the use of psychological defenses and lifestyle solutions to anxiety later. Before continuing, however, we must see how the metapsychological models in Figures 7.1 and 7.2 are clinically operationalized by examining family pathology that imparts anxiety and discussing the influence of gender stereotypes on the development of the defensive lifestyle solutions to anxiety.

Family Pathology and Gender Stereotypes

Family pathology and its product, the disturbed behavior of family members, fill the news with stories occasionally too horrible to contemplate. Spouses and children are beaten, sexually abused, abandoned. Children are often unwittingly forced into behavior to meet parental needs for control and dependency without regard for the child's developmental needs. Cold, abusive, anxious, unnurturing, unpredictable, dependent parents who demand love and conformity invariably create an environment in which children cannot learn to develop trusting and secure attachments (Allcorn, 1992; Horney, 1950, p. 18; Miller, 1990). These parental actions promote both basic and neurotic anxiety and make it difficult to develop adequate self-esteem.

Figure 7.3 integrates many possible parent/child interactions and outcomes. The figure illustrates that parental attributes, actions, and unconscious relationships with the child create predictable chilhood developmental outcomes focused on fears of abandonment and engulfment and possibly a stifling sense of responsibility driven by guilt. These anxiety-filled outcomes are shown to lead to the development of the three basic lifestyle solutions to anxiety—each of which, as mentioned, contains its own internal psychological conflicts that undermine any lasting adjustment to self and the interpersonal world.

Social norms are another source for learning low self-esteem. Our society contains many well-accepted norms about how children and adults, males and females, should be treated. As feminists have pointed out, our society encourages the treatment of females as less worthy than males, thereby encouraging women to have feelings of low self-esteem (Chadorow, 1989; Sanford and Donovan, 1984). Males, in contrast, are held in higher regard than women, which encourages them to learn that they are of value. This belief supports the conclusion that men are less likely to suffer from feelings of low self-worth. Yet men have feelings of low self-worth imposed on them in much the same way as women do (Osherson, 1986). Boys

Figure 7.3. Family of Origin.

Parental Attributes

Type 1: Unloving	Type 2: Overly Loving	Type 3: Needing Love
• Powerful	• Powerful	• Powerless
• Controlling	• Controlling	• Permissive
• Critical	• Manipulative	• Nonjudgmental
• Punitive	• Withholding	• Laissez-faire
• Not available for caring	• Excessively caring	• Requires caretaking

Relationship to Child

Does not want child	Needs child for self-fulfillment	Child wanted for caretaking

Parental Actions

• Autocratic	• Subtly controlling	• Unassuming
• Remote	• Invasive	• Not controlling
• Absent	• Constantly there	• Unoffensive
• Physically and emotionally brutal	• Manipulative and withholding	• Always in need of nurturance
• Judgmental and critical	• Minimizes need for child to develop	• Guilt used to control child

Psychodynamics

Parents need to feel powerful and in control of child and wanted or needed by child	Parents need to feel loved and certain they will be taken care of by child

Childhood Outcomes

• Abandonment a threat	• Engulfment a threat	• Being consumed by needs of others
• Overt parental control	• Covert parental control	• Threat of overcontrol
• Fear and insecurity when acting for self	• Stifling attention	• Stifling sense of responsibility and guilt
	• Limits ability to act for self	• No limits on behavior

Defensive Types

Type 1: Self-Effacing	Type 2: Expansive	Type 3: Resigned	Type 1: Self-Effacing	Type 2: Expansive	Type 3: Resigned

Note: Adapted from: Allcorn, 1992.

and men are equally likely to be held in low regard by friends, both male and female. They are just as vulnerable to having their feelings hurt by remote, critical parents who do not encourage their personal development. They, like their female counterparts, may spend the balance of their lives coping with anxiety and associated feelings of powerlessness, worthlessness, and inferiority. When it comes to coping with these feelings, however, significant differences in socialization arise. At the risk of oversimplification, we may say that women are encouraged to passively accept feeling worthless while men are expected to fight back against these feelings and overcome them.

Men are expected to be brave, to act courageously even at great personal risk, and to suffer in silence. They must be prepared to compete, achieve, and succeed. Personal weakness, illness, and failure are abhorred. Men must be willing to devote themselves to their work and their families. They are expected to have few feelings and needs. These expectations, when combined with feelings of low self-esteem, create an ominous mix of psychological dynamics that lead men to suppress the desire to be cared for, as well as fear and anger that they may not measure up (Osherson, 1986). Like their fathers before them, however, many are compelled to try to compensate—and try they do. They become the single-minded entrepreneurs and achievers we are encouraged to admire. They become the men who are driven to work sixty, seventy, or more hours a week and do not always play by the rules. Achievement becomes an end in itself—an end that they hope will make them feel better about themselves.

Women in contrast, are expected to be nurturing, self-sacrificing, sensitive people (perhaps less so in the past few decades) who are willing to give up their point of view and suppress their self-interest in order to maintain peace and take care of others. They are not expected to accomplish great feats or act competitively to achieve. Rather, they are encouraged to compensate for feeling powerless and worthless by assuming caretaking and utilitarian family roles. They become the women who selflessly sacrifice for others in order to be valued (Beattie, 1989; Wegscheider-Cruse, 1985).

In sum, then, the male stereotype dictates that men should learn to compensate for feelings of worthlessness and inferiority by controlling others through aggression, competition, and achievement. They are encouraged to overcome feelings of low self-esteem and to ignore that their energized efforts to master it by dominating others and achieving success alienate others and are, in some ways, self-defeating. In this regard they are encouraged to develop excessive self-esteem in their flight from feelings of deficiency and low self-worth. In contrast, the female stereotype dictates that women are to learn to be passive and compensate for feelings of low self-esteem by controlling what others think and feel toward them via self-sacrifice and the assumption of roles of nurturance and dependency. Like men, they are not encouraged to acknowledge feelings of worthlessness and their equally control-oriented behavior, which is in many ways self-defeating. Self-sacrifice and subservience are not likely to foster a positive self-appraisal, however, and may therefore be considered a lifestyle solution to anxiety that is consistent with maintaining feelings of low self-esteem. We now turn from discussing self-esteem and explore what can be done to ameliorate the effects of low self-esteem.

Supervising Employees with Low Self-Esteem

The first step in learning to supervise employees who have low self-esteem is understanding what self-esteem is. This step leads to the second—gaining empathy and compassion for these employees and their compulsive hidden agendas aimed at controlling basic and neurotic anxiety. Supervisors must appreciate that employees' efforts to control their anxiety through the use of psychological defenses and domination or self-sacrifice cannot be approached directly without creating more anxiety and more defensive responses. Understanding their deep need for control—something that everyone feels to some extent from time to time—permits one to ask how supervisors can support and correct these employees without compromising the employees, themselves, and others (Levinson, 1968).

This discussion focuses on employees who have persistent feelings of low self-esteem. Many of the suggestions, however, apply equally well to others who occasionally experience low self-esteem. These troubled employees, it should be noted, may also possess other dysfunctions that arise from feelings of powerlessness and worthlessness: substance abuse, phobias, hypochondria, stress-related illness, and many types of dysfunctional interpersonal behavior including poor interpersonal skills and poor control over impulses. The presence of such problems may signal chronic low self-esteem as well as further aggravate the problems it creates in the workplace.

Regrettably there are few easy things a supervisor can do to encourage employees to truly feel better about themselves and, therefore, less compulsive. The discussion of family pathology and the list of dysfunctional psychological defenses and lifestyle solutions is a sobering warning. Overcoming these major problems and interpersonal solutions to anxiety should not be presumed to fall within the purvey of supervisors, however—at the minimum, the origins of the problems are clinical in nature. Moreover, if a superior ends up feeling as though he must take care of an employee to make him feel good about himself, the supervisor may end up compromising himself, his principles, and his relationship with other employees. No matter how hard one tries and how good one's intentions are, these efforts are likely to end in failure. Months of soothing reinforcement may be undone by the slightest hint of criticism, imposition of formal authority, or lack of attention. This eventuality is frustrating and makes supervisors feel ineffective. The basis of the frustration is the supervisor's belief that he can *make* the employee feel better about himself. But a supervisor cannot continually prop up an employee's self-esteem. For employees who possess very low self-esteem, failure is not a question of if but when. This is not to say that the other employees cannot benefit from efforts to bolster their self-esteem—they can, and efforts should be made to do so.

Given these dynamics, there are actions a supervisor can take to avoid wasted effort while nurturing employees' self-esteem. The following guidelines for supervisors are primarily directed toward employees who suffer from persistent feelings of low self-esteem and use the three lifestyle solutions to combat anxiety.

• Give praise when it is merited. Do not change supervisory style to accommodate the expansive person's need for approval, the self-effacing person's need for caretaking attention, or the resigned person's wish to be left alone. Avoid ongoing efforts to prop up the employee's self-esteem that may make it appear that the supervisor favors the employee. Remember that an employee's many needs can become a seductive force that prompts rescue fantasies.

• Similarly, give criticism in a nonthreatening way that maintains self-esteem when it is merited (Hamilton, 1990, pp. 230–233). Do not fear hurting the person's feelings. Accept the fact that employees who suffer from low self-esteem will overreact to criticism and to uses of power and authority even when wielded in the most thoughtful way. The supervisor may be encouraged to feel that he is a brutal, insensitive, uncaring person and, if made to feel sufficiently anxious, may become defensive and insensitive. The supervisor may come to dread having to offer criticism and direction as a result of the expansive person's vindictive and perfectionist responses, the self-effacing person's hurt feelings, or the resigned person's feelings of being coerced. Eventually the supervisor may not offer correction when it is merited. When the supervisor comes to feel this way, the employee has won the encounter. The employee has gained control of his anxiety by controlling the supervisor, and the supervisor may feel that he is no longer effective.

• The employee who readily personalizes the behavior of others will inevitably develop conflicted relationships with others— who, it will be asserted, are aggressive, untrustworthy, imperfect, competitive, insensitive, unprofessional, coercive, and willing to invade one's privacy and disrupt one's peace of mind (Cermak, 1986, p. 20). If confronted, the employee will offer a list of documented grievances—others are never perfect. Any attempt to intervene in these relationships is fraught with difficulty, however, and it may prove to be impossible to achieve an acceptable outcome. The expansive person may simply have to get even. The self-effacing person may persist in the relationship despite feelings of being abused. The resigned person may remain withdrawn and unavailable for future interaction. Supervisors must recognize this reality if they are to avoid feelings of personal failure. Others may feel it is not their responsibility to safeguard the person's self-esteem; perhaps they can, at best, be sensitized to the need to be more thoughtful in their interactions. The employee should be reminded that others are doing their best and he has a responsibility to learn to deal more effectively with others and events. He might be encouraged to visit the office of employee assistance if the problems are significant and influence the performance of work.

- Expansive and resigned employees may be exceptionally resistant to receiving direction—indeed, they may openly combat it or retreat from it. Painful interactions with others in positions of authority will remind the employee of detested parental authority figures. As a result, the supervisor may become the focal point for the transference of many pain-filled childhood feelings. Supervisors may well find that they cannot get the person to follow instructions or to change behavior that undermines the supervisor's reputation and performance. Correcting these dynamics can be difficult and may even require help from human resource professionals. Pointing out the resistance will be greeted with defensiveness. The supervisor must be patient, persistent, consistent, and sympathetic. The employee must learn that the supervisor is different from detested images of parental figures.

- Direct confrontation is not likely to be successful. The employee will respond to confrontation with feelings associated with prior life experiences where power and authority were abused and criticism abounded. Efforts to discuss problems will lead to disorienting responses such as counterattacks, tears, or withdrawal. Direct confrontation should be used with care and as part of a larger plan of intervention.

- Counseling may paradoxically be both well received and rejected. The employee wants approval and caretaking attention while simultaneously wishing to avoid criticism, change, and encroachment into his personal space. A supervisor who takes a personal interest in helping the employee may find a bottomless pit of need for approval and positive interactions. But, strangely, he may also find that his best efforts at changing the employee's feelings about himself and his behavior have little effect. Counseling and coaching should be incorporated within a comprehensive intervention strategy.

- When the employee's behavior becomes dysfunctional, referrals to employee assistance will be greeted with resistance. The employee will feel that he is just fine or is being personally attacked by the suggestion. The expansive person may claim that others are causing the problem. The self-effacing person may be relieved that someone cares enough to make the recommendations, but he will not overcome his inertia and act on the suggestions. The resigned person may respond by arguing that it is none of the supervisor's business. Before endeavoring such a referral, it is wise to visit employee assistance to learn how to approach the employee for the referral.

• Progressive discipline and the threat of reassignment or termination will reinforce the employee's belief that he is powerless and worthless. The supervisor is likely to feel guilty and anxious about contemplating discipline that will inevitably be greeted by vindictive, tearful, or withdrawn responses. Persistent dysfunctional behavior must be addressed, however, and if all else fails, the supervisor should be prepared to offer progressive discipline. Consideration should be given to transferring the person to a position that suits his defensive temperament. Staff positions involving limited supervision and limited interactions with others might well capitalize on the person's skills and knowledge. In any case, the expansive person's aggression should not be rewarded by being "kicked upstairs," which rewards his behavior and reaffirms his idealized self-image.

• Supervisors must be prepared for the employee's nimble use of psychological defenses. The employee may switch rapidly between one defense and another, and continued distress will lead to a gradual escalation of their use in unyielding ways. Coping with an array of defenses will succeed only if the employee is enlisted in an effort to reflect upon what he is saying, thinking, feeling, and doing. The supervisor must also possess sufficient insight and skill to hold the defenses up for scrutiny and, hopefully, understanding. But the supervisor must not become an "armchair Freud" and presume to interpret the defenses. The lifestyle solutions to anxiety are signals that the employee is trying to control the supervisor and the situation. Compulsive and unthinking reliance on the solutions—which, as mentioned, resemble personality types—is more difficult to respond to than the psychological defenses. The employee's sense of self will feel endangered. Although the best course may be to consult a human resource professional, understanding the solutions can help the supervisor avoid being controlled by them.

• Tough love means not yielding to the many subtle (and sometimes not so subtle) demands of employees but letting them know you care. Avoiding enabling behavior can be a lose/lose situation: the employee is not rewarded, admired, or taken care of; the supervisor feels detested by the employee for not doing so. This approach can, however, be successful if one is prepared for its difficulties.

• Another simple behavior modification approach is the use of nonrewards (Allcorn and Allcorn, 1991). In this case the employee may frequently present behavior that needs to change. The expansive person may be critical, aggressive, or manipulative; the self-effacing person may be passive and dependent; the resigned person may be energetic and withdrawn. Rather than appearing defensive, caretaking, or angry and critical, the supervisor provides no appearance of feeling. No rewarding response is offered. Eventually the employee learns that the various types of behavior he customarily relies on to control self-esteem by controlling others are not working—and eventually he may give them up in favor of more authentic behavior. There is, of course, always the possibility that the employee will become more agitated. In this case the supervisor may use one of the intervention strategies discussed earlier.

In sum, then, dealing with employees who have chronically low self-esteem is, without a doubt, one of the most demanding and unrewarding tasks a supervisor must face. This discussion has not explicitly addressed the personal and work-related dysfunctions of employees who are compelled to overachieve in order to receive approval and demonstrate self-worth. In many instances this behavior may be well received by the supervisor. But to the extent it creates personal and family suffering as well as interpersonal problems at work, it will have to be dealt with in the same way as other problems of low self-esteem.

A Few Hypotheses

Low self-esteem is a problem in the workplace that may well be overlooked for the obvious reason that it is commonplace and difficult to deal with. If supervisors are not careful, however, these employees end up in control of the employee/supervisor relation-

ship. Apart from exploring these problems, this chapter also forms
the basis for a number of testable hypotheses about human behavior
in large organizations (Diamond and Allcorn, 1985b):

- Organizations may become top-heavy with employees who consistently rely on the masculine expansive solution to anxiety.
  These employees will strive for mastery at virtually any personal
  cost and are compelled to fight their way to the top.
- Organizations may become middle or bottom-heavy with employees who consistently rely on the feminine self-effacing solution and the gender-neutral resigned solution to anxiety. As
  the self-effacing and expansive solutions complement each
  other, their workplace effects are intensified.
- The effort to implement organizational change will be resisted
  by employees with low self-esteem. Change will be felt to
  threaten the interpersonal networks that help to stave off feelings of powerlessness and worthlessness.
- The preoccupation with controlling self and others in order to
  maintain security and self-esteem may be extended to trying to
  control the design of work and the organization and may even
  be extended to the customer/client interface. Every effort will be
  made to create a controlled, stress-free work setting.
- The interactions among people who consistently rely on one of
  the defensive solutions to anxiety are predictable. (See Diamond
  and Allcorn, 1985a, 1990.)

In sum, the models in Figures 7.1 and 7.2 provide researchers and
managers with testable hypotheses for action research and a comprehensive perspective for appreciating human behavior in the
workplace.

References

Allcorn, S. "Leadership Styles: The Psychological Picture." *Person-
nel,* 1988, *65*(4), 54–56.
Allcorn, S. *Superstars in Resistant Organizations.* Westport, Conn.:
Quorum Books, 1991.

Allcorn, S. *Codependency in the Workplace.* Westport, Conn.: Quorum Books, 1992.

Allcorn, S., and Allcorn, J. "One-Minute 'Non-Rewards' for Counterproductive Behavior." *Supervisory Management,* 1991, *36*(2), 10.

Argyris, C., and Schon, D. *Organizational Learning: A Theory of Action Perspective.* Reading, Mass.: Addison-Wesley, 1978.

Basch, M. *Understanding Psychotherapy.* New York: Basic Books, 1988.

Beattie, M. *Beyond Codependency.* New York: Harper & Row, 1989.

Benjamin, J. *The Bonds of Love.* New York: Pantheon, 1988.

Bowlby, J. *Attachment and Loss.* Vol. 1: *Attachment.* New York: Penguin, 1969.

Brockner, J. *Self-Esteem at Work.* Lexington, Mass.: Lexington Books, 1988.

Brody, S., and Axelrad, S. *Anxiety and Ego Formation in Infancy.* New York: International Universities Press, 1970.

Cermak, T. *Diagnosing and Treating Co-Dependency.* Minneapolis, Minn.: Johnson Institute, 1986.

Chadorow, N. *Feminism and Psychoanalytic Theory.* New Haven, Conn.: Yale University Press, 1989.

Coleman, J. *Abnormal Psychology and Modern Life.* Glenview, Ill.: Scott, Foresman, 1964.

Diamond, M. "Resistance to Change: A Psychoanalytic Critique of Argyris and Schon's Contributions to Organization Theory and Intervention." *Journal of Management Studies,* 1986, *23*(5), 543–562.

Diamond, M., and Allcorn, S. "Psychological Barriers to Personal Responsibility." *Organization Dynamics,* 1984, *12*(4), 66–77.

Diamond, M., and Allcorn, S. "Psychological Dimensions of Role Use in Bureaucratic Organizations." *Organizational Dynamics,* 1985a, *14*(1), 35–59.

Diamond, M., and Allcorn, S. "Psychological Responses to Stress in Complex Organizations." *Administration and Society,* 1985b, *17*(2), 217–239.

Diamond, M., and Allcorn, S. "The Freudian Factor." *Personnel Journal,* 1990, *6*(3), 52–65.

Dyer, W. *Your Erroneous Zones.* New York: Avon Books, 1976.

Freud, A. *The Ego and the Mechanisms of Defense.* New York: International Universities Press, 1966.

Freud, S. *The Ego and the Id.* New York: Norton, 1960. (Originally published 1923.)

Greenspan, S. *The Development of the Ego.* Madison, Conn.: International Universities Press, 1989.

Hamilton, G. *Self and Others: Object Relations Theory in Practice.* Northvale, N.J.: Jason Aronson, 1990.

Hartmann, H. *Ego Psychology and the Problem of Adaptation.* New York: International Universities Press, 1958.

Hartmann, H. *Essays on Ego Psychology.* New York: International Universities Press, 1964.

Horney, K. *The Neurotic Personality of Our Times.* New York: Norton, 1937.

Horney, K. *Neurosis and Human Growth.* New York: Norton, 1950.

Josselson, R. *Finding Herself: Pathways to Identity Development in Women.* San Francisco: Jossey-Bass, 1987.

Klein, G. *Psychoanalytic Theory.* New York: International Universities Press, 1976.

Kofodimos, J. "Why Executives Lose Their Balance." *Organizational Dynamics,* 1990, *19*(1), 58–73.

Korman, A. "Hypothesis of Work Behavior Revisited and an Extension." *Academy of Management Review,* 1976, *1,* 50–63.

Levinson, H. *Executive.* Cambridge, Mass.: Harvard University Press, 1968.

Levinson, H. *Psychological Man.* Cambridge, Mass.: Levinson Institute, 1976.

Masterson, J. *The Search for the Real Self.* New York: Free Press, 1988.

May, R. *The Meaning of Anxiety.* New York: Washington Square Press, 1977.

Miller, A. *Banished Knowledge.* New York: Doubleday, 1990.

Neilsen, E., and Gypen, J. "The Subordinate's Predicaments." *Harvard Business Review,* 1979, *57*(5), 133–143.

Osherson, S. *Finding Our Fathers.* New York: Fawcett Columbine, 1986.

Reich, W. *Character Analysis.* New York: Farrar, Straus & Giroux, 1972.

Rosen, V. *Style, Character and Language.* New York: Jason Aronson, 1977.

Rycroft, C. *A Critical Dictionary of Psychoanalysis.* Totowa, N.J.: Littlefield, Adams, 1973.

Sandler, J., and Freud, A. *The Analysis of Defense.* New York: International Universities Press, 1985.

Sanford, L., and Donovan, M. *Women and Self-Esteem.* New York: Penguin, 1984.

Schwalbe, M. "Autonomy in Work and Self-Esteem." *Sociological Quarterly,* 1985, *26*(4), 519–535.

Shapiro, D. *Neurotic Styles.* New York: Basic Books, 1965.

Shapiro, D. *Autonomy and Rigid Character.* New York: Basic Books, 1981.

Sullivan, H. *The Interpersonal Theory of Psychiatry.* New York: Norton, 1953.

Wegscheider-Cruse, S. *Choicemaking.* Deerfield Beach, Fla.: Health Communications, 1985.

Part Three

Managerial
Programs
and
Practices

8

Redirecting Ego Energy: The Overly Expansive Executive

Robert E. Kaplan

THE SORT OF EGO ENERGY with which I am most familiar as a researcher and practitioner is that of the corporate executive. With my colleagues Joan Kofodimos and Wilfred Drath I gained this familiarity from an intensive study of senior managers that used a feedback-based service as an opportunity to learn about executive character and development (Kaplan, Drath, and Kofodimos, 1991). What has consistently impressed me about these people is the enormous energy that the large majority of them bring to their work. Typically, they have a lot of energy to accomplish things, to distinguish themselves, to take on increasing responsibility, and to advance their careers. Of the various ways this energy can be managed—that is, channeled by the executives themselves or their organizations—the one that interests me most is self-development. How can executives, at or near the pinnacle of their organizations

I would like to thank the following for their helpful comments on an earlier draft: Chris Argyris, Bill Drath, Tim Hall, Rebecca Kaplan, Rick Ketterer, Charles Palus, and Robert Shaw.

and careers, grow and develop in such a way that they expend their abundant energy more productively and more constructively?

What is ego energy? Since novelists are among the best psychologists, let's start with what the protagonist of Saul Bellow's *Henderson the Rain King* says. A fifty-year-old strapping lug of a man on a quest to find some peace in his tumultuous life, Henderson observes that "all you hear from guys is desire, desire, desire, knocking its way out of the breast, and fear, striking and striking" (p. 297). That, it seems to me, is one simple way of defining ego energy—fears and desires. Ego energy, for me, is the emotional energy we spend in avoiding certain things and seeking certain other things.

In my experience, executives often mix a desire to succeed with a fear of failing. Even those very successful, seemingly self-assured, senior managers who appear to have an uncomplicated need to achieve may privately harbor a considerable fear of failure. One executive set me straight in an interview when I reflected back to him that he had a strong need to succeed. "No," he said. "I am motivated by a fear of *not* succeeding." He explained, "I worry and I worry about worrying." In fact, desire and fear correspond closely. To the extent that an executive covets success, to that extent he or she abhors failure.

As my colleagues and I struggled in the early years of our research to find out what energizes executives, we concluded that what they fundamentally wanted was *mastery*—mastery defined as being on top of their jobs in terms of competence and control. We later concluded that in fact they were fundamentally seeking a sense of personal worth and that mastery was their primary way of achieving it.

The question of managing ego energy arises because organizations succeed or fail depending on whether they can enlist their employees' effort and energy. People work for the organization's purposes to the extent that they make an emotional investment in their jobs and the organization. Much of the management literature over the years has been concerned with how to heighten the motivation of workers or managers. In executives the challenge is often the opposite: how to contend with a need to achieve so strong that it begins to cut back on itself.

For executive development to be effective when the person has an excessive need to achieve, our experience has been that it is not enough to change behavior. It is also necessary to work with the executive in altering his or her emotional investments. If development means a significant and sustainable change, then it appears that the change must occur not just at the steering wheel but to some extent in the design of the vehicle itself.

The Executive's Need for Development

I have adopted the term *expansive* to describe the intense drive to achieve and succeed. As the word suggests, expansive executives want to push back the boundaries of what is possible, and they will expend a great deal of energy to do that. They resist limits—in what they personally can do and in what their organizations can do. Although sometimes shy outside a work setting, they are prepared to intrude on the territories of the people around them to get a job done. It has been said of Mario Cuomo, for example, that "he fills his space—and some of yours, too," They are inclined to push the limits—the limits of what people think can be done and the limits of the energy invested in making improbable things happen. In a world that can be bureaucratically stifling, these executives find a way to engage in institutional heroics. Ross Perot is perhaps the epitome of the heroic institutional leader pushing back the envelope and defying the odds—with his daring rescue of two of his executives imprisoned in revolutionary Iran, his attempt to rescue General Motors, and his numerous other take-matters-into-your-own-hands exploits.

It is interesting to discriminate between those expansive executives who perform effectively and those who do not. What makes the difference? We have found the difference to reside in the *strength* of the drive to mastery—the extent of the emotional energy invested in attaining mastery. When expansiveness is strong but within bounds, it is constructive and productive for the organization. But taken to the extremes of too much or too little, it becomes a problem. Table 8.1 delineates the characteristics of executives with too much, too little, and more or less the right amount of expansiveness.

This chapter focuses on the overexpansive type because lead-

Table 8.1. Degrees of Expansiveness.

Dimension	Too much	In moderation	Too little
Aspirations for organization	Sets organization's sights too high, sets too many objectives	Sets ambitious but attainable objectives for organization	Sets organization's sights too low
Aspirations for self	Very competitive; has to win at everything, be right about everything	Very high (but not excessive) standards for self	Not competitive enough
Balance	Works is almost one's whole life	Some kind of balance	Is work a high enough priority?
Ego	Big ego; self-aggrandizing	Confident but not excessively	Modest; self-deprecating
Need for recognition	Huge	Large but not unlimited	Modest
Influences on others	Pushes others too hard; aggressive	Pushes others hard, but not abusive; assertive	Doesn't push others hard enough; not assertive enough
	Fills own space and some of yours too	Fills own space but respects your boundaries	Doesn't fill own space
Sharing influence	Too controlling, can't let go	Holds up own end but able to empower	Empowers to a fault
Openness to influence	Poor listener, hard to influence	Open to influence, listens adequately	Exceptional listener, too accommodating
Treatment of people	Bad; insensitive	Acceptable; considers people's needs	Very good; compassionate, caring, sensitive
Popularity	May be unpopular but often admired for sheer talent, persistence, results	Not unpopular; respected	Popular; admired as a person

Table 8.1. Degrees of Expansiveness, Cont'd.

Dimension	Too much	In moderation	Too little
Judging/ accepting	Intolerant; own way is the only way	Critical yet able to see shades of gray	Very accepting of people, to the point of being uncritical
Constructive criticism	Defensive; externalizes	Reasonably open	May be too quick to take responsibility

ership development for them represents an interesting case of redirecting ego energy. Later, primarily by way of contrast, I discuss the underexpansive type. The moderate category is well represented in the executive population but is treated here only as a direction in which executives on either end of the continuum can move.

Extremely expansive executives are described by the people around them as "driven." It is as if they are possessed by their urge to excel. They have lost control of themselves to it. Being driven means in many cases that these people are in perpetual motion. They have great difficulty sitting still. They will do nearly anything to attain mastery. One executive was described in these terms by a close friend: "With him there are no limits. There are absolutely no limits. I think it comes from athletics—from being a star athlete— where you push the limits back. He'll say: 'You want to become a brain surgeon or you want to run marathons? Let's figure it out.' His attitude is there is no problem that can't be solved." He pushed himself, his organization, his body to the limit. This tremendous force in him was a great asset at work and at home but also a great liability.

Even though it may not be apparent to the casual observer, or indeed to the person in question, the truly driven executive of this kind is, fundamentally, anxious about self-worth. Expansive executives are not the only people with doubts about themselves. But they are distinctive in the way they respond to that insecurity—by proving their worth through high achievement, stunning success, and high position.

Acute concern about one's worth seems to prompt extremely expansive executives to go to extraordinary lengths to allay that concern, and this is how the drive to mastery becomes self-defeating. As we will see in the following case study, in the process of building up something, these executives inadvertently tear things down. In the process of moving things forward, they slow down progress. It is always ironic, sometimes tragic. The wife of one such ultra-expansive executive worried that her executive husband was heading for a fall: "Tragedy is the fall of a figure from a lofty position because of a flaw. I would hate for that to happen to him because of the things he doesn't pay attention to—mainly, relating to people." How can driven senior managers escape the irony that they care so much about winning, prevailing, triumphing that they undermine themselves and the organizations they lead?

Moderating Extremes: The Case of Tim Foley

For extremely expansive executives, development involves a moderation of extreme behavior. From being overly aggressive, they may become demanding without being abrasive or abusive. From being so dominant that they transgress into other people's territory, they may learn to occupy their place fully without invading that of others. From being too controlling, they may learn to turn over responsibility appropriately. From being poor listeners who are hard to influence, they may become reasonably open to ideas and influence. Limited empathy may give way to a better appreciation for what other people—especially people different from them—think, feel, and need. Insensitivity to other people's needs may change to reasonable consideration. Extremely expansive executives may cease making work their whole life and strike a balance between work and the rest of life. They may go from having aspirations without limit for their organization to having a sense of what can realistically be achieved. All these changes in behavior represent a shift from too much expansiveness to strong yet moderated expansiveness—a developmental shift from overabundance to the right amount required by the situation.

Before considering how, at a deeper level, ego energy is redirected in line with these adjustments of behavior, let us consider the case of an executive who experienced this kind of development. Tim Foley, a line executive who had spent most of his twenty-seven-year career in his present company, had risen to a high position of considerable responsibility. (This case is based mainly on one executive, but to protect this person from possible repercussions some material is drawn from a similar executive.) Although he brought exceptional intensity to his work, his wife and family had always been important to him too. Yet his intense drive, which he credited with the success he had enjoyed, had always presented problems to some of his co-workers. The drive had not diminished with his ascension to the executive suite. Fundamentally he had a good heart, but it was hidden from those who did not enjoy his friendship or his high opinion.

What many people experienced was the hardness of his personality. He was variously described by his co-workers as "hard working," "hard charging," "hard driving," "hard-edged," and "hard on people." Although he had his supporters and had assembled a good track record, his detractors felt that he was only moderately effective, mainly because he obtained results at a human cost. (We came to these conclusions on the basis of an elaborate assessment of Tim Foley's leadership and character. More on the method later.)

Then, against the odds, Tim went through an ameliorating transition over the course of three years. The odds were against him because the problems in his style were clearly ingrained and quite a few people doubted he could change. Yet a superior was later to admit: "I was wrong about Tim. He was able to change." Although Tim Foley was demonstrably still the same man he had been, and although he had by no means eliminated the problems, he had clearly changed and the majority of people around him, at home and at work, believed the change was for real and believed it would last. (We drew this conclusion on the basis of interviews with twenty-two co-workers, five family members, and Tim himself. The chief research question in these interviews was: What, if any, change have you observed in Tim Foley in the last three years?)

No single cause seemed to account for the change, but there were three leading explanations: an intensive assessment and development program; a new job he took soon after receiving the feedback, which presented him with a clean slate; and a natural process of maturation. As a result of the transition, Tim was widely seen as a more effective manager. Evaluating him three years after the assessment and development program, his co-workers rated him an average of two points higher on a ten-point scale of effectiveness. What changes in his behavior were associated with this jump in effectiveness?

Co-workers reported two broad kinds of stylistic change: he was less hard on people, and he seemed to be less controlling and more open to influence. On the first count, he was widely seen as more sensitive, less intimidating, more appreciative of people with styles different from his. Although he had been recognized as a leader who got results, his approach had been largely one-dimensional. He had been almost single-mindedly results-oriented and very aggressive—sometimes too aggressive—in driving for results. A superior who had seen him as a strong leader later explained: "My definition of a leader is in all regards, not just pure numbers. He was known for the numbers he got, but you'd have to bandage everyone. He got great results but no one was here to play tomorrow." Another co-worker observed that he had become "more sensitive to people." Someone else felt that "he is really working the people side of the management of his business more than he has in the past." Perhaps unwittingly, he had made a habit of putting people on the defensive—especially people who operated differently from him. But now he was seen as somewhat more tolerant and patient.

On the second count, he began to control his subordinates less while granting them more influence with him. He now listened better. A peer commented: "Where he would have dismissed things, now he's trying to keep his mouth shut and listen." Another way the change manifested itself was that he now gave his direct reports, senior people in their own right, more latitude. He had become "less directive." A subordinate said: "He's trying harder not to meddle, not to dig too deep. He'll say, 'This is your show; run it.' His level of detailed probing has diminished. So I'm feeling better about the controlling aspect." Another subordinate said: "He gives me a lot of leeway and allows me to run my own show." His peers saw the change, too. One of them commented: "I give Tim credit for allowing them to run free." Another one said: "He's doing a really fine job of not getting in the way and at the same time showing the appropriate level of interest." Thus he became more effective because he created less interference. He got out of his subordinates' way and he cut down on the noise he had been creating by not treating people well.

Moreover, certain corresponding changes seem to have taken place on the inside as well. Without actually talking with Tim about how he felt, several people detected a greater comfort with himself. One superior asked: "Did he become at peace with himself? It feels like that: the guy is more at ease with himself." A number of people said that he had "mellowed." Tim, too, felt that he had changed, including his feeling about himself. He felt more confident. There were indications that his self-esteem had grown. Less obvious, but just as important, his trust in himself evidently had increased. In a sense it all came down to trust. In the past he had difficulty trusting others—hence the control, hence the hard treatment. A perceptive person had said at the time: "There is an element of trust that he withholds." Someone else had said: "I think Tim has a high skepticism of motives; I'd like him to be more trusting." And associated with his inability to fully trust others had been his inability to fully trust himself.

Reflecting on his newfound ability to empower, Tim told us: "It's a hard thing to give up—to take your fingers off every switch and let someone else push the switch." He now realized one reason why he had kept his fingers on the controls: "I was always questioning my abilities. Was I good enough to do the task? If you aren't in perfect control, that little ghost tends to pop up. You've got to have faith that you're in more control than you were before and you have to have the confidence in yourself and in your abilities to do that." Trust and confidence in himself went hand in hand with his trust and confidence in others.

Seeing how many things in his life were connected, he could now look back on his childhood and see how a lot of this probably came about. His mother, for example, had been hypercritical and, while holding him to a high standard, had systematically undermined his confidence in himself and put him perpetually on guard. He had felt painfully inadequate. No achievement at the time could alter this feeling. A starter on his high school's state championship baseball team, he skipped the team party because he felt unworthy. As a young man still in his teens he had a choice, he now felt looking back, of giving up on himself or "building a shell around myself." Inside he remained, like all human beings, vulnerable and, because of the harsh treatment he had received, perhaps a little more vulnerable than others. But the shell protected him. And when he became a manager, he led with that armored part of himself. That is what most of his co-workers had felt in dealing with him. Only in the recent past had he felt comfortable enough to soften his hard approach at work.

Redirecting Ego Energy

Tim Foley's experience illustrates what we have found in our research: executives' patterns of leadership behavior are rooted in basic character; their behavior is patterned not just by conditioning or habits but also by basic beliefs or assumptions about how they have chosen to position themselves in this world so as to support a sense of self-worth. Such beliefs channel emotional energy—or ego energy—and direct it into actions assumed to benefit the self. The personality theorist George Kelly (1955) posited that personal constructs, which are similar to what I mean by beliefs, "channelize" behavior. For executives to make a significant and lasting change in the way they lead requires, in my view, a shift at two levels: outer/behavioral and inner/emotional. I would not argue that change at one level must precede change at the other. Both levels of change are essential; each supports and plays off the other.

The type of development I see possible for the typical executive is a redirection of some emotional (or psychic or ego) energy from self-satisfaction through individual achievement to self-satisfaction through relationships. Development, then, redresses an imbalance. Extremely expansive executives, highly specialized and distinctly lopsided, move from being dominated by one part of themselves—the mastery-seeking part—to allowing the emergence of another part—the capacity for strong relationships. The shift that Tim Foley underwent earned him greater balance and range managerially. Several people volunteered that they now saw him as "broader" and a "more complete manager" because he had added an important dimension to his leadership.

The shift from a near-exclusive concentration on mastery to some kind of balance between mastery and relationships is a change in what one desires and also a change in what one fears. In other words, overrelying on mastery stems not just from a great desire for mastery but also from avoiding intimacy. The heavy investment in mastery is overdetermined by a fear of intimacy. To invest more in relationships, then, requires us to overcome some of our inhibition about close relationships. We learn to feel safer with other people, more secure with them, more sure of our worth in their eyes, more trusting that we will be treated well.

The sort of shift we are talking about can be understood as differentiation in the sense that the individual no longer operates along such a narrow band but adds previously latent capacities to his or her repertoire. The shift involves differentiation in a second sense as well. Executives become clearer about who they are as individuals. This is a result of self-reflection that breeds a greater appreciation of one's strengths and a reconciliation to one's weaknesses. It is also a result, more profoundly, of greater self-acceptance. One knows oneself—where one begins and where one leaves off—and is more comfortable with that knowledge. It is not self-satisfaction but self-acceptance. This kind of self-differentiation distinguishes the person more clearly from other people. But instead of making the person unavailable for relationships, it actually puts the person in a better position to come together successfully with other people (Levinson, 1978). Differentiation of this kind actually enables integration.

One Way to Redirect Ego Energy

Over the past several years my colleagues and I have evolved a fairly unusual and, we think, innovative development program for senior managers—the program Tim Foley went through—that has helped executives redirect their ego energy. This is a program for executives with serious performance problems as well as a program for executives with merely a need for fine-tuning. Most of the executives who have taken part in the program are overendowed with expansive tendencies, but some have been underendowed.

The program originated independently at the Center for Creative Leadership and at Kiel Rimmer International. In its full-blown version it is generally reserved for senior managers because of the considerable expense involved, but there is no reason why certain elements of the program or its overall whole-life perspective could not be used with managers at lower levels. There is strong evidence that the program works, at least in some cases (Kaplan, 1990). The program is not a one-time event but runs for months or even years in connection with other events in the executive's life. Although a major impetus for change is the initial assessment that culminates in a great deal of feedback, the program is more than "getting feedback."

One way to describe the assessment is as developmental biography. If an authorized biography is one commissioned by the subject, or someone close to the subject, to tell the story of the person's life in favorable terms, then developmental biography is one commissioned by the person to take an independent view for the sake of the person's development. The material comes primarily from interviews with co-workers (superiors, peers, subordinates), family, and friends. Co-worker ratings as well as several psychological tests such as the Myers-Briggs and the Adjective Checklist are also used. The resulting report is by no means a complete story of the executive's life, but it goes beyond typical feedback for executives in treating their leadership in the context of their lives as a whole. In addition to giving quite a full picture of the executive at work (based on co-worker ratings and the interview data), the feedback report includes a sketch of the person's private life (based mainly on interviews with present family members and friends) and a sketch of the person's original family (based primarily on interviews with members of that family or childhood friends). The executive is interviewed on these topics as well.

We are aware that this design breaks a taboo against involving the family in a management development program. The reason we include the family is to get a reading on the executive's behavior and character at home. If similar patterns show up in both spheres, the executive is more likely to believe the accuracy and relevance of the assessment. The other reason we include the family is that if the executive is to grow and change, the family and especially the spouse must be a source of support. If it is uncommon to collect data from a manager's present family, it is even more uncommon to collect information from the original family. In "taking a history," we help executives to see the shape of their character by uncovering clues as to what shaped them originally.

Given the highly personal nature of the program, we give the assessment report only to the executive. The executive is of course free to share the information with anyone he or she chooses. Most of them give the data on leadership to a trusted co-worker or two selected to help—and committed to help—the executive make use of the results. Another ground rule is that, with certain exceptions, we do not identify who said what in the report. When there is an exception, we ask that person's permission. Even when data are reported anonymously, we advise respondents that a certain response may be identifiable on the basis of what they say or how they say it.

This is obviously a high-impact intervention that gains its power from the large quantity of information collected, from gathering information in three spheres of the person's life, from combining quantitative data (including several psychological tests) and qualitative data, and from the power of extended verbal descriptions. Perhaps the most powerful aspect of the program is having three groups of perceptive people characterize the executive in their own words.

The rationale for offering so comprehensive an intervention is to create conditions for significant growth and change. Executives may have to do more than simply modify their behavior. They must also come to terms with the emotional needs that drive their behavior. It is not easy to get through to adults in general; it is even more difficult to reach proud executives with a track record and a high position to justify their attachment to the way they are (Kaplan, Drath, and Kofodimos, 1991). More modest interventions, while they have the advantage of running less risk and staying safely within the bounds of conventional management development, have less impact. If the awareness they create is merely intellectual, the changes will be skin-deep and short-lived. This comment by a peer of an executive trying to change in response to feedback is not uncommon: "People have seen his attempts at recent behavioral changes, but they don't see the changes as genuine. There's a disconnect between the way he's behaving and how he really feels. He was given some feedback and asked to make some changes, so people saw him behave differently, but they didn't believe his inside and outside were aligned." It is not just behavior but also emotional energy that has to be channeled differently.

What are the benefits of such an exercise? One benefit that accrues to virtually all participants is awareness—both intellectual and emotional. As a result, executives see the consequences of their actions more clearly and the effect on their actions of their emotional needs. A benefit that accrues to certain participants—for example, Tim Foley—is what I have called a "character shift" (Kaplan, 1990). By no means a total change in the person's makeup, it is a reordering or rebalancing of the inner world. It is a shift in the person's array of emotional investments, an alteration in how the person allocates emotional energy. It is also a change in the person's beliefs about the worth of various emotional investments. The executive stops climbing the career ladder long enough to reappraise the value of the ladder itself (Levinson, 1978). One participant characterized this type of development in the following way: "I heard [in the feedback] that I needed to behave differently. What I found in the next few weeks was that there was a side of me that hadn't found a place in business. I needed to unlock that place. Rather than *act out* a difference—that would have been shallow—I had to *be* different. That was difficult. Parts of me had been well developed, but other parts had been suppressed. . . . I'm a healthier person now." This sort of shift is often accompanied by a greater appreciation of the connection between the executive's character as leader, spouse, parent, and friend.

For some time I believed that the power of the assessment to stimulate this development stemmed chiefly from the criticism acting as dissonance between the executives' beliefs about themselves and their actual experience. Lately I have come to appreciate the curative effect of praise. One participant, reflecting several years later on the feedback's effect, commented that the single thing that most affected him at the time was the affirmation he received. (He had received his share of criticism and taken it seriously.) Another executive, reflecting the morning after getting the feedback, said how pleasantly surprised he was that his strengths, primarily intellectual and analytical, were recognized universally: "These things I admire in others, but I was insecure about them in myself. There's nothing that I would rather have people say about me. It's probably too important." What is significant here is not that he felt good but that, assured that he possessed these strengths in abundance, he could free up energy for other things. "What this says to me is that I don't need to try so hard to do this—because it's the image I wanted to have (and have achieved)." He was preparing to reallocate some of the heavy emotional investment from intellectual/analytical pursuits to other matters—namely, relationships. Approval is important to the development of senior managers because of their tendency to go to counterproductive extremes in response to their doubts about themselves and their capabilities.

While the assessment is a way of getting executives moving, by itself it is not sufficient to get them to their developmental destination. Insights must be translated into action. In fact, progress is the result of an interplay between insight leading to action and action leading to further insight. To encourage this mutually reinforcing cycle, coaches—external consultant, boss, colleague, spouse, friend—have a role to play. In addition to providing moral support, coaches can help the executive design and learn from experiments. Training can also help the executive develop new capacities to act— to listen, to make a speech, to negotiate, to run a meeting.

This kind of development is not a one-time event—a sudden revelation that immediately rectifies the executive's performance problems. Typically, it is a process of evolution that plays out over several months or even years, as developmental activity ebbs and flows with events in the person's life. One way to keep the executive moving is to repeat the assessment process, on a much smaller scale, from time to time. Six months after the executive receives the original report, it helps, for example, to survey co-workers on progress made and progress still to be made.

The program's power to create a disequilibrium in the person that can lead to profound change is a source of risk that must be carefully managed. Most participating executives absorb the impact of the assessment data without undue difficulty. For a few weeks they introspect more and have more frequent personal conversations than usual. They tend to be self-conscious, even painfully so. One executive likened the experience to having his fingertips sanded. The period following feedback is more or less unsettling, varying in duration and intensity with the executive's makeup and circumstances (Kaplan and Palus, 1993).

Broadly speaking, there are two basic precautions. The first is to make sure that anyone unprepared to handle the unsettling effects of the program does not participate. The prospective participant and his or her spouse must make an informed choice to take part in the program; the people (superiors, human resource executives) who nominate executives in the first place must be well acquainted with the program; the professional staff must do their part by screening out, with the aid of psychological tests like the MMPI, potential participants who are unsuitable for the program. Executives who are fundamentally unstable are unsuitable, but so too are executives whose *situations* are unstable in some way—their marriage is breaking up, they have lost their job, and so on. This program is not for everyone. Or as one former participant put it: "This is not for the timid or for anyone unwilling to accept the need for growth."

The second precaution is to ensure that those who do participate receive support along the way. The participant and his or her spouse must be prepared for the rigors of the feedback experience and, more important, they must be supported during and after that experience. For these functions to be performed properly, a great deal depends on the quality of the staff. At the risk of sounding elitist, let me emphasize: not every management consultant or clinical psychologist can do this. The work requires a blend of cross-disciplinary skills and opposing personal qualities: expertise in both management development and personal development; strength of character to hold one's own with high-powered executives; and empathy and maturity, which means that the client's needs always come first. The relationship between the professional staff and the participant is the key to the executive's safe and beneficial participation.

The professional staff does not necessarily do it all. In fact, the staff's function is as much to enlist the involvement of other people in the executive's work life or personal life as it is to provide a direct service. The professional staff plays a broker role, which includes referring the executive to therapy if that course seems advisable.

Moving Ego Energy in the Other Direction

So far the chapter has focused on executives who are excessively expansive—those whose basic development need is to moderate the tendency to make themselves into instruments of mastery. But there is in our experience a small percentage of executives whose development needs run in the other direction. These executives possess the very qualities that their overly expansive counterparts lack. They are excellent listeners, they are responsive to their people's needs ("people-sensitive"), they do not have a problem turning over responsibility to subordinates, they do not have "ego problems," they are not regarded as "driven," and so on. What they need is to become more demanding of their people, hold them more accountable, be more decisive. The subordinates of executives like this actually appeal to them to take charge—"be the boss"—more often. Executives who are not expansive enough have a big emotional investment in humanitarian virtues like altruism and being a "good person" and have a strong aversion to such managerial vices as overaggressiveness, unilateral control, machismo, and arrogance. What they could benefit from is less dedication to selflessness and more access to personal power—meaning a greater capacity to express their anger, to be impatient, to take stands, to show passion, to have a sharper edge.

If development for overexpansive executives means containing their restless energy, development for underexpansive executives entails releasing the energy held in check by their inhibitions and compunctions. One staff executive, who was so reluctant to be the center of attention that he did not take the initiative with his line executive clients, freed himself to come forward. Another executive operated within a highly restricted zone of acceptable behavior that he set about to expand. A line executive of this type worked far too hard because he felt freer to make demands on himself than on his subordinates. He had some success in modifying his beliefs about what was legitimate behavior. Another line executive tended to leave his subordinates wondering where they stood with him because he avoided telling them clearly what he did not like about their performance. He discovered that when he let his people know precisely what he felt about their work, including his dissatisfaction, they were energized. In general, underexpansive executives are challenged to learn to contain themselves less.

Curing the Energy Crisis

Ego energy needs to be managed to the extent that it is inappropriately applied to the situation. We have found that executives spend too much ego energy attaining mastery and being recognized as masterful, even relative to the heavy demands of their senior jobs. Ironically, they care so desperately about excelling that they diminish their excellence. They seize upon some aspect of their job—for example, intellectual/analytic tasks—and invest in performing these tasks superbly at the expense of other tasks—for example, forming strong relationships. The out-of-proportion investment in mastery is a distortion: while the adjustment meets some of the person's needs, it neglects and frustrates other equally important needs. In parallel fashion, other people think the executive is successful in some respects but at too high a cost in other respects. To the extent that the self one tries so desperately to be is at variance with the person one actually is, that self is, in a sense, false.

Development that eliminates the distortions in an executive's performance helps to reapportion that person's ego energy. The pattern of emotional investment begins to align with what the executive needs and what other people need. Moreover, the executive stops trying so hard to impress. The desire to live up to one's idealized image begins to wane, and the fear of failing to do so fades. And, perhaps, the executive stops leading so much with the hard part of his or her personality. One executive who had changed in this way commented: "I don't have to waste energy trying to be something I'm not." Frances Hesselbein, the executive director of Girl Scouts of America, learned a similar lesson: "It is not hard work that wears you out but the repression of your true personality, and I've found a way of working that does not demand that." This new adjustment allowed her to be remarkably energetic and at the same time calm. The transition is analogous to acquiring a fifth gear that makes it possible for high-achieving types to move at high speeds but low RPMs—with much less wear and tear.

References

Bellow, S. *Henderson the Rain King.* London: Penguin, 1959.

Kaplan, R. E. "Character Change in Executives as 'Re-Form' in Pursuit of Self-Worth." *Journal of Applied Behavioral Science,* 1990, *26*(4), 461–481.

Kaplan, R. E., Drath, W. H., and Kofodimos, J. R. *Beyond Ambition: How Driven Managers Can Lead Better and Live Better.* San Francisco: Jossey-Bass, 1991.

Kaplan, R. E., and Palus, C. J. "An Unusually Potent Development Program for Executives: A Prescription for Good Practice." In preparation, 1993.

Kelly, G. A. *A Theory of Personality: The Psychology of Personal Constructs.* New York: Norton, 1955.

Levinson, D. J. *The Seasons of a Man's Life.* New York: Ballantine Books, 1978.

9

Mobilizing Ego Energy:
Managerial and Leadership Practices

William P. Ferris

Eᴄᴏ ᴇɴᴇʀɢʏ ɪs ᴛʜᴇ ᴄʜʀᴏɴɪᴄ ᴅᴇsɪʀᴇ to define oneself through behavior in a way that demonstrates to others that one is valuable and unique. The ultimate deployment of ego energy in an organization can be either a powerful asset or a ruinous liability. Managerial and leadership practices usually make the difference. These practices will determine whether positive or negative ego energy will drive the behavior elicited. If the practices are designed to assist the development of self-esteem, and thus to release positive ego energy, then the resulting ego-defining behavior will be calculated to achieve organizational and personal goals at the same time, thus coordinating goal attainment. But if practices are designed to gain compliance through fear, intimidation, secrecy, perpetuation of injustice through coercion, and other tactics that debilitate employees' sense of self, pride, achievement, and justice, negative ego energy will be generated. Employees will give their personal goals top priority. They will meet secrecy with secrecy of their own. They will pursue personal objectives out of earshot and eyesight of managers whenever and wherever possible. Their attainment of organizational objectives will become incidental to their attainment of personal objectives—or, worse for the organization, calculated to interfere with organizational objectives.

Thus the ego energy of employees, when tapped in the service of organizational objectives, can unleash powerful forces in the promotion of higher quality and productivity. When it is not tapped carefully, it can work in just the opposite way, demoralizing some employees and ultimately undermining higher quality and productivity. The effect of such negative ego energy is very hard to remediate. Too many corporate executives (as well as corporate policies) tap ego energy in a way that is counterproductive to corporate goals, and too few increase the flow of positive ego energy within the corporation. This chapter differentiates between managerial strategies that increase the flow of positive ego energy and their negative counterparts which, although they appear effective, in fact increase the flow of negative ego energy. In the process, we will examine a model that helps describe the distinction. Abundant examples and a detailed case study further illustrate the differences.

Understanding Ego Energy

First let us clarify the concept of ego energy. While ego energy is present in all aspects of everyday culture, this chapter is concerned specifically with the organizational environment.

This "chronic desire" cited earlier has its roots in the Freudian notion of ego as the organizing center of a person's experience and planning—the sense that a person exists apart from all other people, the "I am" of individual human consciousness (Freud, 1961). It is a "chronic" need because it is present throughout one's existence, though perhaps in a reduced way as one grows older. Its development in psychological thought can be traced through the work of many psychotherapists, including Erik Erikson, who wrote several books on ego, identity, and what he called the epigenetic principle that "anything that grows has a ground plan, and that out of this ground plan the parts arise, each part having its time of special ascendancy, until all parts have arisen to form a functioning whole" (1968, p. 92). His theory of the life cycle of human identity explains how one's identity proceeds in stages until it culminates ideally in the fully functioning mature adult (Erikson, 1968, 1980).

This development occurs within each person's environment—the setting in which the self grows—but especially the environment relating to work and love.

Existential psychology (see especially May, 1977, 1983) has made a point of differentiating between the self—or simply "being"—and the ego in its contention that being precedes ego and only after the infant's self-awareness emerges can the ego emerge— the part of the self that reasons about the relationship of the self to all else. In fact, it is precisely the anxiety caused by the infant's initial realizations of separation from the mother, as well as generalized fear of further separations throughout childhood, adolescence, and into adulthood, that creates the energy that drives the need for ego development, or self-identity. Extending this view to the work organization, those responsible for managing organizations are in a position either to help subordinates manage this anxiety or to exacerbate it. By this point, the anxiety may include not only the fear of separation from the organization but also a generalized fear of a kind of "death" of individuality that occurs when managers cause subordinates to feel that they must conform excessively, that their jobs are overwhelmingly routinized, or that their initiatives to improve things are ignored. Moreover, there may be anxiety related to fear of making mistakes or the ambiguity of what is expected of one. When managers enhance feelings of individuality among subordinates, thus lowering anxiety to manageable levels, they can expect ego development to proceed in a way that benefits the organization. That is, they can expect subordinates to find that by coordinating their personal goals with the goals of the organization they can engage in behavior that helps them feel valuable and unique.

How then does a person develop such feelings of value and uniqueness (or individuality)? Self-esteem—one's sense of self-worth, of liking oneself—is at the heart of the answer. Much work has been done on the origin of self-esteem (see especially Brockner, 1988). Dependent initially on a great many factors involving the person's relationship with the mother or nurturing parent figure, it continues its development through success and failure in school and throughout childhood. It comprises two aspects: the feelings of others about a person (reputation, prestige, social validation) and one's own feelings about self-competence—skill or ability as measured by one's own standards. It is global in the sense that an overall valuing of the self exists; it is specific in the sense that one can feel very good about oneself with regard to a specific task but very poorly about oneself in other areas. Generally, those with low self-esteem achieve at lower levels. Disagreement exists about how much self-esteem can be influenced after childhood, but it seems clear, for example, that if specific self-esteem can be raised in connection with specific tasks in an organizational environment, then global self-esteem can be slowly raised.

In humanistic psychology, self-esteem is connected for well-functioning individuals with Maslow's (1987) fourth level in the hierarchy of needs—the need for self-esteem. Without fulfillment of this need, argues Maslow, it is impossible to proceed to the culminating fifth level of fully functioning self-fulfillment, which he calls self-actualization. The work of Nathaniel Branden of the Institute for Self-Esteem goes even further in characterizing self-esteem (and its related concept cluster including sense of worth, self-confidence, and self-respect) as "the ultimate *ground of consciousness*, ground to all particular experience" (Branden, 1983, p. 5; see also Branden, 1971). In this vein, nothing is more significant to a person's sense of self-confidence, which is of critical importance to effective performance. High self-esteem virtually requires setting high goals and an increased chance of goal attainment; increases in self-esteem release positive ego energy. Low self-esteem leads to discouragement and the safety of low goals or no goals at all; decreases in self-esteem lead ultimately to dysfunctional anxiety. In order to thrive at a high level, an organization must have a critical mass of members whose sense of self is driven by the positive ego energy available when self-esteem is high. Yet self-esteem is only one factor affecting ego development and the development of the whole self.

People need to be seen as recognizably different from others in the field while at the same time being identified, at some level, as a member of the field. Defining the uniqueness of the self in this way within an organization requires a behavioral demonstration. In other words, in a work setting it is not enough to simply think of oneself as defined without taking into account the perception of others in the environment. Can others differentiate between me and others who do what I do? Is there behavior ascribable to me that helps them make this definition? Otherwise, how is it provable? How can I be sure their impressions are not simply conveyed to me for reasons other than the truth? If I can point to particular conduct—behavior that helps them arrive at their conclusions—I have more confidence that they are basing their opinions on something real when they differentiate between me and others. This is not to suggest that one's self-esteem depends on comparing oneself to others in the workplace. Rather, it is to point out that one's work performance must be recognized for its unique contribution to the organization if one is to feel satisfied of achieving the self-definition and sense of value to other employees that will eventuate in the continuous release of positive ego energy. Through all this, it must be borne in mind that the people being described are members of an organization. People do not necessarily wish to define themselves as so unique that they do not share any characteristics with other members. In fact, their challenge is to define themselves as unique within a group—which by definition is a paradoxical notion because the group defines itself by its similarities rather than by the differences of its members. Thus organizational members are all in the same "field," that is, part of the same organization or group within an organization. The importance of feedback in the workplace becomes apparent in connection with this entire process.

Issues of self-definition are even more important for those members cast in leadership roles within the organization. One of their primary goals is to stand out from the others so they can direct and control in their own particular way. Respect and esteem are qualities they strive to attain. Moreover, as leaders they are engaged not only in the task of self-definition but also the task of creating the environment for other members to define themselves. Based on his research in interviewing some ninety effective leaders from American business and government, Warren Bennis (Bennis and Nanus, 1985; Bennis, 1989) concentrates at length on the importance of self-esteem, or what he calls the positive deployment of self-regard, as a prerequisite for effective leadership. In this view effective leaders must know themselves, which means differentiating who one is from what others think or want one to be. Thus managers must define themselves before they can create the conditions that will result in positive ego energy.

Finally, Bandura's (1986) notion of self-efficacy is of use here. (See also Gist and Mitchell, 1992.) Self-efficacy involves the capacity to know to what degree I am capable of engaging in an effort that will lead to a performance I can predict. If my ego tells me that I am not capable—or if my self-esteem is so low that I am afraid no amount of effort will result in an acceptable performance—then I probably will not attempt it. Although I might attempt it halfheartedly or because I am afraid of incurring my boss's displeasure or losing compensation or even termination, this kind of effort rarely leads to the most successful performance. Even if I am quite sure that I can produce acceptable or even excellent performance, I still may not make the attempt. Vroom's (1964) expectancy theory predicts that my motivation depends not only on my assessment of the probability that effort will lead to successful performance but also the probability that the performance will result in certain outcomes I value. Thus it is up to management to buttress my self-esteem so that I am confident enough to perform, to assure me through actions, promises, or policies that certain outcomes will be connected to successful performance, and to help me understand the value of these outcomes. If all these conditions are met, then I will probably marshall positive ego energy to undertake the task. If these conditions are not met—if I must undertake performance under duress or if the likely outcomes involve the withholding of penalties or only weakly valued outcomes—I will be unlikely to perform. Indeed, I may marshal negative ego energy and ignore organizational goals or pretend to perform or even sabotage organizational goals to get even.

From the leader's point of view, then, the conditions conducive to effective marshaling of positive ego energy must be present at all levels in the organization. Clearly, upper management must not feel threatened: it must have sufficient ego strength and sufficient self-esteem, itself, to feel secure enough to provide these conditions. Of course, upper management must also have a clear idea of how to manage the ego energy field. Let us examine a model that may shed some light on this problem.

Toward a Workplace Model

At this point it seems appropriate to introduce a visual representation of the flow of ego energy within the self—the central piece in the completed model. This model illustrates the interaction among the four psychological senses: sense of self, sense of achievement, sense of pride, and sense of justice. These four senses hold the key to the deployment of ego energy by the self. They are the mechanism through which the ego looks at the self. Consequently, they are instrumental in providing a direction for the behavior that results from the ego's analysis. It will be useful for us to visualize the ego's analysis of the self through these four senses because we will then be able to associate specific managerial practices with each of these senses and to see how such practices result in the release of either positive or negative ego energy.

The Four Psychological Senses

The flow of ego energy in the workplace depends on the interaction of the four senses shown in Figure 9.1—the senses of self, achievement, pride, and justice. These are *senses* in that they involve the ego's way of experiencing various aspects of the self. This experience comes about through an inner reasoning or perception that may involve the use of language or may be much more intuitive. Management practices, policies, and decisions are observed and absorbed by the ego, which then responds to them after filtering their meaning. People consciously and subconsciously ask such questions as: What do they want me to do? How do they want me to do it? Can I do it? If I do it this, that, or the other way, what will the impact be? What does all this mean with regard to how they think about me? What does it tell me about my relationship with management and my fellow employees? How will I look doing it? Will it help me get where I want to be? Is what they are asking right? In sum, what does it all mean for me and how should I respond? Now let us look at the interaction of the four senses.

Each of the four senses represented in Figure 9.1 focuses on a critical part of employees' egos. In reality, of course, these elements interact in a holistic manner within the ego. For purposes of

Figure 9.1. Paradigm of Ego Energy's Evolution Within the Ego State of the Self.

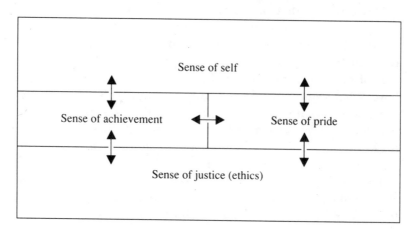

representation, the model allows us to visualize them separately within the ego. Later, it will allow us to consider the impact of specific managerial practices in connection with the development of ego energy. The arrows between each box represent the interaction among the senses as a particular practice is considered by the ego. As noted earlier, the model assumes that people normally wish to define themselves as unique and valued members of their organization. The flow of energy within the ego contains cognitive, affective, and evaluative functions as the ego attempts to recognize what is happening, perceive how the self feels about what is happening, and evaluate the meaning of what is happening in terms of the self. Inasmuch as we are primarily concerned with organizational functioning here, the evaluative function is quite important. This is the function that depends on individual self-esteem. It asks such questions as: Do I feel good about my performance? Will a particular action that I am contemplating make me feel good about myself? How am I coming across to others? Do they value me?

At the top of the figure is the concept of members' sense of self—generally self-awareness—which refers to the need to define oneself, especially insofar as that idea implies a full investigation of who one is actually as well as potentially. In the middle is the sense of pride, which responds strongly to the ego's need to be unique and valued. Also in the middle is the sense of achievement or performance that members need to feel when they do their work—which refers by implication to the other side of defining oneself, the side in which one is defined by one's achievements and feels satisfied as a person by having achieved in certain ways. At the base of the model is the sense of justice or ethics that all members have—a sense that considers whether a certain act is right, whether it fits properly into how they view the way things ought to be—and which can affect their morale as they consider their place in the organizational field. Although the model shows each of these concepts as equal, it should be borne in mind that the senses exist in a dynamic state within the actual self, each one expanding and contracting from moment to moment, as the behavior/feedback loop progresses. Let us consider each of the four senses referred to in the model in turn.

Who am I? This has been a philosophical question since well before the work of Freud on ego and the subsequent work of Erikson. Thus the *sense of self*, fixed at the top of the model because it is preeminent, focuses strongly on seeking identity. It represents the part of the self that attempts to define the self in relation to the rest of the environment. An organizational setting normally accelerates self-definition because it is rich with behavioral requirements, other people with whom a myriad of differing relationships are required, and evaluations of all kinds. This self-definition can be accomplished in concert with organizational goals or totally apart from them. In fact, self-exploration itself can be encouraged within an organization or discouraged. Regardless, members will engage in self-oriented and self-seeking behavior. Taking this into account, the best management practices will harness the members' natural identity seeking and use it in some way that benefits the organization. Such practices as providing opportunities for individual contribution to an organizational goal, delegating important organizational responsibilities, and fostering successful experiences for employees will encourage a strong sense of self that ultimately benefits the organization. The alternative for upper management is to see employees leave company concerns aside as they define themselves on company time and with company resources or to see them mindlessly perform their work while looking forward to going off-duty for self-exploration.

The *sense of pride* comes into play as a result of the self-evaluation of the person's behavior as perceived through the sense of self. It is differentiated from high self-esteem in that the latter involves the evaluation of people's expectations about themselves that allow them to attempt certain kinds of behavior at which they think they will be successful. The sense of "pride in one's work," on the other hand, results from observation of the effect of one's behavior on others or on oneself when that effect is perceived as essentially positive. It constantly modifies one's sense of self through its reciprocal relationship with self-esteem, which plays a central role in the flow of both positive and negative ego energy throughout the ego state. But bear in mind that a wide variety of meanings as well as positive and negative connotations have been associated with pride. In the medieval Christian sense, for example, pride is the opposite of humility and the deadliest of the Seven Deadly Sins. In Western literature, excessive pride, the Greek notion of *hubris,* inevitably causes the downfall of the tragic hero, who until this point has been a highly respected community member. Pride can also be defined as a raw emotion, which can be perceived as either appropriate or inappropriate (for example, team pride versus narcissistic pride in one's good looks). In the study of ethics, however, pride is often considered a virtue that can help one pursue a moral ideal of behavior. (See, for example, Gert, 1989.)

Because pride can be defined in such a variety of ways, one must be clear in describing how it is useful in relation to our subject. The pride referred to in connection with a sense of pride is what most managers mean when they encourage the "taking of pride in one's work." It alludes to a person's need to do work that is respected, to have self-respect, and to be respected by others who matter to the person. When we suggest that it is wise for upper management to encourage a sense of pride in employees, we mean the kind of pride that leads to positive ego energy—in other words, a satisfaction that one has attained or even exceeded the standard of excellence. Such practices might range from giving awards or bonuses for work that exceeds stated goals to fostering pride by publishing material that reflects the best side of the organization in comparison to its competitors or as it helps its community. Even an organization's advertising slogans (for example, Ford's "Quality Is Job One") can permeate its members' consciousness and increase their sense of pride. In both his speeches and in the books about him, W. E. Deming has been stressing this need for years (Deming, 1992; Aguayo, 1990). Finally, this kind of healthy pride must be grounded in a strong positive self-esteem. Self-esteem and its concept cluster of self-confidence, self-worth, and self-respect all comprise the critical psychological base needed to stimulate the flow of positive ego energy so that organizational members can perform at a high level.

Sense of pride and sense of self are clearly linked, but what is their relationship to *sense of achievement* and how is such achievement to be measured? Following McClelland (1961 and later), achievement can be seen as the performance of work at a high standard of excellence. This standard is not established by measuring the work of fellow employees. Rather, it should be established by what management (or a highly respected outside authority) could reasonably expect employees to accomplish. It would be a mistake to measure work on a social comparison basis. Such measurement would violate the need for self-identity itself: how is one to be unique or even different if one's achievement is characterized by similarity to others' achievements? One's achievement must be valued by the organization, yet it must be identifiable as one's achievement. Though some totalitarian societies have disagreed, trying to repress individual initiative and recognition, such societies have not flourished for long. The best achievement is not measured by the attainment of one's peers but rather by a standard set by the achiever or other achievers. There is less threat to one's sense of pride, less chance of dysfunctional anxiety (separation from one's peer), if direct social comparisons are minimized. The most compelling reason managers should avoid such social comparisons is that they do violence to sense of self: "The greatest barrier to achievement and success is not lack of talent or ability but, rather, the fact that achievement and success, above a certain level, are outside our self-concept, our image of who we are and what is appropriate to us" (Branden, 1983, p. 3).

Whether we study self-esteem or self-efficacy, it seems clear that achievement is limited only by self-concept and a willingness to make the effort. Thus upper management should be heavily invested in facilitating employees' decisions to achieve in a way that benefits the organization as well as themselves, creating a win/win situation. Achievement can also come in a win/lose situation, in which case the organization seems always to lose since some of its members lose. This would be the case if achievement were accomplished at the expense of other employees or at the expense of some loss of self or pride to an achieving employee. In fact, the delicate balance between the senses of pride and achievement should be evident as it becomes clear that harm to one seems inevitably to affect the other. Both involve standards and behavior and how the results are seen both by the self and by others as perceived by the self. Of course, harm to either sense also affects one's sense of self, suggesting once again the holistic nature of the components of the ego state. At this point one might add that McClelland and many others have found that such achievement is facilitated by setting challenging but attainable goals, providing immediate feedback, maintaining a resource-rich environment, and encouraging moderate risk taking. Upper management should take these conclusions into account in its effort to develop the state of ego energy for achievement.

At the base of the model is the employees' *sense of justice*, which is to be found in their individual ethical systems. This sense has been developing since their earliest childhood experiences and perceptions of not being treated fairly. In fact, a great many employees, when asked what trait they admire most in a supervisor, will respond: fair treatment of subordinates. Nevertheless, much behavior may not seem to carry an ethical component; indeed, moral ideals may be hard to find in certain actions. Yet many employees are trying to develop themselves and their self-pride according to moral rules they have either developed for themselves or learned from respected sources (parents, teachers, religion). And even when they themselves are not following the rules, they are often quite aware when upper management is not following moral rules either. Such violations (or perceived violations) will upset their sense of justice or equity—whether the violations are to themselves, other employees, or even other stakeholders such as customers, clients, vendors, or, lately, the environment. If these unjustified violations or perceived violations are not satisfactorily explained, members are quite likely to withhold their efforts, redirect energies, and engage in other behavior not ideally suited to the attainment of organizational objectives. Perceived injustice profoundly affects the senses of pride and achievement, an interaction symbolized by the internal two-way arrows in the model. Such injustices do harm to a person's sense of pride and cause employees to devalue achievement that benefits the organization. In sum, when organizations are highly respected for their ethical behavior and employees are treated equitably and with respect, more ego energy is available to be used positively.

Positive and Negative Ego Energy

Although the concepts of positive and negative ego energy have been briefly described, we need to be a bit more precise before introducing the completed model. The ultimate goal, of course, is to use the model to distinguish between techniques of management that promote corporate objectives and those that are mistakenly thought to assist such objectives but actually work against them. For our purposes, positive ego energy is the energy that is self-directed by each employee to help him identify himself within the organization and which concomitantly helps the organization achieve its own objectives. Negative ego energy is the energy focused by employees on the establishment of their personal ego identity—without any particular regard to organizational objectives or, worse, with the express goal of violating organizational objectives. In the model, the flow of the two types of ego energy is symbolized by the arrows.

The Model Completed

Figure 9.2 presents a final look at the model. It shows how managerial practices are processed through the ego states of employees who then respond through ego-defining behavior to achieve some combination of organizational and personal objectives. The nature of the practices will determine whether positive or negative ego energy

Figure 9.2. Flow of Positive and Negative Ego Energy in the Organization.

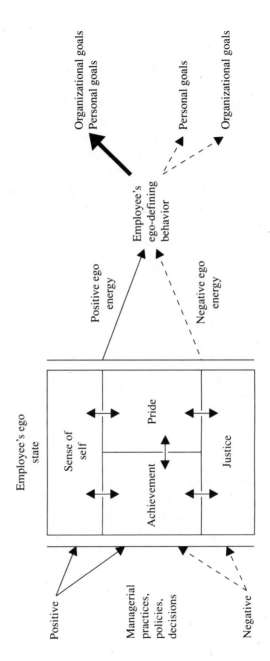

drives the behavior elicited. The top half of the model represents the flow of positive ego energy through the use of solid arrows; the bottom half shows negative ego energy with dashed lines. If managerial practices are designed to assist the development of self-esteem, thereby releasing positive ego energy, the resulting ego-defining behavior will normally be calculated to achieve organizational goals as well as personal goals. Employees will try to coordinate the goals. And given the encouragement to their senses of self, pride, achievement, and justice, they will expect to succeed. Thus the model in Figure 9.2 ultimately shows a double arrow to reflect the coordinated seeking of organizational and personal objectives. Organizational goals are shown on top because employees generally give them priority.

Alternatively, if practices are designed to gain compliance through tactics that undermine their senses of self, pride, achievement, and justice, employees will give their personal goals priority. Organizational goals will become incidental. They may even make it their personal objective to sabotage various organizational objectives. This is why the model following the creation of negative ego energy in Figure 9.2 shows personal goals on top and organizational goals on the bottom along with a diverging arrow instead of a double arrow.

Positive Practices

Based on the model described here, Table 9.1 shows common management practices that lead to the encouragement of positive ego energy. Table 9.2 shows the employee behavior that can be expected to result from such positive ego energy. Note that the management practices all include creation of an environment conducive to employees' individual growth as fully functioning adults seeking to fulfill their potential. Some practices, especially those centered on the encouragement of pride, require an environment wherein the organization takes pains to show it values individual uniqueness as well as the specific contributions of project units and functional teams. Teams in particular, valuable for their crucial benefits of synergy and cooperation, are given a clear sense of recognition and identity within the organization. Many of the practices concerned

Table 9.1. Management Practices Encouraging Positive Ego Energy.

Practices That Encourage Self-Exploration

- Policies that offer the chance to coordinate personal and organizational goals (professional development seminars, education, desired job rotation)
- Allowance of maximum autonomy to employees in performing their jobs
- Plans that involve employees in decisions on benefits and other aspects affecting personal life away from work
- Personal/career development programs, workshops, facilities
- Tuition reimbursement plans

Practices That Encourage Achievement	Practices That Encourage Pride
• Programs that encourage employees to create, modify, and improve the service or product as measured against a standard of excellence	• Team performance-based pay or standard pay steps
• Setting of challenging but attainable goals for employees	• Regular one-time bonuses for team accomplishments
• Provision of a resource-rich work setting	• Facilitation of association with respected organizational members
• Regular, systematic, concrete feedback systems	• Assurance of high task significance
• Employee involvement programs, quality circles, TQM, continuous improvement programs, employee empowerment initiatives	• Opportunity to work with respected product or service
• Training and workshops to improve knowledge, skills, and abilities important to work	• Promotion based on competence and respect of others
	• Opportunity for employee's initiative (frequent chances to be first, unique, or recognized in the workplace for ideas or behavior that is valued by organization)
	• Leadership opportunity in some area for every employee

Practices That Satisfy Ethical Sensitivity

- Ethical codes
- Workshops on ethics
- Just, equitable, and consistent treatment of employees, customers, clients, other stakeholders
- Sensitivity to environmental concerns
- Public and private attention to fulfillment of legal obligations
- Consistent model of ethical behavior

Table 9.2. Common Employee Behavior
Resulting from Positive Ego Energy.

Self-Exploration Behavior

- Given the chance to coordinate personal and organizational goals, employees pursue both kinds of goals more diligently.
- Given maximum autonomy in doing their jobs, employees find new and better ways to complete assignments.
- Given the chance to be involved in decisions on benefits and other aspects affecting personal life away from work, employees concentrate on work at hand.
- Given the opportunity to use career development workshops and facilities, employees spend more time at work.
- Given tuition reimbursement plans, employees improve selves by going to school.

Achievement Behavior	Pride-Generating Behavior
Employees:	Employees:
<ul><li>Attempt to create, modify, and improve service or product as measured against a standard of excellence</li><li>Commit to goal achievement</li><li>Explore both environment and available resources thoroughly</li><li>Make use of feedback to facilitate goal achievement</li><li>Willingly contribute to work tasks and attempt to carry out improvements cooperatively</li><li>Willingly attend training and workshops to improve knowledge, skills, and abilities important to work</li></ul>	<ul><li>Help each other and engage in cooperative teamwork</li><li>Make extra effort so their team will look good (such as voluntary overtime)</li><li>Pursue association with respected organizational members</li><li>Take more care with tasks when task is significant</li><li>Attempt more self-improvement when promotions are based on competence</li><li>Show high initiative when management shows it is valued; offer new ideas and suggestions</li><li>Demonstrate leadership where opportunity is provided</li></ul>

Ethical Behavior

Employees:

- Are more careful in trying to follow ethical codes
- Willingly attend workshops on ethics
- Waste little energy on seeking justice when equitable treatment of members, customers, clients, and other stakeholders is perceived
- Show sensitivity in the work setting when the organization does
- Obey laws and policies more carefully when management encourages it

with self, pride, and achievement can be expected to create Hackman and Oldham's (1980) three critical psychological states for employees: meaningfulness of the work, responsibility for outcomes of the work, and knowledge of the actual results of the work. The practices concerned with encouraging achievement are grounded in the research of McClelland and his colleagues in their attention to conditions necessary for optimum fulfillment of the need to achieve. The inclusion of organizational goals that allow for the coordination of personal goals—as well as the focus on trying to help employees with their personal goals—reflects an increased attention to employees' concerns outside their work. This policy has the advantage of clearing away many outside obstacles to work success while at the same time showing that management cares for employees as people. Open two-way communication between upper management and all other employees is characteristic of management practices in all four cells.

It is worth paying special attention to the cell at the base of Table 9.1: practices that satisfy ethical sensitivity. The link between moral reasoning and individual behavior is well established (Biasi, 1980). Most adults are at the second of Kohlberg's (1971, 1984) three levels of moral reasoning, the conventional level. At this level they are concerned with conforming to what society expects of them, a consistent set of rules and codes that apply equally to everybody. Thus corporate ethical codes and consistent policies reinforced with workshops and management's behavior are likely to result in employees' behavior that adheres to corporate policy. With employees at the preconventional level, where behavior is guided only by satisfaction of personal needs, management's efforts will have little impact. For employees at the postconventional level, however, where behavior is heavily influenced by personal philosophy grounded in universal ethical principles without regard to social expectations, there will be little need to consider how to deal with a corporation that is perceived to be ignoring its moral responsibility and no need to go over the head of their superiors when they perceive injustice. Thus, with ethics attended to in the base of the ego state model (Figures 9.1 and 9.2), excessive energy does not have to be focused on circumventing management decisions, on contemplated or actual whistle-blowing, or on resentment at decisions that are perceived as unjust. (See, for example, Brockner, Derr, and Laing, 1987.)

The ego-defining behavior to be expected from pursuit of these management practices favors the organization as shown in Table 9.2. Employees' ego energy is directed, naturally, to defining themselves as valued organizational members—instead of being more valued than their peers. They seek to achieve goals and standards—instead of attempting to avoid disfavor or punishment. They think of the organization as being on their side and themselves as members— instead of seeing the organization as the enemy and themselves as guerrilla fighters.

Negative Practices: A Corporate Example

Table 9.3 shows management practices which lead to ego-defining behavior that does not favor the organization. Table 9.4 describes the behavior that results in such a negative environment. Ranking employees against each other, as is frequently done in some performance appraisal systems, forces them to show each other up or to sabotage each other's efforts so they will benefit at the expense of their peers in the ranking system. It also spawns arguments over how people are ranked and by whom. Merit systems have the disadvantage of this latter problem, too. Incentive systems of most kinds, unless team-based, have the same shortcoming. Commission-based systems result in arguments over territories, over who gets access to which potential customers, over how much of a commission should be paid when help is involved or prices are cut. W. E. Deming contends that all commission compensation should be done away with; in places where it has been eliminated, more teamwork has occurred, selling energy has remained the same, and customers have benefited (Deming, 1992; see also Aguayo, 1990). Piecework, another incentive system, suffers from the perennial problem of "busting the rate," whereby employees intentionally hold down productivity in order to keep the base rate low. Pay secrecy, another common managerial practice, results in resentment—and members try to find out what the others make anyway. The policy of written warnings or even termination for any employee caught trying to find out another member's salary seems the ultimate in

Table 9.3. Management Practices Encouraging Negative Ego Energy.

Self-Oriented Practices

- Upper management engaging in personal projects on company time
- Loafing, gossip, wasting company time by upper management
- Failure to explain rationale behind decisions
- Quibbling with subordinates
- Office romance, affairs
- Sexual harassment
- Excessive executive pay and perks

Practices That Discourage Achievement	Practices That Discourage Pride
<ul><li>Any practice that entices employees to achieve by encouraging them to compare themselves to each other</li><li>Secrecy regarding pay</li><li>Most merit pay systems</li><li>One-upmanship in arguments (win/lose mentality)</li><li>Lack of vision, mission, organizational goals (or failure to express them)</li></ul>	<ul><li>Employee ranking systems</li><li>Many incentive compensation systems</li><li>Cronyism, nepotism, old boy network</li><li>Requirement of unquestioning loyalty</li><li>Most merit pay systems</li><li>Arbitrary decisions and behavior</li></ul>

Practices Perceived as Unethical or Unjust

- Violation of laws (OSHA, EPA, civil rights, fair labor)
- Unfair treatment of employees, customers, clients, other stakeholders
- Violation of ethical codes
- Inconsistency in following internal policies

motivation through fear. As Branden suggests, "Fear sabotages mind, clarity, efficacy [and] undermines the sense of self-worth" (1983, p. 72). Yet how can members discover what is rewarded in an organization unless they discover how their peers are compensated? If along the way they discover, as they inevitably do, that there is a gross inequity, then they are involved in occupying themselves and their ego energy in attempting to expose it or attempting to right it—behavior found at the base of the model under justice-seeking behavior. None of these compensation practices advance organizational objectives.

**Table 9.4. Common Employee Behavior
Resulting from Negative Ego Energy.**

Self-Oriented Behavior

Employees:

- Engage in personal projects on company time
- Appropriate company supplies, equipment, resources for personal use
- Loaf, gossip, waste company time
- Worry about layoffs, terminations
- Fail to communicate with superiors
- Quibble with boss, peers
- Engage in office romance, affairs
- Engage in sexual harassment (or ignore it)
- Become diverted by office betting pools or similar activities

Self-Oriented Achievement Measuring	Self-Oriented Pride Building
Employees:	Employees:
• Generally exaggerate their work in comparison with peers and colleges through persuasion tactics with superiors	• Make others look bad to enhance themselves
• Undercut contributions of other employees	• Promote their personal image continuously
• Try to find out others' compensation	• Engage in self-ingratiation with their boss and others
• Try to discover others' rank within department	• Protect the boss due to misplaced loyalty
• Engage in one-upmanship in horseplay or argument (win/lose mentality)	• Expose the boss by going over his or her head
• Sabotage efforts of other employees and the organization	• Argue about their own or others' compensation
• Place personal opportunities above organizational goals and pursue them at organization's expense	• Complain about management decisions and behavior

Justice-Seeking Behavior

Employees:

- Occupy their time in worry and discussion about injustices they see around them
- Worry about others' imminent termination as well as their own
- Discuss unethical, immoral, and illegal organizational behavior outside the organization
- Report illegal organizational behavior to outside authorities

Apart from poorly designed compensation practices, perhaps one of the most deleterious of management practices resulting in negative ego energy is the use of favoritism, cronyism, nepotism, and the old boy network to fill jobs, give plum assignments, award raises, and generally provide opportunities for self-definition. Besides the well-chronicled resentment of minorities, these practices result in an exaltation of loyalty as an organizational value. Employees defend and cover for bosses, peers, and subordinates to the detriment of competence and achievement. While loyalty has traditionally been a well-respected human value, it can be the enemy of organizational growth and creativity and control unless it is carefully monitored. Yet careful monitoring is exactly what loyalty is supposed to make unnecessary. If productivity and quality are to be preeminent organizational goals, the place of unswerving loyalty must be painstakingly analyzed.

Perhaps the saddest of these management practices is actually a management abdication—lack of clear vision, mission, and clearly articulated organizational objectives. When an organization is perceived as lacking direction, employees design their own direction. Freed from the burden of knowing exactly what the organization is trying to achieve, they decide to achieve in their own personal way (or not to achieve at all). This practice degenerates into self-oriented personal behavior that is designed to define themselves to each other without organizational interference. Such behavior includes using organizational resources—materials, machines, time—to their own advantage. Informal leaders spring up and vie for power and the chance to define themselves in the absence of formal leadership. The organizational environment then becomes a convenient staging ground for defining oneself to one's peers, and an informal organization may supersede the formal one. Alternatively, employees may drop out of the formal and informal organizations and prepare on the job for their lives off the job. Employees are not bothered by conscience in any of these situations. They feel that since management has abdicated in the matter of justice, the law of the jungle prevails—it is survival of the fittest. This final abdication of ethics can occur apart from the problem of lack of vision. Any of the negative practices can bring it on.

Negative Practices: A Corporate Example

Company A is a giant of the defense industry located in the northeast. It has just given an organizational climate survey to one of its divisions' four thousand salaried employees, many of them engineers. Looking at the results, the company decided that it could not share them with the employees. Employees know why: the results reflect a severe morale problem. This morale problem cannot be due to cutbacks in the defense industry, for employees in other corporate divisions have received the results of their climate surveys. The main reason for the morale problem can be found in the annual employee ranking process that begins in March and ends in June every year. Employees report that animosity, discontent, and mistrust reach their zenith at this time.

A typical group of seventy engineers is headed by four different supervisors. Each supervisor has a team of ten to twenty employees. By June, each team member must be ranked within the team. Then the supervisors hold a showdown meeting and argue for their rankings as their managers attempt to rank all engineers from 1 to 70. Raises are awarded according to quadrants: 7 percent for the top quadrant, 5.5 percent for the second, 4.5 percent for the third, and 3 percent for the bottom. Promotions and dismissals are also guided by these rankings. Every June, employees are sent performance reviews that cite the rankings. As the time between April 1 and June 30 represents the first quarter of the next appraisal period, the effects of this process profoundly affect the first part of the subsequent review period. It is not surprising that the environment is electrically charged for the first half of every calendar year. But how are these rankings determined by the supervisors?

Supervisors have many different ways of determining their rankings. Seniority can play a role, as can obvious or unusual technical competencies. So can the old boy network. Many supervisors have a difficult time with their decisions and do not like the system any better than their engineers. In an effort to be fair, they are reduced to bean counting—anything that is countable, no matter how contrived or meaningless, is counted because it helps supervisors rank employees against each other. Accordingly, an engineer had better be at his desk during one of the four "attendance checks" at 7:20 A.M., 11:45 A.M., 12:15 P.M., and 4:15 P.M. The number of overtime hours per week can also be critical, as it appears to be a popular method of determining who deserves a high ranking. Consequently, everyone is working hard to tell their supervisor their whereabouts during one of the four attendance checks. Meanwhile, many are coming in early and leaving late (but not doing any real work in these overtime hours). These hours are not compensated unless they exceed five hours a week and are approved. High praise goes to engineers who put in four and one-half hours of overtime per week.

Most puzzling is the report that the performance appraisals do not predict where one will land except for differences between the bottom and top 10 percent. All the ratings tend to be in the "satisfactory" category; "outstanding" and "unsatisfactory" are both quite unusual. Perhaps most alarming in terms of the application of ego energy, one group held a private meeting in which they all met and thrashed out who should get what ranking. In other words, in what must have been a highly demoralizing experience, some engineers sat at a meeting and agreed that they should be ranked in the bottom quadrant—one even agreed that he should be last. They then filed the rankings away and awaited the official results from their supervisor. With the exception of the engineer who was ranked first by the team and the supervisor, the rest of the official rankings were exactly opposite to those of the informal team meeting. Given an environment like this, is it any wonder that negative ego energy is rampant? Employees are doing personal business in their office on "overtime," ingratiating themselves with their bosses at every turn, and lying to their supervisors about when they get in from the road. In other words, the process of ranking employees against each other—a negative management practice described as discouraging achievement and pride in Table 9.3—results in self-oriented achievement-measuring and pride-building behavior as described in Table 9.4. In short, employees attempt to inflate their own performance, undercut that of their peers, discover their own and others' rankings, and continually ingratiate themselves with their managers.

What, exactly, does management gain from demanding this kind of ranking? It is touted as an incentive to increase motivation among the "professional" engineers. It may make layoffs easier to accomplish (though employees are not usually laid off in strict conformance with the rankings due to the need to keep people with special competencies and knowledge). It makes promotions easier (though the top engineers are not always the ones promoted). And it is presumed to be a "pay-for-performance" compensation system—the fairest way to determine raises, according to the managers. From an objective point of view, however, it is difficult to see how this system can be responsible for anything other than squandering and misdirecting the ego energy of a large number of engineers on whose technical and creative talents we have rested a great many of our hopes as a nation.

Positive Practices: A Corporate Example

At Company B, another giant defense contractor located in the northeast, an entirely different kind of program is causing the positive deployment of ego energy among its engineers. Starting at the top, this contractor, which is roughly the same size as Company A, has implemented a "Continuous Improvement Program" (CIP). The company has announced that its two-year goal is to compete for the Malcolm Baldrige Award and that all members can help achieve this goal. Company B has not necessarily had a stellar history of encouraging cooperation among its employees. In fact, the CIP is to some extent a reaction to Company B's own morale problem. Despite some misgivings and mistrust, however, the company has now embarked on a program that has allocated twenty-three employees, mostly engineers, to the role of "facilitator." As facilitators they are responsible for creating teams that get special training in cooperative behavior and are given a particular task by upper management to accomplish within a certain time. These tasks, which are in addition to each team member's normal duties, usually involve improving process, quality, and production. Many involve engineer-led work teams making recommendations to middle and upper management at formal meetings called by employees with high school educations for managers with graduate degrees. Clearly the teams are functioning at a level beyond quality circles. They are autonomous and have the power not only to recommend change but also to implement their ideas as a self-managing work team. Having engaged in management practices that encourage achievement and pride (Table 9.1), management now reaps the benefit of employee behavior that is productive, creative, and cooperative (Table 9.2).

Observation of the teams has revealed genuine enthusiasm from employees who are now working overtime and weekends willingly. There is much interest in improving quality and showing superiors how things could be better. Unions are feeling a definite power loss—an issue that will have to be dealt with carefully—but employees on these teams are finding pride in wearing special tee shirts and gaining an identity for themselves. There is personal meaning to be had by making a big company sit up and take notice of better ways to do things. As described in the self-exploration cell of Table 9.2 and suggested by the concept of ego energy itself, employees are seeking to define themselves as unique and valued within their environment by finding new and better ways to complete assignments and pursue organizational goals.

Much has been written (Goodman, 1986; Hackman, 1990; Manz and Sims, 1989) about how work groups like those being formed throughout Company B, especially self-managing work teams, can provide exactly what is needed within an organization to improve quality and efficiency. There are many caveats—or "trip wires," as Hackman calls them—to worry about, too. One of the biggest problems is that the teams can become too isolated from the main business of the organization. However, they can also provide opportunities for leadership from within. And, most important, they can create a highly receptive environment for the deployment of positive ego energy. We should spend more time learning how to integrate such groups into the production process so that we can take greater advantage of this energy. We cannot afford to let it go unchanneled or simply attribute it to the personal leadership style of one particular leader.

Guidelines for Leaders

Milton Moskowitz (1985), in his description of the hundred best companies to work for, found the following traits to be typical:

- Supervisors and subordinates are made to feel part of a team.
- Open communication is encouraged by supervisors and subordinates.
- Supervisors and subordinates stress quality and are made to feel good about what they are doing.
- Distinctions in rank are reduced.

These four traits imply the necessity of cooperation, two-way communication, reinforcement of self-esteem, and reduction of personal comparison—all among the qualities suggested throughout this chapter in connection with the ego energy model. While it is impossible to create a list of guidelines that is both short and comprehensive, it is worthwhile listing the major considerations for leaders who wish to encourage positive ego energy. Recalling the definition of ego energy as the chronic desire to define oneself through behavior in a way that demonstrates to others that one is valuable and unique, a set of principles can be formulated. These principles reflect the practices that encourage positive ego energy listed earlier in Figure 9.3. Naturally, they assume that employees have the knowledge and skills to carry out their basic job responsibilities effectively.

1. Reinforce the organizational value of each employee to each employee.
2. Recognize the uniqueness of each employee and communicate this recognition to the employee.
3. Allow employees maximum autonomy in the performance of their responsibilities as well as the opportunity to exercise leadership in some aspect of their jobs.
4. Afford employees opportunities to enhance personal growth and self-exploration.
5. Furnish challenging but attainable standards of excellence to measure achievement, and forgo temptations to measure achievement by comparing employees to each other.
6. Make it a point to use input from each employee, and credit employees with their input.
7. Arrange explicit opportunities for employees to cooperate with each other—in teams, for example.

8. Maintain open two-way communication with each employee, both with regard to their tasks and to the relationship at hand.
9. Treat employees, clients, customers, and other stakeholders in a just, equitable, and consistent manner and with full attention to all legal and moral obligations.
10. Provide a clear vision, mission, and set of goals for the organization and communicate its essence to all employees.

These principles cover the essence of ego energy by definition, and they do so in all four cells of the employee's ego state—senses of self, achievement, pride, and justice. Moreover, they focus on the end result of the ego energy model, which is to facilitate the coordination of personal and organizational goals. Finally, they steer managers away from some of the mistakes that can stimulate negative ego energy.

Can we be certain that organizations whose leaders assiduously follow these guidelines will function at a higher level and be more profitable over the long run than those who do not? At this point, not enough research is available to guarantee that conclusion. We need studies that explore the intensity of the employee's need to be valued and unique and to correlate these needs with the fulfillment of challenging but attainable organizational objectives. For the model's value to be assured cross-culturally, we also need research that includes employees from cultural backgrounds different than those found in the United States. This is not to say that the guidelines should be put on hold. We have a fair amount of behavioral science research as well as a variety of case evidence that suggests the model's value. The extended cases cited earlier are just two of the many that could be brought to bear on the subject.

Toward a Win/Win Solution

Two sets of managerial practices have been described in this chapter. Each leads to a different set of behavior and culminates in a very different kind of goal-seeking behavior when understood in the light of the model. Positive managerial practices lead to positive ego-defining behavior and thus to the achievement of organizational and personal objectives simultaneously: a win/win situation. Negative practices lead employees to focus on personal objectives; organizational objectives are attained by default or as a by-product (if not subverted). It seems clear that leaders should want to take advantage of the natural potential for positive ego energy to help them improve organizational functioning. Many are engaging in practices that release such positive energy to one degree or another. Many others, whether they realize it or not, are engaging in practices that release negative ego energy. They are violating their employees' senses of pride, self, achievement, and justice.

The case studies of managerial practices at two companies suggest the differences between positive and negative practices and their results. Despite a generally poor outlook for the defense industry at this time, Company B is coping fairly well. Company A, however, is afraid to give out its own climate survey results and its engineers report that many of them have résumés out.

Although the ten guidelines for leaders are neither exhaustive nor entirely validated, they do capture the essence of the ego energy model and are suggested by a great deal of research on self-esteem, identity, and successful organizations. Moreover, a great many case studies appear to validate them. For those in power, the choice seems clear: they cannot serve themselves better than to utilize positive ego energy if they wish to achieve their organization's objectives.

References

Aguayo, R. *Dr. Deming*. New York: Simon & Schuster, 1990.

Bandura, A. *Social Foundations of Thought and Action: A Social-Cognitive View*. Englewood Cliffs, N.J.: Prentice-Hall, 1986.

Bennis, W. *On Becoming a Leader*. Reading, Mass.: Addison-Wesley, 1989.

Bennis, W., and Nanus, B. *Leaders: The Strategies for Taking Charge*. New York: HarperCollins, 1985.

Biasi, A. "Bridging Moral Cognition and Moral Action: A Critical Review of the Literature." *Psychological Bulletin*, 1980, *88*(1), 1–45.

Branden, N. *The Psychology of Self-Esteem.* New York: Bantam, 1971.

Branden, N. *Honoring the Self: The Psychology of Confidence and Respect.* New York: Bantam, 1983.

Brockner, J. *Self-Esteem at Work.* Lexington, Mass.: Lexington Books, 1988.

Brockner, J., Derr, W. R., and Laing, W. N. "Self-Esteem and Reactions to Negative Feedback: Toward Greater Generalizability." *Journal of Research in Personality,* 1987, *21,* 318–333.

Deming, W. E. Speech and question and answer period, Amherst, University of Massachusetts Fine Arts Center, April 22, 1992.

Erikson, E. H. *Identity, Youth, and Crisis.* New York: Norton, 1968.

Erikson, E. H. *Identity and the Life Cycle.* New York: Norton, 1980.

Freud, S. *The Ego and the Id.* Vol. 19 in Standard Edition. London: Hogarth, 1961. (Originally published 1923.)

Gert, B. *Morality: A New Justification of the Moral Rules.* New York: Oxford University Press, 1989.

Gist, M. E., and Mitchell, T. R. "Self-Efficacy: A Theoretical Analysis of Its Determinants and Malleability." *Academy of Management Review,* 1992, *17,* 183–211.

Goodman, P. S., and Associates. *Designing Effective Work Groups.* San Francisco: Jossey-Bass, 1986.

Hackman, J. R. (ed.). *Groups That Work (and Those That Don't): Creating Conditions for Effective Teamwork.* San Francisco: Jossey-Bass, 1990.

Hackman, J. R., and Oldham, G. B. *Task Redesign.* Reading, Mass.: Addison-Wesley, 1980.

Kohlberg, L. "Stages of Moral Development as a Basis for Moral Education." In C. M. Beck, B. S. Crittenden, and E. V. Sullivan (eds.), *Moral Education: Interdisciplinary Approaches.* New York: Newman Press, 1971.

Kohlberg, L. *Essays in Moral Development.* Vol. 2. New York: HarperCollins, 1984.

McClelland, D. C. *The Achieving Society.* Princeton, N.J.: Van Nostrand, 1961.

Manz, C. C., and Sims, H. P., Jr. *Super-Leadership.* New York: Berkeley, 1989.

Maslow, A. *Motivation and Personality.* New York: HarperCollins, 1987. (Originally published 1954.)

May, R. *The Meaning of Anxiety.* Rev. ed. New York: Norton, 1977.

May, R. *The Discovery of Being.* New York: Norton, 1983.

Moskowitz, M. "Lessons from the Best Companies to Work For." *California Management Review,* 1985, 27(2), 42-47.

Vroom, V. *Work and Motivation.* New York: Wiley, 1964.

10

Fostering Self-Efficacy: Guidelines for the Diverse Workforce

Mary Cianni, Beverly Romberger

TECHNOLOGY, THE ECONOMY, the political arena, and global competition are powerful forces driving organizations today. Concurrently, the changing demographics of the workforce are creating an added dimension to organizational transformation. In light of the dramatic and rapid change occurring within organizations, employees must use ego energy to chart their own organizational courses. Ego energy represents the power to maintain control over one's inner world and sustain a level of self-confidence and belief in oneself, especially during periods of organizational chaos and restructuring.

To succeed in today's corporate environment, one needs not only requisite management and technical skills but also a resilient perception in one's ability to accomplish personal and organizational goals. Bandura (1977) has called this belief "self-efficacy." Self-efficacy is a person's judgment of his ability to perform a task—namely, confidence in one's ability to mobilize motivation, cognitive resources, and courses of action needed to meet situational demands (Wood and Bandura, 1989, p. 364). Thus an important precursor of ego energy is self-efficacy. To stay motivated, to sustain the requisite self-confidence, and to remain in control of our inner world, first we need to believe that we have the internal capabilities to manage these new challenges.

Not only does the construct of self-efficacy have important implications for individual performance, but it enhances organizational effectiveness as well. Empirical studies demonstrate the role self-efficacy plays in predicting and improving work performance in a variety of domains (Gist and Mitchell, 1992). Indeed, research has shown self-efficacy to be a better predictor of subsequent performance than past behavior (Gist, 1987). Self-efficacy has also been linked to the range of career options one considers (Betz and Hackett, 1981) and to receptivity of retraining by midcareer managers (Hill and Elias, 1990).

This chapter describes an exploratory study that uses oral history to explain how corporate experiences may affect efficacy beliefs of male and female managers from diverse racial and ethnic backgrounds. We also review self-efficacy theory with special reference to organizational behavior by presenting the oral history findings and offer recommendations for both managerial and corporate actions that may enhance the development of positive self-efficacy. Through the oral histories, we hear in the managers' own voices how one organization influences their beliefs about themselves. While gender differences in self-efficacy beliefs have been investigated, no research has addressed racial or ethnic differences. Thus, these stories help us to understand how managers from diverse backgrounds may respond differently to similar organizational experiences. Furthermore, the recommendations should aid human resource managers and other leaders in their efforts to optimize the talents of their diverse workforce.

Organizational Experiences and Self-Efficacy

A Fortune 500 financial services company agreed to participate in a study of organizational experiences with a special emphasis on women and minorities. The study's purpose was to discover the various experiences women, men, and minorities had in their organizational lives. Oral history was chosen as the research method because of its potential to elucidate the organizational experiences of the various groups by providing rich detail. Oral history refers to the collecting of people's spoken memories of past experiences. This methodology allowed the researchers to hear the managers express in their own words the experiences they viewed as important. Without a predetermined sequence of questions, managers were free to follow their own paths of reminiscences and tell their stories. Oral history affords a more detailed understanding of managers' perceptions of self and others.

Using the corporate human resource information system, we composed a list of randomly selected managers. Managers were grouped according to position, gender, and race or ethnic background. We then sent letters to a hundred selected managers asking for their participation in an oral history study of daily experiences in a corporation. Confidentiality was assured and volunteers were asked to respond directly to the researchers. Thus all names and job titles have been changed in the narratives.

Forty-three managers volunteered (a 43 percent response rate). Sixteen managers were selected to represent different line and staff areas, levels of management, and organizational tenure. Equal numbers of male and female managers participated. Four minority men (two black and two Hispanic), three minority women (two black and one Hispanic), four white men, and five white women participated. (One white woman was incorrectly classified as a Hispanic female because of her husband's surname.) All sixteen oral histories were collected during a one-week period by the two investigators. Each researcher was assigned an equal number of managers from the different demographic groups. Interviews were tape-recorded and then transcribed.

To investigate the factors associated with self-efficacy, we conducted a content analysis of the transcriptions. The narratives were analyzed to determine what the managers reported concerning organizational experiences related to self-efficacy. All sixteen managers told stories regarding sources of self-efficacy. While the generalizability of the findings is limited, the stories are useful and vivid illustrations of ways in which organizations may influence self-efficacy beliefs.

What Is Self-Efficacy?

The construct of self-efficacy is derived from social cognitive theory, which posits that behavior, personal factors, and environmental events interact to influence each other (Wood and Bandura, 1989). Efficacy is the conviction that one can successfully execute behavior required to produce certain outcomes (Bandura, 1977). Gist and Mitchell (1992) highlight three aspects of self-efficacy important to organizations. First, employees make judgments about their ability to perform a specific task from information derived from themselves, the work itself, and others in the work environment. Others serve as powerful sources of self-efficacy information. Second, as a dynamic construct, efficacy judgments may change as information and experiences are gained. Organizational interventions—certain training methods, for example—can enhance aspects of self-efficacy. Third, people with the same skills may perform differently depending on whether their efficacy beliefs enhance or impair their efforts. Employees who believe they can successfully complete a task will perform better than those who expect failure. Simply having the appropriate background and experience for an assignment may not be the only determinant of success.

Sources of Self-Efficacy

Self-efficacy is developed from four sources of information: mastery experiences, vicarious experiences (modeling), social persuasion, and physiological or emotional arousal (Bandura, 1977). While efficacy can be strengthened through these experiences, ultimately it is the employee's own assessment of these experiences that determines self-efficacy (Bandura, 1982).

The most effective way for employees to gain a strong sense of self-efficacy is through mastery experiences (Wood and Bandura, 1989). By having the opportunity to accomplish tasks through effective performance, people enhance their efficacy expectations. Successful performance strengthens their belief in their ability to perform a particular task. The perceived self-efficacy may then generalize to similar situations (Bandura, 1977). Efficacy becomes resilient by repeated accomplishments based on a certain level of perseverance: easy successes increase the likelihood of discouragement when confronted with failure; failures create self-doubt (Wood and Bandura, 1989). Therefore, ensuring that managers' preparation includes the necessary challenges which build resilient efficacy expectations may shape their subsequent performance. If women and minorities are assigned managerial positions for affirmative action without the prerequisite training or experience, for example, their efficacy expectations may be lowered as a consequence (Barclay, 1982).

The content analysis revealed no stories by the black female managers reflecting mastery experiences. The other managers reported at least one example of a mastery experience: the opportunity to complete an assignment successfully which led to a feeling of accomplishment and enhanced belief in oneself. John, a forty-five-year-old black manager, was "the first black accountant in the company . . . and the first black assistant manager." He talked about the opportunities he had that other black people in the company did not experience. He attributes his successes to his belief in himself, which was enhanced through successfully completing assignments:

> I don't think I failed in any assignment that I've had. Failing wasn't part of the picture. And I think that really comes internally. . . . It's an overabundance of confidence in myself. . . . I think my number one confidence is knowing I can get people to do a good job. . . . I've always managed people to get the best out of them.

Liz, a thirty-eight-year-old Hispanic assistant manager, described her early professional development as working on many projects that expanded and honed her skills. These special projects, which increased her self-confidence, were assigned by her supervisor. By gaining experiences to strengthen her skills, she was able to move successfully into a leadership role and improve the unit's performance:

> He forced me to do more than I thought I was capable of doing. . . . There were opportunities constantly

challenging me. He was always making opportunities
available to me. . . . Then I had been looking for
more challenge, different responsibilities. . . . And he
basically created a couple of projects that he wanted
me to take the primary role in and come through successfully. . . . So then I inherited another unit along
the way. . . . And one of the strongest skills that I
would say I developed is motivating people. And I got
recognized for that. An outstanding achievement
award for turning the unit around.

Tim is a thirty-year-old white officer who works directly with
corporate clients. His career training illustrates how mastery experiences lead to performance accomplishments:

I learned quickly. First by concentrating on things I
already had some skill base in. And I quickly assim-
ilated that stuff and was able to perform at a level
where I didn't really need to be supervised. When it
came to other areas, I needed to be coached in that. To
go out with experienced people and see firsthand what
works, what doesn't work. . . . So it was a learning
process. Very challenging work. After about the first
year, I got my chance to lead a project team. . . . After
that I was basically turned loose to consult on my
own.

Efficacy expectations can also be strengthened by observing
proficient models (Bandura, 1977). While modeling is perceived to
be less influential than mastery experience because it leads to beliefs
that are more susceptible to change, effective models contribute to
efficacy expectations by allowing people to observe how others,
similar to themselves, handle various situations effectively. Seeing
others succeed through sustained effort raises observers' beliefs
about their own abilities. Seeing others fail despite high efforts
lowers observers' assessments of their own abilities and undermines
their efforts (Wood and Bandura, 1989). Since high-ranking women
and minority managers often have increased visibility in an orga-

nization, their successes and failures may send powerful messages to others in lower-level positions about the likelihood of success. Several women and minority managers in our study revealed that they believed they would achieve a management level only as high as the highest-ranking woman or minority had attained.

The stories about modeling differed according to gender. Female managers, regardless of race or ethnicity, spoke primarily of the lack of models. Male managers recounted stories about the men they observed and then tried to emulate. The white men appeared to have sufficient models that allowed them to choose a model appropriate to the situation. Jerry, a forty-nine-year-old officer, discussed the assortment of role models:

> As far as role models, everyone was a potential role model. [I'd say] "All right, who's the one I should use as my model in how to be successful in this? Who's the one I should use?" The guy I thought was most interesting, by virtue of his being the boss, was the vice president at the time.

Joe, a twenty-nine-year-old Hispanic assistant manager, spoke about a person who was a role model for him because Joe noted similarities between them. The common factor was not ethnicity but the fact that they had once been peers:

> One particular individual I was friends with because we started out as peers. I had more experience than he had. He's division head now. But he's made his. Over beers I said, "Hey, how do you do this?" And he said you walk into the guy's office and you say in two years I want to be there. I don't know if I can do that. . . . I'm not as brassy, I guess, as him. Maybe that's what I'm learning, how to be like that. . . . There are still a lot of things I don't know.

John, the black manager with twenty-five years at the company, spoke about the scarcity of black role models: blacks who have advanced through the ranks to high-level positions. John's one role model is an assistant vice president, the same level to which John aspires. He discounted black officers who came from other companies. Their experiences were viewed as different from his since John is a long-term employee:

> I think assistant vice president is a good spot. I like that. I don't know that I will be able to break the barrier to make it to the vice-president level. It's not that I'm not qualified. But I don't know if I'm going to live long enough, or my career will extend long enough, to knock down those barriers to get there. Some of that's changing. We've got [black] senior vice presidents. . . . But again, those were brought in. They didn't work their way up the ranks through the company levels. So I set my goal as assistant vice president.

Female managers told stories concerning the lack of female role models. Ellen, a thirty-seven-year-old customer service manager, talked about the shortage of women in higher-level management positions. She also spoke of her fears that the few women who did succeed may not help other women:

> I think in some cases women are being promoted as tokens. But there are not a whole lot of role models in this company for a woman who wants to get ahead or be an officer. And even women who are in that position, they are very tight. I don't sense that they're going to share with subordinates. . . . Instead they feel, phew, I made it. And I've done it myself, and now you're going to have to do it yourself, lady. I don't feel that there is a sisterhood as there is an old boy network.

Ellen also discussed at length women at her level of management whom she labeled successful because of what others said about them. She learned from observing their behavior.

Diane, an assistant manager, spoke of being female and black and the consequences in terms of role models similar to herself:

> As I look at the corporation in terms of people that look like me and where they are, there are very few. I don't see that really changing. I see maybe a few more people, not enough to really make a whole lot of difference. So when they start to make efforts [to promote women and minorities], the only thing about that person that's going to look like me is that she's female. That's it.

Social persuasion, another source of self-efficacy beliefs, is viewed as less effective than mastery experiences and modeling (Bandura, 1977). Realistic encouragement from others can result in the exertion of greater effort, which if coupled with task performance may then lead to greater self-efficacy and achievement. But if the conditions that promote effective performance are absent and failure ensues, the persuader may be discredited and the person's perceived self-efficacy may also be lowered (Bandura, 1977).

Managers, regardless of gender, race, or ethnicity, told stories of the encouragement they received from others. For some managers, persuasion was linked to the opportunity to gain direct experience that validated the support. For other managers, encouragement was not connected to a specific task or challenge.

Liz, the thirty-eight-year-old Hispanic assistant manager, exemplifies how social persuasion linked to task performance can lead to feelings of accomplishment:

> A couple of successes [occurred] before PCs came along. Our area created this program and in its infancy we were going to be involved with it . . . and nobody wanted to touch it. . . . And basically I was the first person to pilot that. And I was like the boss. . . . That was an accomplishment I felt proud of because I didn't give up on it. But somebody had to push me to take that risk. I wasn't willing to do it myself.

So a lot of times that's how it was. People would volunteer you.

Bill, a thirty-one-year-old white computer specialist, also
described how his boss encouraged him, gave him new tasks, and
supported his movement into new job areas. Carol, the thirty-five-
year-old white supervisor, spoke of a boss who provided encouragement as she assumed increased responsibility. Celia, a forty-one-
year-old black technical manager, spoke of the encouragement she
received from superiors on her ability to advance. This persuasion,
however, is more of a general and gentle urging:

> I am finding that I would like to be an officer. My
> immediate senior management is saying that I have
> the goods to do that. I don't have the college back-
> ground, and they would like me to have that. So
> they're pushing me to at least sign up for some
> courses. . . . They say, "Celia, if you want to move up
> to the next step, this is what you have to do." . . . I
> don't know if you'd call it nurturing, because they
> really don't. They just say it and leave it. If you pick
> up on it, fine; if you don't, fine.

Tim, the white male assistant director, recounted numerous
stories of encouragement he received from higher-level managers.
He described in detail how his advancements would occur and how
senior managers believed in his ability to make it to the top:

> I've been told that I'll be a director at this time next
> year. That's just recognition for performance. . . . So
> that makes me feel good. Is that success? I don't know.
> I could do something to screw it up. I don't think that
> will happen.

Emotional arousal is the least influential source of information regarding efficacy expectations. Emotional or physiological
states influence self-efficacy. People may assess their ability and the
likelihood of effective performance in relation to the degree of stress

and anxiety they experience (Bandura, 1977). Reducing stress levels has a positive change on efficacy expectations. Because women and minorities often feel lower levels of acceptance in corporate environments, they may experience higher levels of anxiety in the workplace.

Several male managers who had been with the company for more than twenty years expressed feelings of anxiety related to changes brought about by restructuring. One manager spoke of waking up at 4:00 A.M. wondering what would happen next. And yet they continue to work, recognizing that in many ways they have little control over the outcome. John, the black manager, expressed it this way:

> Having gone through all these changes, still I try to do the best job that I can, recognizing that someone else can do the same job. And recognizing that a lot of times it's a numbers game and if I get caught up in the numbers, I'll be on the outside looking in. Realizing that a lot of it is politics.

Management Implications

The narratives reveal that managers in this financial services company were aware of organizational experiences that have been determined to influence efficacy expectations. They described situations that caused them to feel confident about their abilities as well as situations that detracted from their belief in their ability to succeed.

Racial and gender differences were present in two categories of stories: mastery experiences and modeling, the two powerful sources of self-efficacy. Black female managers related no stories of mastery experiences. Women, regardless of race or ethnicity, offered few examples of role models in this organization. No differences regarding social persuasion emerged among the various racial, ethnic, and gender groups. Stories portraying aspects of emotional arousal were not prevalent among the oral histories with the exception of a few managers who spoke about the anxiety connected with the continual restructuring.

While we recognize that our study has certain limitations, the stories provide examples of how organizations influence self-efficacy. By understanding the sources of self-efficacy and ways that organizations serve as sources of efficacy expectations, corporations can create environments conducive to growth and well-being for all members of the diverse workforce. Because efficacy judgments change as new information and experiences are acquired (Gist and Mitchell, 1992), organizations can intervene by design to enhance managers' beliefs in their capabilities.

Managerial Actions

Managers have the capacity to aid in the development of efficacy expectations. Through their managerial functions, they are positioned to furnish mastery experiences, to serve as role models, to provide exposure to models similar to their employees, to encourage the development of new skills, and to reduce stress. Table 10.1 summarizes the source of efficacy expectations and the related managerial actions that can facilitate self-efficacy.

Mastery is enhanced by guiding employees through experiences in which gradual accomplishments are acquired. Managers can arrange employee assignments in a hierarchy to improve the likelihood that positive self-efficacy results as employees achieve progressive challenges. Ensuring that employees have the requisite training and experiences to handle challenging goals will aid in the mastery of these experiences. Furthermore, elucidating the specific tasks necessary to complete each assignment will provide employees with valuable information to assess their capabilities for performance. Bandura and Schunck (1981) found that incremental subgoals increased performance and self-efficacy as well as interest in the task.

In concert with task assignments, managers play a critical role as coaches by guiding employees through the mastery experiences and providing the necessary feedback. Giving specific comments on task performance leads to increases in both efficacy expectations and subsequent performance (Gist, 1986). But managers need to know when to intervene and when to allow the employee to complete the task independently. Intervening in task perfor-

Table 10.1. Sources of Self-Efficacy and Management Guidelines.

Source	Management guidelines
Mastery experiences	
• Specific task performance generalizing to similar situations	• Guide employees through experiences (coaching role) • Offer challenging goals
Modeling	
• Proficient models • Similar models	• Assign experienced mentors
Social persuasion	
• Realistic encouragement linked to task performance	• Encourage performance on specific assignments • Provide specific feedback
Emotional arousal	
• Stress and anxiety impeding efficacy expectations	• Assess contribution to unnecessary stress • Work with human resources to reduce job stress

mance must be approached cautiously. The degree of coaching needs to be monitored as well as well timed. Resiliency of self-efficacy depends on persevering when setbacks are encountered, learning from mistakes, and viewing obstacles as challenges rather than self-deficiencies. Therefore, to abort employees' efforts prematurely may undermine personal accomplishments (Wood and Bandura, 1989). Managers need to assess when intervention is appropriate for both the employee and the work unit and must learn to view mistakes or failures as opportunities for learning. Furthermore, managers must help employees understand the coaching role and must ascertain how different employees respond to their intervention.

Senior-level employees may also be trained to serve as coaches to new or inexperienced colleagues. This tactic has two distinct benefits. Experienced employees will acquire new skills at a time when promotional opportunities are becoming more limited. Junior employees may view coaching by a colleague as less threatening and thus less anxiety-producing.

As part of the performance appraisal process, managers can gain information about employees' perceptions of strengths and weaknesses and then work with them to assign realistic goals to address areas of improvement. By providing the opportunity to gain mastery experiences, they may enhance goal achievement. Belief in oneself intensifies and sustains the effort needed to realize challenging goals (Bandura and Cervone, 1983), such as those established during the performance review.

The oral history findings suggest an area of further investigation: whether or not black female managers receive fewer opportunities for mastery experiences. Managers need to determine how tasks are delegated and whether there is discrimination against any group. Often there is a tendency to assign tasks to experienced personnel who can easily and competently complete them. This practice may inadvertently limit developmental opportunities for others in the work group, particularly women and minorities who may have less seniority.

Exposing employees to similar role models enhances efficacy expectations. Managers can assign new or junior-level employees to work with more experienced employees to gain exposure to proficient models for the various job situations they will encounter. Since women appear to have less access to female role models, managers should work to expand the networks and connections with successful women managers in other units or within the profession itself. The lack of successful role models is a similar concern of minority managers. Providing women and minorities with successful role models whenever possible may lead to enhanced efficacy expectations.

A relatively easy way for managers to affect efficacy expectations is through encouragement—realistic encouragement. Furthermore, persuasion is most effective when linked directly to performance. Thus specific and timely feedback is more effective than general words of encouragement. The oral histories did not reveal racial, ethnic, or gender differences in the nature of social persuasion in this organization. Even so, managers may want to assess their own behavior regarding their encouragement of women and minorities. For example, opportunities for informal feedback and encouragement are often unavailable to women and minorities who may be excluded from informal interactions with supervisors and managers (Cianni and Romberger, 1991).

Emotional arousal may interfere with employees' beliefs in their ability to accomplish tasks. Activities designed to reduce stress and tension in the workplace should be implemented. Much employee stress today stems from the continual downsizing and restructuring that have become common organizational occurrences. As the tempo of organizational change increases, managers need to be trained to manage change effectively. Understanding how each employee responds to change and the nature of the response required can help to lessen the resultant stress. Some employees require additional information about proposed changes, for example, while others may need an opportunity to vent anger and frustration. Managers should also appraise their management style and its possible contributions to unnecessary stress and tension in work units. Human resource professionals can assist managers to understand how their behavior may negatively affect employees.

Women and minorities often feel lower levels of acceptance in corporate environments (Cianni and Romberger, 1991) and thus may experience higher levels of anxiety. Those practices in the corporate culture that exclude rather than include women and minorities must be exposed. Many companies are implementing cultural audit surveys (Cox, 1991) to assess the unique factors in their organizations that alienate women and minorities. Audit data enable organizations to design interventions which increase the probability that all members of a work unit will feel accepted. Before managers can change their behavior, however, human resource professionals must facilitate the process by which managers come to recognize underlying assumptions that may prohibit them from providing the diverse members of their work units with a full range of developmental experiences.

Organizational Interventions

Organizations have abundant occasions for enhancing the efficacy expectations of their members. Table 10.2 lists the organizational

Table 10.2. Organizational Actions and Workforce Diversity Issues.

Organizational actions	Diversity issues
Mastery experiences	
• Effective training programs • Career planning programs • Management development: coaching • Risk-taking environment	• Access to developmental opportunities • Preparation for promotion
Modeling	
• Training using behavior modeling approaches • Mentors and role models	• Diverse role models in training videos • Enhanced visibility of successful women and minorities • Participation of women and minority professionals in networks
Social persuasion	
• Feedback from training • Effective performance appraisal system	• Support groups for women and minorities • Equitable feedback and appraisal systems
Emotional arousal	
• Stress management programs • Change management programs • Conflict management programs	• Valuing diversity initiatives • Reducing culture clashes

actions related to self-efficacy as well as specific issues relevant to the diverse workplace.

Training and development offer numerous occasions for direct application of self-efficacy theory. Training programs designed to allow participants opportunities to model behavior and gain feedback on their own performance enhances self-efficacy (Gist, 1987). Therefore, the training instructors should use training to provide mastery experiences, role models (either real or simulated), feedback and encouragement, and nonthreatening learning environments.

Through effective and well-designed training programs, opportunities for mastery experiences can be increased. Management development programs can teach managers to be more effective coaches—leading others to master new skills and gain important developmental experiences. Career planning programs can assist by pinpointing an employee's skill needs and interests. Individual career development plans can guide managers in assisting employees to grow professionally. Career path models can provide information on the critical mastery experiences by cataloguing the experiences necessary to advance to higher positions. But corporate leaders must first stimulate an atmosphere that fosters and rewards risk-taking behavior, thus enabling employees to take advantage of new development opportunities.

Equal access to learning experiences must be provided to all employees. Projects and assignments labeled as "developmental opportunities" should be analyzed to ensure that women and minorities are fairly represented. Providing opportunities for increased visibility through special projects can also boost employees' chances for advancement. Women and minorities must have the proper developmental assignments and receive the requisite training before they can be promoted. Training programs provide convenient and effective vehicles for modeling. Behavioral modeling techniques have been integrated into many training programs, such as performance management modules. By using a behavior modeling approach, training can also serve as a mechanism for feedback and encouragement. Furthermore, simulated models have been shown to be effective in enhancing efficacy expectations. Developers of training programs should ensure that diverse role models are represented in training videos.

Mentors provide an array of benefits (Kram, 1985)—as models of effective behavior, for example. But since mentors tend to choose protégés who are similar to themselves (Kanter, 1977), they may exclude women and minorities from access to effective modeling. Mentor programs that pair women and minorities with similar role models are effective in enhancing efficacy expectations. If female and minority mentors are not widely available in the organization, featuring the accomplishments of women and minorities may serve as a viable substitute. Supporting the involvement of women and minorities in professional organizations and networks can also increase access to professional role models.

Performance appraisal systems that provide realistic encouragement and identify task assignments leading to success are effective tools for using social persuasion to enhance efficacy expectations. Sanctioned support groups for women and minorities can foster a supportive work environment.

Attention to tension and stress in corporations is increasingly important today as the pace of internal and external change quickens. Employee assistance programs that include interventions for stress management are now in great demand. Furthermore, helping managers to become more proficient in managing change may attenuate the anxiety created by corporate restructuring. Conflict management skills can improve a manager's ability to handle intergroup conflict resulting from increased competition for limited corporate resources.

Training programs devoted to managing or valuing diversity promote learning about the diverse members of the organization and acceptance among diverse groups (Cox, 1991). These interventions can reduce stress for all employees as the ability to work together improves. Aspects of the corporate environment that result in "culture clashes" can be identified and then attenuated so that unnecessary discomfort can be avoided.

Toward Optimum Performance

Self-efficacy theory provides corporations with guidelines for ways to equip people with the competencies, the internal capabilities, and the resilient belief in themselves that will allow them to enhance their well-being and accomplishments. This belief in one's ability to perform critical tasks is a vital component of ego energy and may sustain internal strength and motivation during turbulent organizational times.

Listening to the voices of employees from various gender, racial, and ethnic groups provides insight into the steps required to enact organizational change. While our study includes only sixteen oral histories, limiting its generalizability to a broader group of managers, the findings suggest that differences in efficacy experiences may be a critical area for exploration. The stories provide rich detail about ways in which one group of diverse managers respond to their organization. Clearly we need further research on the application of self-efficacy to organizational performance as well as the effectiveness of the recommended strategies for various employees.

Organizations have limited resources today as they work to improve their competitive positions. Allowing all corporate members, male and female, white and nonwhite, to achieve optimal levels of performance and realize their full potential is a prerequisite to individual and, hence, organizational success. Specific actions to improve utilization of a diverse workforce are available at both the managerial and organizational levels. Recognizing that organizations can either enhance or impede self-efficacy is a pivotal first step.

References

Bandura, A. "Self-Efficacy: Toward a Unifying Theory of Behavioral Change." *Psychological Review*, 1977, *84*, 191–215.

Bandura, A. "Self-Efficacy Mechanism in Human Agency." *American Psychologist*, 1982, *37*, 122–147.

Bandura, A., and Cervone, D. "Self-Evaluative and Self-Efficacy Mechanisms Governing the Motivational Efforts of Goal Systems." *Journal of Personality and Social Psychology*, 1983, *45*, 1017–1028.

Bandura, A., and Schunck, D. "Cultivating Competence, Self-Efficacy and Intrinsic Interest Through Proximal Self-Motivation." *Journal of Personality and Social Psychology*, 1981, *41*, 586–598.

Barclay, L. "Social Learning Theory: A Framework for Discrimination Research." *Academy of Management Review*, 1982, *7*, 587–594.

Betz, N. E., and Hackett, G. "The Relationship of Career-Related Self Efficacy Expectations to Perceived Career Options in College Women and Men." *Journal of Counseling Psychology*, 1981, *28*, 399–410.

Cianni, M., and Romberger, B. "Belonging in the Corporation: Oral Histories of Male, Female, Black, White and Hispanic Managers." *Academy of Management Best Paper Proceedings*, 1991, 358–362.

Cox, T. H. "The Multicultural Organization." *Academy of Management Executive*, 1991, *5*, 34–47.

Gist, M. "The Effects of Self-Efficacy Training on Training Task Performance." *Academy of Management Best Paper Proceedings,* 1986, 250–254.

Gist, M. "Self-Efficacy: Implications for Organizational Behavior and Human Resource Management." *Academy of Management Review,* 1987, *12,* 472–485.

Gist, M., and Mitchell, T. R. "Self-Efficacy: A Theoretical Analysis of Its Determinants and Malleability." *Academy of Management Review,* 1992, *17,* 183–211.

Hill, L. A., and Elias, J. "Retraining Midcareer Managers: Career History and Self-Efficacy Beliefs." *Human Resource Management,* 1990, *29,* 197–217.

Kanter, R. *Men and Women of the Corporation.* New York: Basic Books, 1977.

Kram, K. *Mentoring at Work: Developmental Relationships in Organizational Life.* Glenview, Ill.: Scott, Foresman, 1985.

Wood, R., and Bandura, A.. "Social Cognitive Theory of Organizational Management." *Academy of Management Review,* 1989, *14,* 361–384.

Part Four

Organizational
Transformations

11

Using Ego Energy
in an Electric Utility

Robert B. Marshall, Jo-Anne I. Pitera,
Lyle Yorks, Stephen T. DeBerry

WE BELIEVE ORGANIZATIONS seeking successful transformation must use strategies and techniques that promote employees' ego energy and foster its growth. Redeployment is a technique for transformational change designed to streamline and improve corporate functioning by following the advice of management expert W. E. Deming (Aguayo, 1990) and "restoring power to the individual." The goal of the process is to place the right people in the right jobs in order to ensure efficient and effective planning, production, and performance.

Florida Power and Light (FPL), the fourth largest investor-owned electric utility in the country, was one of the most recent of many organizations to undergo redeployment as described here. Although it is too early to determine the ultimate degree of success, preliminary indicators suggest a positive outcome. At least one such indicator was the company's rapid restoration of service following the unprecedented destruction of Hurricane Andrew. We believe the success of FPL's redeployment depended, in part, on the company's ability to nurture ego energy among its employees. This, in turn, began transforming the corporate culture in a positive way. This chapter describes the redeployment process and explains why it is effective for managing ego energy.

Ego Energy: What It Is and How It Works

In psychological metatheory, the ego is defined as the executor of the person—that is, the motivational and organizational modulator of the individual. Traditionally, the ego is associated with the reality functions of the self, especially as they relate to work and play (Hamilton, 1988). In terms of work productivity, the energy that the ego identifies with and invests becomes a crucial variable. Related concepts from the literature of psychology are locus of control and attachment theory. Ego energy is a measure of employees' personal involvement in their work. In relation to corporations or organizations, ego energy refers to the degree to which the employee's motivational, organizational, and productive capabilities are identified with the organization. The greater the degree of identification, the greater the potential for both personal and organizational success. The concept is basically an ecological perspective (DeBerry, 1993) that relates the microscopic level (the worker) to the macroscopic arena (the corporation). The more a person's ego is invested in the work, the greater the benefit for the individual, the task, and the organization. Positive ego energy relates to a secure feeling of attachment, a strong locus of internal control, and, in terms of the task at hand, a sense of meaning, involvement, importance, and satisfaction.

The healthy, adaptive ego seems to parallel today's ideal corporate culture, while an unhealthy, rigid, or weak ego parallels a nonadaptive culture. The greatest (corporate culture), as the Hindu sage would say, is in the smallest (individual ego energy of each employee). According to extensive research by Kotter and Heskett (1992), an adaptive and flexible corporate culture is required for success in the changing global marketplace while nonadaptive cultures are doomed to failure. Citing a study of two hundred major corporations, they conclude (p. 143):

> Cultures that are not adaptive take many forms. In
> large corporations, they are often characterized by

some arrogance, insularity, and bureaucratic central-
ization, all supported by a value system that cares
more about self-interest than about customers, stock-
holders, employees and good leadership. In such cultures, managers tend to ignore relevant contextual
changes and cling to outmoded strategies and ossified
practices. They make it difficult for anyone else, especially those below them in the hierarchy, to implement new and better strategies and practices. . . . In
corporate cultures that promote useful change, managers pay close attention to relevant changes in a
firm's context and then initiate incremental changes
in strategies and practices to keep in line with environmental realities. . . . These values emphasize the
importance of people and processes that can create
change. Such a value system, when expressed in written form, often sounds either hopelessly idealistic or
hopelessly vague to the point of almost uselessness.
Yet, that very system is the key to excellent performance because it energizes managers and gets them to
do what is needed to help firms adapt to a changing,
competitive environment.

The postmodern world represents an arena in which rapidly
accelerating events and changes result in novel interactions and
emergent circumstances never previously encountered. As the shift
toward global community becomes more entrenched, the postmodern quality of life affects every person and every community. The
critical element of postmodernism is the acceleration factor. Information, especially as it relates to the business climate, can be trans-
ferred and used almost immediately due to rapid advances in
technology. The postmodern business world reflects an environment in which financial decisions in Tokyo immediately affect the
corporate atmosphere in Wisconsin. Paradoxically, in such an interconnected world, the feelings and actions of certain people can
have marked effects. This creates an organizational climate in
which the worker's personal investment (ego energy) has increased

importance. In true ecological fashion, the outcome of the whole has become increasingly identified with the success of its parts.

According to Kilmann and Covin (1988), the predictable, protected marketplace of yesterday that made the corporate world seem stable has been replaced by a world marketplace that appears dynamic and turbulent. What made organizations successful in the past no longer applies. To keep pace with changing world dynamics, corporations must now be more flexible, creative, adaptive, innovative. Such an overwhelming change in approach requires a total reexamination and transformation of organizational structure. This transformation implies that new ways of thinking, perceiving, and behaving are necessary for all members of the organization. Simple linear extrapolation, so common in the past, is no longer sufficient for success. Change must affect the organization at the level of corporate culture. Culture, a term from anthropology and social psychology, implies the total environmental context of a group. At an organizational level, culture may best be viewed as a group reflection of the collective attitudes and behavior of individual employees. This is expressed as the manner in which the work gets done and how the employees relate to customers and to each other.

Transformation is no easy task—especially for large corporations with strong corporate cultures (Kotter and Heskett, 1992). Change threatens the ego of each employee, which in turn affects the productivity and climate of the organization as a whole. If sufficient attention is not paid to the ego needs of all concerned during the transformative process, a wholesale decline in ego energy can send quality and productivity into a tailspin from which recovery may not be possible.

Downsizing, a common response to the recent economic climate, was seen initially as a transformative strategy that boosted stock prices and enhanced company profits. The experience of companies who have used this method suggests that it certainly should not be the only focus of a restructuring. Despite initial "profit boosts," this strategy alone is not effective. Eastman Kodak, for example, one of the first to jump on the downsizing bandwagon, has experienced slumping profit margins since 1982. Their stock today is lower than it was in 1986. Boroughs (1992) analyzes several companies that have undergone downsizing over the past few years and concludes that "there is no way you can just downsize yourself into profitability."

Traditional downsizing models can do great damage to individual ego energy—which in turn damages corporate culture, tending to make it even more rigid and less adaptive. Though this is not the intent, it can occur, in true boomerang fashion, because individual ego energy is damaged rather than nurtured. Even employees who survive the downsizing may feel like victims, subject to the whims of management that does not appear to be managing the restructuring process according to objective and legitimate business criteria. They may also feel betrayed by a company that, in their view, had a "social contract" to care for them for life in exchange for their loyalty and now appears to show no concern or compassion.

A damaged ego accounts for overrigidity, narcissism, borderline personality states, and the inability to deal successfully with external conditions. (See Blanck and Blanck, 1986; Hartmann, 1958; Young-Eisendrath and Hall, 1991; Rosenberg and Kaplan, 1982). This is mirrored in the damaged corporate culture that results. A healthy ego, on the other hand, results in more flexible, dynamic coping strategies and is strengthened by successfully dealing with change. This may also reflect in the culture of the organization. Successful transformation may best be described as a metamorphosis from ossification to a dynamic process where outmoded practices are discarded for positive alternatives.

What determines the difference between ego damage and ego enhancement during restructuring? One relevant dimension is locus of control—a concept from social psychology developed by Julian Rotter (Fiske and Taylor, 1991) that can be traced back at least to Gordon Allport's work on defense mechanisms and self-esteem as well as to research in attribution theory. Locus of control relates to the degree to which a person attributes success or failure to personal actions compared to external circumstances. A person with an external locus of control feels that the outcome is based primarily on uncontrollable environmental variables; a person who displays an internal locus of control attributes success or failure to self. Imagine a classroom situation where two children take a spelling test and both receive high scores. A student with an internal locus of control

will feel that the high score was obtained because of the study time
devoted to the test. This conclusion results in enhanced self-esteem
and the desire to continue studying and achieving. A student with
an external locus of control will feel that the high score was acquired because the test was easy. This will have a negligible or
negative effect on self-esteem.

Evidence indicates that an internal locus of control correlates
with high achievement, positive attitudes, and good health (Fiske
and Taylor, 1991). This finding seems to suggest that organizations
would be wise to recruit and develop employees with a strong internal locus of control. Research also suggests that locus of control
is malleable and that those who anticipate failure are constantly
exposed to low-control situations, continually confusing stimuli,
and are more likely to shift from an internal to an external locus
of control (Rosenberg and Kaplan, 1982). It may be that traditional,
"lean and mean" downsizing practices have the side effect of shifting locus of control in employees, particularly middle management,
to a more external orientation. Extended periods of indecision combined with minimal communication and diminished sense of control over one's position can lead to a negative transformation with
an external locus of control bias.

Just as an infant's difficulties in attachment and bonding
during the early stages of life can result in major personality dis-
orders, difficulties in attachment and bonding between employee
and company can, likewise, result in negative corporate effects.
Withholding of ego energy, inertia, passive/aggressive behavior,
and fear of future risk taking are correlated with disturbances in
attachment. Damaging one's corporate culture by striking blows to
employee attachment can be fatal—for in today's marketplace, risk
taking, ego involvement, and high-energy contributions from all
employees are crucial to success.

Traditional downsizing practices often violate employees'
attachment in at least two ways. First, when some employees are
forced to leave while others remain, the group's identity disinte-
grates. Those who remain are often as traumatized as those who
leave by feelings of guilt and betrayal (Brockner, Davy, and Carter,
1985). Second, forced layoffs are perceived by all employees as a

violation of the "social contract" with the paternal organization that is expected to care for loyal employees for life.

A successful restructuring strategy must account for employees' ego needs in order to maintain and enhance their ego energy. This is best accomplished by maintaining an internal locus of control and boosting the level of attachment of all concerned. This policy results in a healthier, more flexible, and more adaptive corporate culture. The restructuring process must ensure that employees maintain an awareness of what is occurring, a sense of personal involvement, and a healthy attachment to the group—not only those who remain with the company but also those who leave. Using a Redeployment strategy seems to accomplish this objective.

A Four-Phase Restructuring Model

To keep pace with the future, organizations need a paradigm that allows for the increased development of human resources during and after restructuring. Support for this assertion is found in an extensive international comparison of Japanese and American firms (Kagono and others, 1985). The study cited several differences in management strategies that seem to account for the relative success of Japanese companies: a tendency to offer broad rather than specific directions and domains to employees (job descriptions in Japan are far less likely to list specific duties); a focus on adaptive, in-house resource development; an emphasis on developing human resources through education and activation as opposed to financial management; distribution of risk through intra- and interorganizational networks in Japanese firms; and an emphasis on process through inductive, incremental reasoning rather than a logical, deductive approach. In short, quality control is applied to people as much as to things. This policy results in the successful building and enhancing of individual ego energy—which, in turn, enhances the collective energy of the organization. This paradigm transcends the outdated pretechnological notion of a paternal company that employees serve and obey and replaces it with an employee/employer relationship that supports a dynamic, collective corporate identity comprised of the interactive, creative ego energy of each employee. Restructuring large organizations to improve operating efficiency and reduce costs while allowing this type of paradigmatic shift to occur is a difficult but essential task.

One company that seems to have realized this goal of restructuring for success is Sea-Land Services. Boroughs (1992) notes that Sea-Land was different from most companies because of the way it reorganized itself. We suggest that one of the major reasons for the organization's success was the manner in which the transformation process affected the collective ego energy of the corporation. Major organizational change opens a "critical window of opportunity" that, if properly managed, can result in a powerful new realignment with a fresh and energized corporate culture. Sea-Land's human resources strategies helped the organization, among other things, to manage planned change and continuous improvement by monitoring and nurturing employee ego energy. These strategies focused on matching the right people with the right jobs, addressing critical business issues, and openly communicating forthcoming changes. This strategy accounts not only for attachment/detachment states experienced by employees, but also an enhanced internal locus of control that reframes individual changes as potential growth opportunities rather than failures.

Organizational change is, ultimately, driven by individual change. People are the key to success. Satisfied employees keep satisfied customers. As technology becomes the common ground for all players, it is people that make the final difference between success and failure in the marketplace (Barnett, Geweke, and Shell, 1989). Efforts to change organizational culture and achieve transformation must not be motivated purely by financial need. Rather, they should incorporate individual ego energy in a positive way as a legitimate business precept. Corporate change should focus on how employees think about themselves in relation to their jobs, their organization, and their fellow employees; how they define their roles in the organization; and how they define success. To facilitate these changes, the organization must nurture the ego energy of all its employees. Redeployment contributes significantly toward this goal.

Figure 11.1 shows an organizational transformation in four phases. The timelines are derived from the experience at Sea-Land, FPL, and other companies. Redeployment begins during Phase III—when employees are made acutely aware of change and their

Figure 11.1. The Four-Phase Transformation Process.

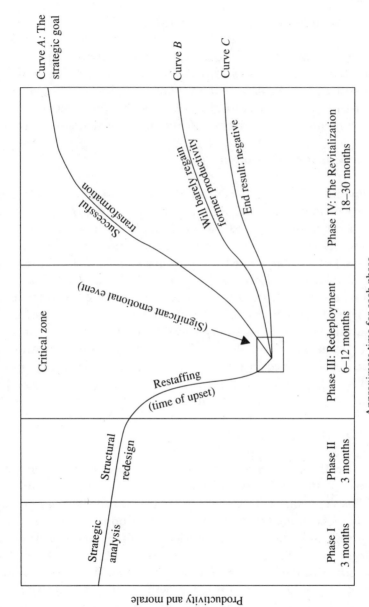

Productivity and morale

Curve A: The strategic goal

Curve B

Curve C

Will barely regain former productivity

End result: negative

Successful transformation

Critical zone

(Significant emotional event)

Restaffing (time of upset)

Structural redesign

Strategic analysis

Phase I
3 months

Phase II
3 months

Phase III: Redeployment
6–12 months

Phase IV: The Revitalization
18–30 months

Approximate time for each phase

Source: **Copyright Marshall Group, Inc., 1993.**

normal routine has been disrupted—and extends into the early stages of recovery as well. Redeployment is a process to assess and realign employee talent to a new strategic direction and organizational design. It usually involves restructuring and may or may not result in the displacement of employees from the organization. Redeployment is strategically driven, not simply a response to cost-saving targets, and strives to use the energy of change effectively.

Phase I: Strategic Analysis

The first phases of this transformation do not affect employees or production. During Phase I, a strategic analysis of corporate and individual needs is undertaken. Groups of senior managers work with selected employees to evaluate the internal and external business factors that created the need for change. Competition, new technologies, deregulation, legislation, and changes in ownership are examples of such driving forces. The result of this participative planning, usually conducted with the assistance of an outside consulting firm, is a new strategic direction and a vision statement for the business. It includes a definition of the corporate culture required to succeed in the new business environment. This process should be conducted openly, and employees should be regularly informed of progress and results.

Phase II: Organization Redesign

Phase II of the structural redesign develops a new organization chart at the macro level that supports the new strategic direction. This step requires an analysis of organizational effectiveness to improve operational efficiency and eliminate unnecessary work. Cross-functional teams work with outside consultants and inside management to develop a design that ultimately leads to defining each position in the new organization. These new descriptions provide the validity for the restaffing that will occur during Phase III, the Redeployment Phase. Again, all employees should be kept apprised of progress through open, regular, and timely communications. For this process to work, there can be no sacred cows.

Robert Kriegel (1991) says that "sacred cows make the best

burgers." He defines sacred cows as systems, strategies, policies, and routines that have become standard operating procedure. Employees take the practices for granted because "that's the way it has always been done." Sacred cows are, in physical terms, entropic— and overcoming entropy allows for smoother, more dynamic functioning. Inertia is greatest from 0 to 1, though, so overcoming sacred cows may be one of the greatest challenges in restructuring. Kriegel recommends that corporations assess their present systems and culture, look for all the sacred cows, and then round them up for a barbecue. Sacred cows are symbols that not only block organizational efficiency but also undermine employees' attitudes. Employees may think: "If you say we must change, but we still have to do some things the old way, then we are not really changing. I don't have more control and I shouldn't be creative or initiate new ideas." Thus, in order to free employees to truly participate in the transformational process, all sacred cows must be scrutinized. Employees at every level should be involved in the search and slaughter of sacred cows, giving employees the power to challenge what might prevent their future success.

Phase III: Redeployment

The last phases of the transformation become highly interactive: they involve managers and employees at all levels. During these phases, the opportunity for creating effective cultural change through building self-esteem, commitment, and ego energy becomes most pronounced. It is as this potentially chaotic third phase begins that Redeployment enters the picture. Phase III must be handled with great sensitivity and attention to detail. An analogy of managing the process might be the *Queen Elizabeth II,* a huge, oceangoing cruise ship, rapidly changing course by 180 degrees during a hurricane. It can be done, but it requires time and an effective captain at the helm and the careful attention and active participation of the entire crew.

A plunge in productivity occurs whenever a workforce experiences a major restructuring. This is evident in Figure 11.1 as the organization enters Phase III. We call the nadir of this curve the "critical zone." During this time, individual employees are affected and stress and anxiety are highest. Management's every action is scrutinized. Many companies falter at this point and never fully recover. We believe this is because their actions have a damaging effect on employees' ego energy.

Redeployment enables the organization to increase its chances of success by managing this critical zone as a rare opportunity to drive positive transformational change. Properly implemented, Redeployment creates a "significant emotional event" that touches every employee. Management now has everyone's attention. Resistance to change becomes minimal. In this atmosphere, a well-managed process may help employees jolt loose from their traditional attitudes and redirect them toward a new set of corporate goals and a fresh working climate. The Redeployment process enables this positive change to occur through a carefully designed and orchestrated set of strategies. At the heart of the process is a simple principle: Strive to maintain the dignity of and respect for each employee, regardless of how he or she is affected by the process. Although the exact methodology depends on the organization, as well as the situation and goals, the process has typical elements.

First is a *steering committee* composed of key managers representing human resources, communications, the legal department, and major business units affected by the restructuring. The committee's role is to guide the design and implementation of the process acting in an advisory capacity to executive management. This element enables management and employees to view the process as participatory and objective. It supports an internal locus of control for employees by allowing them to see the direct influence of their peers on the process. Committee members also serve as role models for other managers and employees as their active and visible participation increases and enhances ego energy. It also serves as a useful mechanism to support attachment to the new vision, for each employee now takes part in focusing this vision. At FPL, twelve employees comprised the steering committee and over two hundred employees were involved in the other teams supporting Phases I and II.

A *zero-based staffing approach* provides for all nonunion employees to be reassessed and redeployed to appropriate positions. Zero-based staffing means, in principle, that all past jobs are eliminated. All potential employees are starting fresh and will be reassessed. This process may sound overwhelming at the level of a large corporation, but experience demonstrates that it can be managed in an orderly fashion. Strict timelines are imposed to avoid extended periods of uncertainty. This procedure also helps to prevent a shift from internal to external locus of control for all those who are affected by restructuring. In zero-based staffing, all salaried employees are reassessed. Thus the group remains intact and the old culture is symbolically put to rest. Lower-level employees do not feel unnecessarily penalized, for they can see that their supervisors are in the same situation as themselves. Everyone is in the same boat. The openness of the process helps to assuage feelings of guilt and remorse among survivors of traditional transformation practices. Zero-based staffing is a key concept because it helps maintain group attachment bonds while at the same time breaking up the old organization and providing an open avenue for restructuring. It also sets the stage for a complete symbolic rebuilding of the organization from the ground up with a new emphasis. A totally new culture can now be created. The message: The old is gone now. Let's begin to build the new together.

A *selection system*, based on the future needs of the business, is now developed. Skill assessment identifies the employees best suited to realize a new corporate vision and new performance standards. An objective model for matching the right people to the "right" jobs prevents the feelings of insecurity caused by a poorly communicated or seemingly random layoff. It also prevents a loss of key talent through the open window of a traditional "early retirement" downsizing strategy. Selection focuses on the individual and makes it clear that the company wants to help each employee find a role suited for personal growth, development, and self-actualization. By so doing, respect for people is communicated and ego energy is enhanced.

A *targeted, voluntary severance plan* determines severance eligibility on an individual basis. This element seeks to assure that only those employees whose skills are not required in the future are eligible to leave the organization. It supports the dignity of each employee by providing options and helping eligible employees make informed choices. While employees eligible for the plan may or may not like the situation, they become actively involved in a process that will define their future. Full details concerning their options and decision-making support services are provided. Management plays a nonauthoritarian, facilitative role. This aspect of Redeployment fosters ego energy by allowing individual choice and maintaining an internal locus of control for the employees affected.

A *training plan* prepares managers at all levels to implement the Redeployment program. Active participation, as noted earlier, supports internal locus of control and provides additional opportunities to incorporate the new vision of the organization. Training managers in techniques and strategies allows them to apply the selection process effectually and consistently while modeling new behavior. Modeling brings the redeployment process to each layer of the organization and every employee. This fosters ego energy by reinvolving employees and making them feel an important part of a new organizational vision.

A *communication plan* ensures that employees, customers, and other stakeholders are informed throughout the transformation. Open and regular communication is crucial. These communication processes sustain an environment of trust and support a sense of personal control. Allowing employees to maintain an internal locus of control, as previously discussed, enhances ego energy.

A *business-based framework for recovery* provides a sense of security and structure while still emphasizing the power of change and the value of every employee. This strategy enhances ego energy and assures employees that they are a major part of enabling the organization to realize its goals.

Phase IV: Revitalization

During Phase IV, which may last from eighteen months to over three years, management must continue to support and reinforce the new vision and performance standards. Supervisors must model the desired behavior and establish new human resource systems to strengthen the cultural change. Such systems would include, for example, performance management and compensation. The organization's ultimate goal is to be more successful after the restructuring than it was before. The process should position the organization for the future and make it more competitive in the marketplace. It should also enable employees to be more flexible and more confident in their own abilities, as well as having skills that match the needs of the business. These benefits are realized during Phase IV. Success depends on how well the process was managed during the first three phases. It also depends on management's ability to support employees through their own personal transition.

Employees experience stages of psychological transition (Bridges, 1988) as they reattach to the new organization (see Figure 11.2). During the initial stage of "Letting Go," employees react to the loss of what was commonplace with denial, a tendency to cling to the familiar, and nostalgia for the good old days. In this stage, people become anxious about the future and anxiety manifests itself in apparent confusion. Employees may be angry at the organization for fostering change and angry at management for allowing it. Although this is a normal response expected after restructuring, it is essential for employees to transition as quickly as possible into the next stage: "Chaotic Reorientation." During this second stage, the employee has made an intellectual decision to let go of the past but is not yet ready to commit to the future. This stage is important because people need the opportunity to work through the implication of change on both an emotional and intellectual level. The Chaotic Reorientation stage is just that—chaos because the employee's actions and words may be inconsistent and incongruent; reorientation because the employee is starting to see value in the new and creating bridges between the past and the future. Employees recommit to the new organization when they have worked through the feelings of loss, let go of the old, and taken time out to reorient their thoughts and feelings. In the third stage, "Focused Recommitment," employees are no longer confused; they have a sense of direction and know what is expected of them. They are connected to the new organization and other employees. They are invigorated and have a sense of anticipation about the future. Employees have now created a new frame of reference relative to the change and view the future more positively. Since each employee is unique, there is no specific timeline for this psychological transition. Yet the transition of the majority of employees into the final stage is the driving force behind a successful, revitalized organiza-

Figure 11.2. Stages of Individual Psychological Transition.

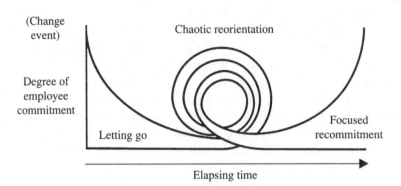

tion. Success depends on how well the process was managed during the first three phases and how quickly employees demonstrate new behavior and apply their skills to the new vision.

Although an organization, too, goes through stages of transition after a restructuring (Bechard and Harris, 1977), the transitions of the organization and its employees are somewhat different and usually do not coincide. (See Figure 11.3.) There are three stages of organizational transition: disorganization when roles, responsibilities, relationships, and procedures within the organization have changed; recovery when new roles, responsibilities, relationships, and procedures have been established; revitalized performance when productivity improves to a level exceeding that prior to the restructuring. Ultimately, the success of the restructuring requires a large majority of employees to progress through their own transition in order for the organization to achieve revitalized performance levels.

Redeployment in Context

Florida Power and Light (FPL), the fourth largest electric utility company in the nation, was the first non-Japanese corporation ever to receive the coveted Deming Award for quality. From a workforce of nearly 15,000, about 1,050 FPL employees accepted voluntary

Figure 11.3. Individual and Organizational Transition Processes.

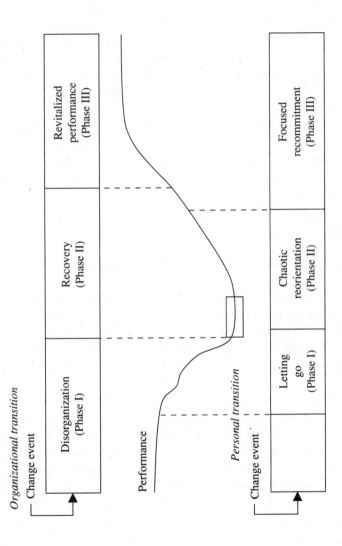

separation packages and another 300 assumed new positions within the company during a 1991 restructuring. The total cost of restructuring was $90 million, with a payback estimated in just over one year. In some cases, layers of management were cut in half from as many as twelve to six. Almost 8,000 positions were redefined with as many employees directly affected by the redeployment process. No lawsuits were filed as a result of the restructuring, and the company has begun its transition from a paternalistic environment where the watchwords were "loyalty and security" to a more flexible and dynamic organization where "efficiency and opportunity" are the key terms. This is because, in part, the redeployment strategies used in restructuring attended, as far as was possible, to the ego energy needs of employees.

Step I

At FPL, as well as other organizations using this four-phase model, the initial planning and analysis (Phases I and II) were completed with a focus on the future needs of the business. Once the planning was completed, it became even more critical to maintain open communications during Phase III: redeployment. Providing timely honest feedback minimized a feeling of "loss of control" to a degree that would not otherwise have been possible. At FPL, video productions explained the redeployment process, the rationale for it, and the step-by-step manner in which it would unfold, complete with timelines and relevant details—thus enhancing the ego energy of all concerned. These tapes, broadcast throughout the working day on FPL's internal video network, were supplemented with written periodic reports. The process was further clarified by regular meetings conducted by managers and supervisors at the work unit level.

The selection process at FPL cascaded down a hierarchical structure. Executive managers were first selected and announced. They, in turn, were responsible for staffing the positions that reported directly to them by using the selection tools and guidelines provided. They looked at all appropriate candidates and decided who was best qualified. Candidates fell into two categories: employees who had been in the same or similar position and other FPL employees who were identified by managers as potential candidates or had expressed interest in the position. This process continued at each level until all positions had been filled.

Before implementing zero-based staffing and making selection decisions, approximately seventeen hundred managers and supervisors were carefully trained at a one-day staffing workshop. This training prepared all managers/supervisors to participate in the four-step selection process. During the first step, managers prepared a one-page position description for each job in their department. The description listed minimum requirements, principal accountabilities, and competencies (skills and abilities) required for success in the position. Core competencies—cited by executive management as critical to success in the new organization—were included for all positions. These core competencies were defined as:

- Multifunctional behavior: the ability to work across disciplines and functions to achieve the common goals of the company—as opposed to simply carrying out orders and being loyal to the department
- Flexibility/adaptability: the ability to respond effectively to change and adjust to shifting directions, priorities, and personalities while noting the implications of changes in the business environment and adjusting to these quickly—as opposed to rigid, expected behavior and ossified, entropic work patterns
- Initiative/independence: the ability to originate actions independently, take calculated risks to achieve results without specific instructions, demonstrate self-starting behavior, and persist to achieve goals—as opposed to a "pass the buck and do what you're told" mentality
- Creativity/innovation: the ability to generate new ideas and approaches to customers and business needs, anticipating change in the environment and responding in advance

Additional competencies tied to position accountabilities were also listed for each position. Competencies were then described in job-specific behavioral terms and weighted in order of importance by individual managers, who were given the freedom to define each competency and assign weights according to departmental needs. A one-page position description format and careful guidelines were provided in the training. Completed position descriptions were re-viewed and approved by the next higher level of management and then forwarded to the compensation department for evaluation and grading. This department assigned a salary band, job code, and title to the position. The descriptions were completed before candidates were evaluated.

Step II

During the second step of the selection process, managers selected the best-qualified candidate for each new position. Careful guide-lines for interviewing procedures and using the company's "em-ployee selection matrix" were provided. The selection matrix ensured that incumbents received consideration for each position. FPL employees from other departments, who had been recom-mended by their managers or who had expressed interest in being considered for other positions for which they were qualified, were also included on the matrix. Managers were given latitude in their decisions. High expectations, as well as faith in management's decision-making ability, were communicated consistently. The goal was to "select-in" those employees who would take the company forward, rather than "select-out" those not qualified. This strategy further enhanced ego energy by demonstrating respect for their abil-ities and allowing them to maintain a personal sense of control.

A useful check and balance in the selection process was the use of review boards. The five FPL review boards, each composed of three employees from various levels in the company, reviewed all selections before they could be finalized. The boards examined doc-umentation for every hiring decision in the company. This was a time-consuming process, but it was justified in order to ensure ob-jective, consistent, and defensible selection decisions. Review board members represented a cross section of company functions, loca-tions, and other employee populations. They worked independently of the departments making the staffing decisions. In the event that a member had a close relationship with a candidate being consid-ered, other members stepped in for that person in order to maintain objectivity. Members of the review board were not there to substitute their judgment for that of management, but rather to keep a keen eye on affirmative action concerns and ensure that the process was managed as intended. As a result, FPL actually improved its minority representation and there was no significant change in the age of FPL's workforce.

Step III

After selection decisions were made and approved, managers informed employees and departments of the decisions. This step required effective communication skills and support for all who were affected by the process. Here the materials and training were especially crucial to success. The training provided guidelines for the process and indirectly helped overcome negative feelings such as guilt, anger, or resentment. Communication of selection decisions is one of the most critical aspects of the reorganization, as during this time egos may be especially fragile and anxiety runs high. All candidates for each position must know the outcome of the decision and have access to the legitimate job-related criteria on which the selection was made.

Training focused on communicating selection decisions in a way that demonstrated respect for individual dignity. It is not simply what one says, but the manner in which the message is delivered, that people remember. Suggestions were offered for every part of the communication: choosing an appropriate time and place, delivering the message, monitoring and managing reactions, acknowledging feelings, and identifying appropriate follow-up actions in each situation. It was during this critical step that special attention had to be paid to each employee so that problems with attachment, feelings of betrayal, or damage to locus of control were minimized and dealt with immediately.

Step IV

During the fourth step, managers, supervisors, and human resources representatives supported affected employees. Employees not selected for positions in a particular organizational unit became eligible for an Enhanced Severance Plan (ESP) and the Internal Placement Program (IPP). The ESP continued salary and benefits for up to one full year based on years of service. Outplacement counseling was available for all employees who chose to leave the company at this time. The IPP allowed eligible employees to apply for vacant positions within the organization. These positions were accessed through a computer-based posting system that presented full details of each position such as duties, pay grade, minimum requirements, and competencies. Employees offered less than comparable positions could turn these down in favor of ESP and IPP eligibility. (A comparable position was defined as being less than fifty miles from the previous job site with a maximum salary range that exceeded the current salary and a midpoint within 15 percent of the old salary midpoint.)

Eligible employees had at least forty-five days to consider their options under the ESP and IPP. These employees attended career decision workshops and financial awareness seminars and were encouraged to explore their options. Complete information about options was available, so everyone was aware of the services and support provided to eligible employees. Each step of the selection process was carefully defined and explained, as well. Employees had access to all information related to the selection decisions that affected them.

Throughout the forty-five-day decision-making period, employees eligible for ESP and IPP were treated with sensitivity, as the company sought to place each person in the position best suited to his or her skills, needs, and talents. During a potentially painful emotional event, such as restructuring, employees have three primary needs to help them maintain self-esteem and internal locus of control: honest information about what is going on and how they are affected; a sense of structure; and support tailored to their personal needs and concerns. The redeployment process addressed all of these needs. More than fifty human resources representatives at FPL were trained to meet with employees who were eligible for ESP and IPP. They met individually with each employee, offered complete packets of information that they carefully explained, made sure all employees understood their options, and told them where to go for additional information. A special telephone hotline, staffed with qualified personnel, was available to counsel affected employees.

Nurturing and supporting subordinates, regardless of the selection decisions, helped both managers and employees cope with loss and change. This process brought them successfully through broken attachment, detachment, and reattachment in a manner that enhanced rather than damaged ego needs. Redeployment channeled negative emotions such as anger, resentment, blame, and guilt into positive outlets such as active participation, involvement, nurturing, and support. It reframed the outcome for everyone as a new and challenging opportunity for personal growth rather than a negative situation imposed by "others" over which no one had control. This strategy effectively directed ego energy and enhanced the opportunity for internal locus of control for every employee involved.

Step V

Once the selection process was complete and decisions were communicated, any employee who felt that the process had not been applied appropriately had a forum for voicing concern. A special appeals board was established to hear the cases of employees who felt they had been treated unfairly. The fourteen-member board had representatives from several departments, including both exempt and nonexempt employees, with appropriate representation of protected-class employees. Three board members constituted a quorum for hearing an employee's appeal. To appeal, an employee who had not been rehired into a current or comparable position made a written request within five days of receiving the ESP or after failing to be selected through IPP. In all, only one hundred and forty-nine employees entered the appeals process at FPL—less than 1 percent of those affected by the process. Of this group, seventy-four dropped their appeal after meeting with their managers and human resources representatives. Of the remaining cases, the appeals board found in favor of management on seventy-two appeals and with employees on three occasions: one employee accepted a comparable job in another area; one employee accepted a noncomparable position but remained with the company; the remaining employee refused multiple job offers, then later accepted a severance package.

With attention from executives, adequate training, and management's commitment to making the process work, FPL passed the nadir. At the end of the forty-five-day critical period, over eight thousand employees had been repositioned in the new organization. Due to a zero-based staffing approach, there were no layoffs—more than a thousand employees who had opted to select ESP left with full outplacement support. The process, which included a dynamic and well-iterated selection system, resulted in no lawsuits. The voluntary severance plan and IPP provided options for employees who were not selected originally. A clear communication plan, as well as a framework for recovery expressed through well-coordinated, high-energy training, greatly increased the odds for successful recovery at FPL.

Reattachment of Employees

The next challenge facing FPL—indeed, any organization that has restructured—is reattaching employees to the new organization and gaining their full commitment to the new vision. Managing the return of the organization to full productivity (see Phase IV in Figure 11.1) is equal in importance to managing the selection process. Even with the checks and balances and the attention to individual ego energy, the restaffing is traumatic. Reattachment to the reorganization does not depend on any single action; it is a combination of leadership, role modeling, behavioral consistency, accurate communications, and time. FPL facilitated this combination by using transition workshops for managers and supervisors as a forum for communicating the vision, sharing expectations throughout the new organization, modeling leadership behavior, understanding phases of transition, and responding to employees' concerns. Senior executive involvement in the workshops as co-facilitators ensured that issues were discussed at the highest level in the organization. Executives had an excellent opportunity to build new connections with those in their business units. These workshops were extensive, consisting of six modules with a variety of activities, discussion, worksheets, and overheads. The same materials were then used by managers as a structured communication with employees in their departments. The workshops pointed out issues throughout the organization that needed management's attention. It was encouraging to note at FPL that the issues had a future focus as managers wondered how to rebuild trust, how to communicate new roles and relationships quickly, how to encourage cross-functional communication, and how to manage careers in a "flatter" organization. Although it is too early to tell whether FPL's actions to resolve these issues were successful, management and employee involvement in rebuilding the relationship between the company and its employees redefined that relationship—from dependence ("FPL will take care of you") to shared responsibility between FPL and its employees in a partnership for maximized performance. The new message was "FPL will support you in ways that allow you to take care of yourself."

Another feature of the Redeployment process at FPL was the use of focus groups after the selection process to monitor employees' concerns and keep management informed of additional needs for promoting the new corporate vision. Twelve focus groups included one hundred and fifty-seven participants from throughout the company, both exempt and nonexempt. "This reorganization was like a wake-up call," reported one employee who now appeared willing to take control of her career. These groups allowed employees to form fresh bonds of attachment by voicing their concerns and working through grief and anger that might otherwise have prevented attachment to the new organization.

Overall, the responses of employees as they discussed the targeted questions in these focus groups indicated the start of a positive recovery. As one employee said, "A bad day at FPL is a good day anywhere else." Most understood the need for restructuring and thought the new approach had streamlined the company and facilitated communication. Many felt more accountable and perceived increased flexibility and autonomy in their jobs. This was seen as a challenging opportunity for creativity and growth.

Indications that certain employees still had not completely detached from the old structure and reattached to the new vision were evident, and concern over a second reorganization was voiced. Many of the concerns resembled the issues from traditional forms of downsizing. However, employees' willingness to openly express concern to their managers, who were willing to listen and confront issues, demonstrated the organization's willingness to reinforce internal locus of control through daily practices. At FPL, it seemed the majority of employees were, if not ready to sail into new waters full steam ahead, at least willing to board the newly refitted ship for the journey.

This is not a perfect world, and redeployment is not a perfect process. Some employees are hurt, and their internal locus of control may be affected in a less than positive way. But the number of employees and managers working to make the new vision a reality seems to be much greater in restructuring that includes redeployment. We believe this is because of the manner in which redeployment enhances employees' ego energy.

Any organizational restructuring is traumatic. People's lives are affected. Although redeployment attempts to place the right people in the right jobs while moderating traumatic effects, it would be unrealistic to expect that everyone passes smoothly through the transition and emerges on the other side unscathed and ready to produce phenomenal results for the transformed organization. This, of course, is not the case. Some employees may still feel insecure, bitter, or detached regardless of the strategy. There is pain associated with any type of change. A few lessons from our experiences at FPL and in other organizations, however, may help to minimize this pain in future applications of the redeployment process.

We learned that it is more important to find the right person for each job in the company than to try to find jobs for people who may not be suited for the new organization. Encouraging job matches that are inappropriate or incompatible does not benefit the organization or, in the long run, the individual. Employees who were offered "less than comparable" jobs several levels below their previous position seemed to have the greatest difficulties. From the perspective of ego energy, this is perfectly consistent as people given lower positions may have suffered greater ego damage. Some of these employees assumed a victim mentality and withdrew, protecting their self-esteem by becoming less involved with the company.

A second lesson was the importance of continuous monitoring and involvement with all employees during Phase IV of the transformation process. Viewing redeployment as the end of the transformation is not enough and can lead to a benign neglect of the human factors that are necessary if the recovery process is to proceed smoothly up the productivity curve. Support, training, focus groups, and regular communication must continue. This view is consistent with the ego energy perspective, in that a loss has occurred and new bonds must form and be nurtured. Not everyone will proceed through feelings associated with loss, detachment, and eventual reattachment at the same rate. Continuing questions, insecurities, and other concerns associated with the process of change will manifest. These cannot be ignored. They must be monitored and dealt with. A successful transformation requires a long-term commitment from the organization to respect and maintain the dignity of every employee.

The final lesson from FPL and other organizations is the most important: although restructuring is implemented to achieve specific business results, achieving these results depends on the employees who remain with the organization. As companies overcome the many difficulties of transformation, it is the employees who stay and want to make a contribution—those who value their relationship with the company and their peers because they are part of a high-performing team—who are the employees that make a difference. This lesson is especially consistent with the ego energy perspective discussed here.

Any process used to restructure or downsize an organization must ultimately produce a base of employees who have a strong sense of self-worth and a commitment to the new company vision. A process increases the chances of success if it enhances employees' self-confidence because they are objectively selected according to what they can contribute, if it offers workable, if not ideal, options that foster a sense of control, and if it involves employees at all levels in building a new relationship with the company based on partnership. Conversely, any process that irreparably damages employees' sense of internal control and severs attachment to the organization offers little hope for a positive future relationship between the company and its employees. This process will inhibit the organization's ability to achieve its business goals. We have observed this in many organizations that restructured with a strict cost-cutting mentality, using traditional methods rather than redeployment techniques.

FPL's restructuring is too recent to evaluate the project's

success. Redeployment at FPL seemed to be very effective, but more time must pass before we can judge the ultimate degree of improvement. Even so, preliminary indicators suggest that FPL is well on its way to a successful future. Customer service tracking studies show that nearly 90 percent of the utility's customers rank its services good to excellent. During 1991, FPL stock actually rose 25 percent to $37 per share, while during the first quarter of 1992 it settled at $33 per share. Another indicator, on an operational level, was the company's ability to restore customer service rapidly following the unprecedented damage caused by Hurricane Andrew. This is promising evidence that FPL's restructuring—which included redeployment—will be at least as successful as the process has proved to be at other organizations. We think the attention given to the ego energy of all employees—which maintained an internal locus of control, facilitated attachment to a new structure, and boosted ego energy—increased the probability of success.

Thus it seems that transformation cannot succeed without fostering positive ego energy. Redeployment, as implemented at FPL, accomplished the critical business task of restructuring the company while keeping the ego energy of employees intact. As one employee commented about the reorganization at FPL: "The company made the best of a difficult situation. This told me they actually *cared* about the outcome of the restructuring, not just about the dollar saving." FPL appears positioned for success in the competitive marketplace of the postmodern world. We predict that further study of FPL and other organizations employing similar restructuring strategies will demonstrate the validity and practicality of the Redeployment approach. By considering and enhancing ego energy, it becomes possible to achieve success on both a financial and a human level.

References

Aguayo, R. *Dr. Deming*. New York: Simon & Schuster, 1990.
Barnett, W., Geweke, J., and Shell, K. *Economic Complexity: Chaos, Sunspots, Bubbles and Nonlinearity*. Cambridge: Cambridge University Press, 1989.

Bechard, R., and Harris, R. *Organizational Transitions: Managing Complex Change.* Reading, Mass.: Addison-Wesley, 1977.

Blanck, R., and Blanck, G. *Beyond Ego Psychology.* New York: Columbia University Press, 1986.

Boroughs, R. "Amputating Assets." *U.S. News and World Report,* May 4, 1992.

Bridges, W. *Surviving Corporate Transition.* New York: Doubleday, 1988.

Brockner, J., Davy, J., and Carter, C. "Layoffs, Self-Esteem and Survivor . . . Consequences." *Organizational Behavior and Human Decision Processes,* 1985, *36*(2), 229-244.

DeBerry, S. *Quantum Psychology: Steps Towards a Postmodern Ecology of Being.* New York: Praeger, 1993.

Fiske, S., and Taylor, S. *Social Cognition.* New York: Random House, 1991.

Hamilton, N. *Self and Others: Object Relations Theory in Practice.* Northvale, N.J.: Jason Aronson, 1988.

Hartmann, H. *Ego Psychology and the Problem of Adaptation.* New York: International Universities Press, 1958.

Kagono, T., Nonaka, I., Sakakibara, A., and Okamura, A. *Strategic vs. Evolutionary Management.* New York: North-Holland, 1985.

Kilmann, R., Covin, T., and Associates (eds.). *Corporate Transformation: Revitalizing Organizations for a Competitive World.* San Francisco: Jossey-Bass, 1988.

Kotter, J., and Heskett, J. *Corporate Culture and Performance.* New York: Free Press, 1992.

Kriegel, R. *If It Ain't Broke . . . Break it!* New York: Free Press, 1991.

Marshall Group. *Restaffing/Transition Manuals.* Scottsdale, Ariz.: Marshall Group, 1991.

Rosenberg, M., and Kaplan, H. (eds.). *Social Psychology of the Self-Concept.* Arlington Heights, Ill.: Harlan Davidson, 1982.

Young-Eisendrath, P., and Hall, J. *Jung's Self Psychology: A Constructivist Perspective.* New York: Guilford Press, 1991.

12

Using Ego Energy
in a Public Organization

Herbert A. Marlowe, Jr., Ronald C. Nyhan

THE RELATIONSHIP BETWEEN people's level of ego energy and their work setting is a complex topic. Ego energy encompasses a person's interior perceptions and feelings of hopefulness, agency, worth, and potentiality. Ego energy is manifested in physical activity (as shown in the "hustle and bustle" of a dynamic workplace), in emotional investment in the work (as shown by extra hours, sincere arguments, and animated discussions about work), and in the psychological experience of work as stimulating, engaging, and challenging. Numerous variables affect this relationship through a broad range of interaction patterns. Discussion is limited here to three main variables: organizational environment, organizational design, and organizational culture. Three assumptions underlie this chapter. The first is that public organizations are experiencing a massive loss of citizen confidence and an ongoing fiscal crisis. As a consequence the developing image of the public organization is that it is inept. The second assumption is that there is a complex relationship between the external environment of an organization and the ego energy of the people comprising that organization. This relationship is mediated by a number of variables, three of which are the design of the organization itself, its culture, and individual personality factors. The third assumption is that the regaining of public confidence must include as a strategy the redesign of organizations, including culture change, in ways that activate rather than enervate the ego energy of its members. If these assumptions are accepted, a key question is: how can public organizations be redesigned so that their cultures activate ego energy and ultimately challenge and change the image of ineptness?

The analysis of these assumptions is followed by the outline of a work in progress that focuses on how ego energy can be activated to meet a crisis in the first variable—loss of customer confidence—through direct intervention in the second variable—design—with resulting changes in the organization's culture. The outline is intended as an illustration of an approach to meet the challenges of the assumptions with a theory-based methodology for implementation.

Explaining the Loss of Customer Confidence

The litany of voices decrying the weaknesses and failures of public organizations is strong and perhaps growing (Osborne, 1992). While few would argue that public service used to be a fun job with unrelenting spiritual rewards, we should acknowledge a recent substantive change in the self-image and the rewards of public service. The image of government as somehow "broken," as not working well, is a popular image, even among government officials (Pammer, 1990; Walters, 1992).

It is clear that public confidence in government as a problem-solving mechanism is remarkably low (Heise, Gladwin, and McLaughen, 1991). With that lack of confidence has come an associated tendency to deride the public employee as a bureaucrat, as someone who lives off the public with minimal effort, and as a parasite rather than a person contributing to the productive effort of the society (Hubbell, 1991). There has been a concomitant trend for elected officials to engage in staff bashing as a way to vent their frustration over the complexity and seeming intractability of socioeconomic problems (Marlowe and Arrington, 1992). With such an image in place it should come as no surprise that the self-image of the public employee is low. Osborne and Gaebler (1992) report that only 5 percent of Americans surveyed would choose government as their preferred career. Only 13 percent of top federal employees would encourage their children to go into public service as a career.

Coupled with this decline in occupational status are other changes that are proving debilitative to the self-image and ego energy of public agencies and their employees. Chief among these are the ongoing fiscal crises that continually drain the energy and lower the expectations of public organizations (Spitzer, 1991). These fiscal crises restrict the choices available to public managers to where and when to cut back, instead of which problems to address. Furthermore, the perception of public employment as stable is increasingly diminishing as layoffs and furloughs become more prevalent as budget-balancing mechanisms (MacManus, 1992).

Another factor contributing to the loss of ego energy among public servants is the growing complexity of the issues they are asked to solve. Public schools, for example, are asked not only to teach but to assume the role of family and societal problem solver for our children as well. Environmental agencies are asked to design solutions for problems we either did not have or did not recognize a generation ago, often without adequate data to develop model solutions or to be able to determine the ripple effect of those solutions. Human service agencies are asked to solve highly complex social problems with minimal funding, poorly trained staff in many cases, and a public attitude of NIMBY to creative solutions that would affect local communities. While the work of government still has some relatively straightforward and simple elements (such as fixing potholes or animal control), the policy dimensions are only increasing in complexity.

A third factor that challenges the public servant's sense of self-efficacy is the general social malaise and sense of fundamental disorder, including a lack of mission and ideological consensus (Wildavsky, 1988; Dempsey, 1985). Those who work in the public sector are not guarded from the sociopsychological experiences of the general public. Borgmann (1992) has argued that the current public mood is one of sullenness. He contends there is a lack of public will for either self-discipline or self-government—a lack of willingness to engage reality. This results in a posture of debilitation, an inability to engage real joy or real pain, and a lack of vigor and integrity. He further argues that the response of professional and technological leadership is a level of hyperactivity that, while energizing in its focus, is ultimately destructive due to its narrowness and misplaced energies. Similar arguments are put forth by Goldfarb (1991) under the construct of cynicism. Krugman (1992) argues that we live in an age of diminished expectations. While we once expected an ever increasing standard of living, many now would be happy simply to maintain the level they currently have and indeed expect no more. This perspective has been reported in the popular press (Peterson, 1991).

While other external factors could undoubtedly be enumerated, the ones cited here indicate an environment for public organizations that is draining and enervating. The impact of these external factors on people's level of ego energy is mediated by factors unique to the organization and people themselves. It is these factors to which we now turn.

The External Environment and Ego Energy

While the relationship of an organization's external environment to the level of ego energy among its members is multifaceted and not fully understood, it clearly exists. Larson and Lafasto (1989) in their study of successful teams continually illustrate the impact of organizational success and individual self-worth. If public agencies are undergoing a crisis in public confidence as previously argued, there is a strong likelihood that the self-efficacy levels of public employees will be lowered. The relationship between the external environment and ego energy is mediated, however, by three primary variables: organizational design, organizational culture, and individual personality characteristics. This relationship is illustrated in Figure 12.1.

Organizational Design and Ego Energy

One constellation of mediating factors is the design of the organization itself. Design issues include how the organization sets goals,

Figure 12.1. Factors Affecting Ego Energy.

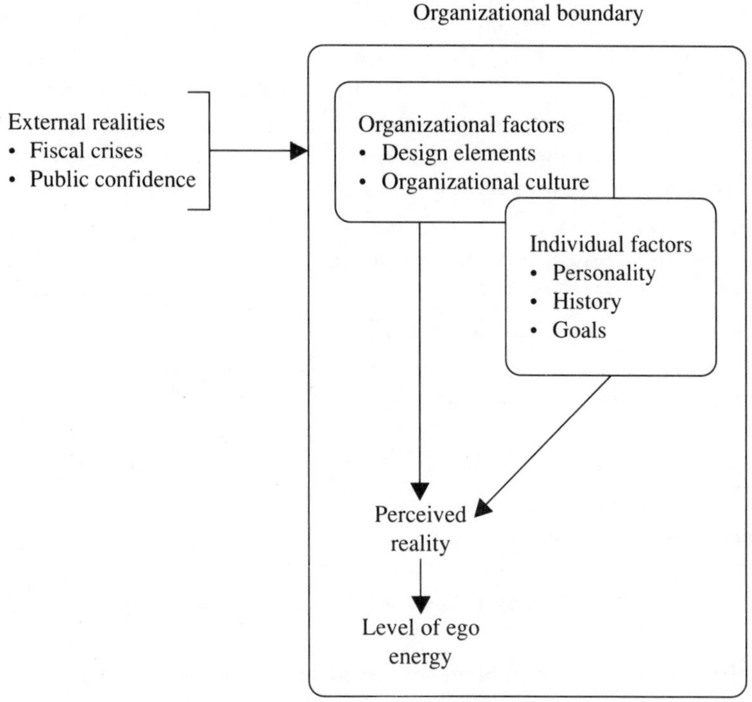

Organizational boundary

rewards performance, makes decisions, structures itself, organizes work, uses capital. Hanna (1988) and Keidel (1990) have argued that design is clearly related to performance. One potential result of good design is the activation of employee energies to achieve the organizational goals. Recently the relationship of organizational design and ego energy has been discussed in terms of empowerment and bureaucracy. Block (1987) has argued that there is a patriarchal contract in bureaucracies that fosters dependency. This contract consists of four elements: submission to authority, denial of self-expression, sacrifice for unnamed future rewards, and the belief that the other three provisos are just. This contract, interacting with myopic self-interest and manipulative tactics, reinforces dependency. Block goes on to argue that an entrepreneurial contract can be created. This contract, in conjunction with enlightened self-interest and authentic (direct) tactics, results in autonomy or empowerment.

Organizational Culture and Ego Energy

A second grouping of mediating variables consists of the factors that comprise the culture of the organization. Explication of the relationship between organizational culture and ego energy is complicated by the fact that these two constructs are abstract symbols of highly complex phenomena. Neither lends itself to simplistic operationalization for empiricist research paradigms. Whatever logical or intuitive relationship we may be able to elucidate is also dependent upon the definition of these terms. Both Ott (1989) and Kilmann (1989) argue for multilevel definitions of culture. Ott delineates a comprehensive definition including symbols, values, underlying assumptions and expectations, artifacts, and work behavior as elements of an organization's culture. Kilmann contends that a useful model for understanding organizational behavior is a complex hologram. His point is that to understand behavior in organizations we must not only be sensitive to overt behavior but also to other realities: culture, assumptions, and psyche. In an empirical work, Marlowe and Nyhan (1992) have found clear relationships between culture and ego energy operationalized as organizational commitment.

One common element among the wide variety of perspectives on organizational culture is the emphasis on collective understandings (Van Maanen and Barley, 1985; Schein, 1985). If interactions between collective understandings and individual schemas and then between individual schemas and ego energy are posited, a logical relationship between culture and ego energy can be established. James, James, and Ashe (1990) posit such a relationship in their discussion of psychological environments and organizational well-being in the workplace. They argue that the construct of organizational culture should encompass a psychological perspective which supplements the anthropological and sociological perspectives that currently underlie the concept.

The ways in which the culture of an organization mediates external events and directly or indirectly affects any one person's sense of self-efficacy are only rudimentarily understood. While empirical evidence is scarce, the position that there is some degree of relationship between culture and ego energy is logically and intuitively defensible.

The Individual and Ego Energy

A third category of mediating factors consists of the personality characteristics and personal history of the people who comprise the organization. Ego energy is the property of an individual in a social context. An individual's history and personality combine to form the perceptual and interpretive framework through which that person interprets the world. To the degree that a person's level of ego energy is influenced by both personal factors and external events and their interpretation, each person will differ in level of ego energy. As an example on the individual level, Noel (1991) studied unconscious processes underlying differences in strategy formation among executives and found differences in strategies that were linked to individual psychodynamics. Hirschhorn (1988) has argued that people in work groups under stress sabotage their leaders as a mechanism to avoid self-blame for organizational failure. Another example of individual mediating variables are the cognitive mechanisms people use to interpret organizational reality. Gioia (1986) has analyzed these factors and their impact on organizational behavior.

Relationships exist between a person's level of ego energy and the perceived reality of the organizational world in which that person is operating. This "perceived reality" can be influenced by individual factors, organizational factors such as design and culture, and the external environment of the organization. While acknowledging the importance of individual variables in the organizational/ego energy interaction, we will not focus here on change efforts aimed at individual psychodynamics. Rather, the focus will be on developing a strategy of organizational redesign to meet the challenges of the external environment and the internal mediating factors.

Strategy for Organizational Redesign

Seven design assumptions and six design elements comprise the overall strategy for regaining customer confidence. The design assumptions explicate a hypothesized relationship between a "psychological/cultural" variable and ego energy. The design elements are components of an organization's framework.

Design Assumptions

The following assumptions underlie the design process:

Assumption 1: Empowerment and participation activate ego energy. If one accepts this assumption as valid, the questions then become: How does one design empowering and participating structures and processes? What structures or processes disempower, and what are the alternatives to these disempowering structures? In what ways can valid forms of participation be facilitated?

Assumption 2: Direct and honest contact between people activates ego energy. This assumption is based on the belief that true encounters between people—even if the encounter is antagonistic—are energizing. Senge (1990) argues that speaking truth is necessary for organizational growth and improvement. Various therapeutic models emphasize the need for "truth encounters" in order to free the person for change (Moore, 1992). The challenge in an organizational framework is how to avoid an impersonalizing or depersonalizing bureaucracy that fosters stereotyped interactions rather than authentic encounters. A further challenge is how to develop an organizational culture that values direct encounter rather than behind-the-back interactions. In short, this is the question of how to develop engagement structures.

Assumption 3: Open conflict, as opposed to hidden conflict, is energizing. This assumption is an extension of Assumption 2 with explicit reference to the issue of conflict. It assumes that continually unaddressed conflict is ultimately debilitating for an organization. It also assumes that while a moderate level of unresolved conflict can be productive and energizing, an inability to resolve conflict is draining. Finally there is the assumption that there is an inverted U relationship between conflict and innovation. The design question is how to design structures that expose and resolve conflict.

The cultural question is how to develop organizational values that promote the exposure and resolution of conflict.

Assumption 4: The consensus development process activates ego energy. Consensus is defined as general agreement or accord. There are several levels of consensus ranging from full unanimity to a general willingness to proceed to a willingness to set aside doubts or disagreements for the sake of the larger group. The consensus-building process involves "truth speaking" and open conflict. If Assumptions 2 and 3 are correct, then the process of seeking consensus is itself energizing. This fourth assumption argues that the achievement of a state of consensus is also energizing. If the assumption is correct, the design question is how to create consensus-building structures and processes in an organization.

Assumption 5: Risk and change under certain conditions are energizing (Sitkin and Pablo, 1992). Scitovsky (1992) argues that pleasure depends on change and variation. Yet there are both positive and negative aspects of change. Too much change may be immobilizing; no change at all is stultifying. A moderate level of change or risk, however, is energizing. The design question is how to create structures and processes that allow an acceptable level of risk within the organization. This can be termed the design of risk-taking structures.

Assumption 6: Holistic or systemic approaches to organizational redesign are more energizing than partial approaches. The term holistic is used in several contexts. It means systemic in the sense that the redesign addresses all elements and levels of the organization. It means consistent in that the redesign effort is congruous and uniform throughout the organization. It means historical in the sense that the past of the organization is considered. It means holographic in the sense that there are multiple perspectives on organizational reality that must be examined in the redesign process (Talbot, 1991).

Assumption 7: Interesting work is energizing. Csikszentmihalyi (1990) has developed the concept of autotelic jobs. He argues that the more a job is like a game—with variety, appropriate and flexible challenges, clear goals, and immediate feedback—the more enjoyable and energizing the work will be. Langer (1989) contends that playlike work fosters what she terms "mindfulness," a focused energy. The design question, therefore, is how to make work gamelike.

Design Elements

At this point the question is: how does one operationally redesign an organization so that ego energy is activated rather than enervated? The approach reported here was to integrate the design assumptions discussed above with the design elements cited by Hanna (1988):

- Decision Making: This element refers to the norms and style of decision making within the organization. The goal of the redesign process was to develop a collaborative, participative style that pushes decisions downward in the organization and empowers people to make decisions.
- Information: This element refers to the type, quality, and distribution of the information the organization needs in order to perform effectively. The goal of the redesign process was to increase the accuracy and range of relevant information.
- Structure: This element refers both to the table of organization and the associated policy and procedures that guide work. The goal of the redesign process was primarily to ensure that the structure facilitates organizational problem seeking and solving. A secondary goal was to flatten and simplify the organizational structure to foster direct contact, lower-level decision making, and more direct conflict resolution.
- People: This element refers to the human capital of an organization. One goal of the redesign process was to provide mechanisms and opportunities to encourage knowledge and skill development. A second goal was to build a climate that fosters organizational commitment and involvement.
- Tasks: This element refers to the actual work tasks and processes of the organization. One goal of the redesign process was to

ensure the necessity, nonredundancy, and simplicity of tasks. A second goal was to ensure clear links among task responsibilities. A third goal was to develop sufficient diversity and challenge in tasks so that work was interesting and fulfilling.

- Rewards: This element refers to a wide range of both formal and informal acknowledgment, incentives, encouragement, and recognition, either monetary or nonmonetary. The goal of the redesign process was to ensure that the formal and informal reward and incentive systems support the desired organizational culture.

All of the design assumptions and elements were incorporated in the overall redesign process.

Redesigning a Public Organization: A Work in Progress

The client in this study is a 4,000-employee county government that is among the fifty largest county governments in the United States. It provides government services to what was one of the nation's fastest-growing counties during the 1980s. Beginning in the 1990s, however, that growth rate decreased dramatically for a variety of reasons. The drop in growth, the national recession, and a variety of long-term trends (some local and some global) all led to a fiscal crisis for the government. The client, faced with expanded requirements for services—particularly criminal justice and fire protection services—and continued budget shortfalls for the next several fiscal years, clearly had to change its services and practices to meet these needs. Given the mood of the electorate, county officials were not willing to raise property taxes to offset the shortfalls, although minor revenue adjustments were acceptable. This combination of factors created a financial and organizational crisis. And this crisis created the punctuation in the organizational equilibrium (Gersick, 1991) required for substantial organizational change. Thus the opportunity to redesign an organization in order to promote ego energy was created.

The proposed solution was to refocus local government using the philosophy and techniques of total quality management

(TQM) to guide the process and implement the needed change in organizational culture. The basic tenets of TQM emphasized by the client were:

- Customer focus
- Process variation
- Employee empowerment

The organization operationalized TQM by adopting a "rightfocusing" process. Rightfocusing was defined by this organization as a collaborative process that redesigns an organization by clarifying its priorities, values, and primary mission; by refining how it does its work; by rightsizing to eliminate unnecessary or low-priority work and reallocate resources to higher-priority tasks; and by strengthening the values of customer service, cost consciousness, employee commitment, and continuous improvement. Rightfocusing begins with prioritizing customer needs, eliminating or simplifying work to do a better job of meeting those needs, and then restructuring the organization (reallocating or reducing resources) to improve services to customers. Unlike downsizing, which focuses on eliminating positions as a way to reduce budgets, rightfocusing concentrates on how to do more and better work with fewer resources. The term *quality* was added to the program title of Quality Rightfocusing to indicate the organization's commitment to using basic principles of total quality management to guide the redesign process. TQM is no more than three simple questions asked over and over: What are our customer's priorities and opinions about our work? How can we change how we work to better meet these priorities with a shrinking resource pool? And how can we engage our staff to work on continuous improvement?

Quality Rightfocusing was presented to the elected officials as a plan for the redesign and continuous improvement of their local government. The goals of the redesign project were to develop a strategic plan to rightfocus county government in order to meet or exceed public expectations of county government, to improve the quality of county government services, to increase the effectiveness of county government, and to reduce the cost of county government. The objectives of the program were to simplify work processes, eliminate unnecessary, redundant, or low-priority work, refine the structure of the organization, and encourage and strengthen customer service, teamwork, continuous improvement, and participatory management as key values in county government.

With these goals and objectives, what would the rightfocusing effort produce? It would provide options for the elected officials in the following areas: major ways of streamlining the work and structure of county government while improving customer service; the investment costs and potential consequences of each option; strategies for building a high level of employee commitment to quality and cost containment; strategies for changing organizational systems to encourage and reward cost savings and productivity improvements; and optional methods for the elected officials to set a priority agenda and maintain a strategic focus on that agenda.

Envisioning the Redesigned Organization

The rightfocusing process began with the development of a shared vision regarding the county government's future. The elements of this vision included a government that focuses its resources on the missions established by the Board of County Commissioners. It would be a flatter, tighter organization that responds quickly and effectively to community needs. It would be a government that invests in its people and rewards them for high-quality performance. This vision was expressed in the following terms:

- Government should be responsive. Citizens should be treated as people, not numbers. When they have a problem it should be resolved quickly. When they call with a problem they should not have to play telephone roulette.
- Government should be efficient. It should not waste the citizen's time waiting for forms or standing in lines. Neither should it waste its own time.
- Government should be managed well. It should use its resources (staff, time, and money) wisely.
- Government should be concerned with doing the job right. "Good enough for government work" should be an attitude of the past. Programs should be thoroughly evaluated and ineffec-

tive programs scrapped. Government programs should not go on forever after they have fulfilled their purpose.

- Government should try to do its job as economically as possible. It should be as concerned with the full costs of a project and with cost effectiveness as any private-sector organization.
- Government should be flexible. It should recognize the uniqueness of citizens' problems and develop unique solutions. The attitude that "we do it this way because we have always done it this way" should be abolished.
- Government should have a sense of direction. Both the staff and the public should understand the long-term goals of government.
- Government should have the confidence of the citizenry. The public should believe their tax dollars are used wisely, honestly, and for maximum impact.
- Government should provide challenging work. It should create a supportive work environment that enables employees to use their full professional potential.

The Redesign Work Plan

The work plan for the redesign process (summarized in Table 12.1) consists of eight self-explanatory elements. This work plan provided an overall conceptual framework for participants in the process.

Decision Making. The redesign efforts were aimed at increasing the amount and quality of participative and collaborative decision making within the organization. Increasing participation in decision making should lead to an increased sense of empowerment. The collaborative nature of decision making should increase the amount of direct contact and direct conflict resolution. While high-quality group decision making should minimize organizational risk, individual risk will increase somewhat as each person would have to put ideas on the table for the group to examine. Collaborative decision making is inherently consensual and holistic. Properly facilitated solutions are of a higher order than simple compromise. To reach higher-order solutions, broader perspectives must be taken. Finally, participation in a decision process that is

Table 12.1. Organizational Redesign Work Plan.

Element	Action	Methods
1.0	Develop top-level understanding and support	Briefings, white paper, readings of *Reinventing Government* (Osborne and Gaebler, 1992)
2.0	Goal-setting workshop	Executive team and department heads: consensus building, goal clarification, additional task teams and specific training needed
3.0	Strategic planning workshops	Follow-up to element 2.0 with lower-level managers; same methods; work plan development
4.0	Departmental workshops	Process analysis and redesign
5.0	Special-focus task teams	Developing county-wide solutions to such issues as management support, incentives, citizen involvement, performance measurement, criminal justice
6.0	Management team workshops	Reviewing and integrating all previous work into a coherent county-wide plan to present to Board of County Commissioners (BCC)
7.0	BCC management team agenda-setting retreat	Delineating the plan for rightfocusing of county government; developing consensus among BCC as to agenda for the next two years
8.0	Implementation	Implementing rightfocusing plan, consistent budget process, and long-term training programs that support the plan

truly open creates a higher level of interesting work (Scitovsky, 1992). In public organizations many of the key decisions center on authority to spend budgeted funds as well as operational decisions. The client organization has developed a plan requiring board approval that would expand the scope of budget expenditure authority.

Information. The information needs of the organization were augmented by the development of the Total Organizational Performance System (TOPS) (Nyhan and Marlowe, 1992). TOPS was designed as a bottom-up system that produces continuous information on the quality of products and services. It empowers employees by assigning them the responsibility for defining quality. It promotes communication among work members as they collaboratively define work quality and between their internal and external customers as they validate quality. Consensus is built through conflict resolution, resulting in definitive performance measures that are shared throughout the organization. TOPS provides comparative feedback on all groups through a common metric that exposes the group to some peer risk but also encourages shared performance and promotes a better understanding of the work group's contribution to the overall organization. TOPS is being implemented in two large departments of the county government at this time. To date, the reception has been positive.

Structure. The organization's structure will be one of the last elements to be examined. It may be changed so that it fits all the other elements of the redesign. The emerging structure may well be flatter—which should lead to increased contact between levels of the organization, less ability to hide conflict, and a greater sense of power for all members. The structure may well be tighter and decentralized, too, leading to a greater degree of accountability and risk. The structure may provide for a greater range of work complexity and job flexibility, leading to a more interesting work environment. The structure should be mission-focused, thereby fostering a broad sense of what the organization is trying to accomplish and weakening parochial perspectives. Finally, the structure should clarify linkages and responsibilities so that it is clear where consensus is needed for action. Also envisioned is the creation of a parallel structure. This parallel structure would be an ongoing mechanism for addressing critical organizational issues that are not addressed by the present structure. This experiment in parallel structure is currently being implemented.

People. The redesign process does not involve the wholesale turnover of employees. What it does try to do is create the opportunity to build a culture that is empowering, open, serious about resolving conflict, supportive of risk taking, dedicated to individual development, and seeking continuous improvement. Such a culture should foster a high level of ego energy.

Tasks. A major thrust of the redesign process is to eliminate unnecessary, redundant, or low-priority work and simplify the remaining work. As this occurs, the work itself will become more interesting. It will become clear which work must be done in teams, thereby requiring increased efforts at communication, conflict resolution, and consensus building. The work that remains should be the critical work of the organization. This process of prioritizing and simplifying work should produce a broader picture of how the work of the organization all fits together. Both the TOPS process and other internal task teams have cited examples of tasks to be simplified. The organization to date has focused on the tasks related to the budgeting, personnel, and purchasing processes for change. Specific proposals have been developed, presented to senior management, modified, and approved for presentation to the policy board.

Rewards. The organization's reward systems are in the process of redesign to reflect individual, work unit, and departmental performance, and the unique organizational variations in work. They are also being redesigned to reflect customer satisfaction, quality, and productivity in a more continuous manner. Finally, they are being redesigned to provide supervisory performance feedback as well as the traditional rating by the supervisor. By providing increased amounts of unique feedback as well as two-way feedback, the new system will create a greater sense of empowerment than the annual performance rating while at the same time increasing the amount of communication within the organization. As the amount of communication increases, conflict will become more open but also more open to resolution. A better feedback system does increase the level of risk. But the fact that the feedback is reciprocal and not focused solely on individual performance should make that level of risk a moderate one. Because the reward system will focus on all levels of organizational behavior, it will be more holistic than a reward system that focuses only on individual performance. Finally, increasing feedback should foster continual efforts at improvement, thereby creating a more interesting work environment. Staff of the client agency developed a set of proposals for new reward systems that was approved by policy makers.

Lessons Learned

As this is a work in progress, the ultimate results are yet to be determined. To date the elected officials have been supportive and the key leaders of the organization have endorsed the effort as their attempt to reinvent government. Middle-level managers are skeptical. The lower-level worker is most likely unaware of the process. The public's focus on the process has just begun with the election of a new board chair who has made reinventing government one of her three goals. To support these goals a retreat has been planned with a national figure in the reinventing government movement. In this retreat the staff's proposals for change will be presented. Also in attendance at this retreat will be advisory committees from the business community. At this point the interest of the new chair, as well as the active support of the new administrator and his deputy, have led to a high level of interest by management staff. The level of ego energy is increasing as people more willingly work on task teams to develop proposals for change, as they speak more positively of the opportunity, and as they begin to use the language of reinventing government.

Lessons have indeed been learned. First, rarely is there one internal or external force that causes sufficient disequilibrium to create a period of intense change—rather, it is the convergence of forces. In this case it took the convergence of a fiscal crisis with a public confidence crisis (expressed by the board), a new administrator and deputy, and the publicized interest of the chair. These forces converging have created the opportunity for change.

Second, in the public sector the scope of change may be different than change in other sectors. The magnitude of the proposed changes, while perhaps radical internally, may not be viewed as particularly dramatic from the outside. The reaction of the business advisory group to the planned changes was simple: This is what you should have been doing.

Third, the pace of change in the public sector is slow unless there is a serious environmental crisis. Even though employees may be unhappy with the current practices, the unknown alternative may require more energy to achieve than they are willing to expend. In essence this is the question of "the lesser evil."

Fourth, consistency of design is extremely difficult to achieve. While it is possible to conceptualize a coherent and internally consistent organizational design, the development of that design is often challenged or blocked by people whose perspective is focused on their personal area of responsibility or interest. And what may be most reasonable from their perspective may not fit at all well with the intended design. Their insistence may be due to self-interest (unions, special interests), professional background, or historical experience.

Finally, the use of a central concept such as ego energy helps to focus the redesign discussion. With a central focus it is possible to ask whether an intended action will raise or lower the level of ego energy. The difficulty with this approach is that improperly used it makes one variable, ego energy, the ultimate criterion. In reality there are many criteria that should guide a redesign process. Balancing ego energy among other valid criteria is a continuous design challenge.

References

Block, P. *The Empowered Manager: Positive Political Skills at Work.* San Francisco: Jossey-Bass, 1987.

Borgmann, A. *Crossing the Postmodern Divide.* Chicago: University of Chicago Press, 1992.

Csikszentmihalyi, M. *Flow: The Psychology of Optimal Experience.* New York: HarperCollins, 1990.

Dempsey, C. "Confessions and Frustrations: Bureaucrats Insisting on High Standards Tell Politicians to 'Get Like Us.'" *Bureaucrat,* 1985, *14,* 3-6.

Gersick, C.J.G. "Revolutionary Change Theories: A Multilevel Exploration of the Punctuated Equilibrium Paradigm." *Academy of Management Review,* 1991, *16,* 10-36.

Gioia, D. A. "Symbols, Scripts and Sensemaking: Creating Meaning in the Organizational Experience." In H. P. Sims and D.

Gioia (eds.), *The Thinking Organization*. San Francisco: Jossey-Bass, 1986.

Goldfarb, J. C. *The Cynical Society: The Culture of Politics and the Politics of Culture in American Life*. Chicago: University of Chicago Press, 1991.

Hanna, D. P. *Designing Organizations for High Performance*. Reading, Mass.: Addison-Wesley, 1988.

Heise, J., Gladwin, J., and McLaughen, D. *FIU/Florida Poll*. Miami: FIU Press, 1991.

Hirschhorn, L. *The Workplace Within: Psychodynamics of Organizational Life*. Cambridge, Mass.: MIT Press, 1988.

Hubbell, L. "Ronald Reagan as President Symbol Maker: The Federal Bureaucrat as a Loafer, Incompetent Buffoon, Good Ole Boy, and Tyrant." *American Review of Public Administration*, 1991, *21*, 237–253.

James, L. R., James, L. A., and Ashe, D. K. "The Meaning of Organizations: The Role of Cognition and Values." In B. Schneider (ed.), *Organizational Climate and Culture*. San Francisco: Jossey-Bass, 1990.

Keidel, R. W. "Triangular Design: A New Organizational Geometry." *Executive*, 1990, *4*, 21–37.

Kilmann, R. H. *Managing Beyond the Quick Fix: A Completely Integrated Program for Creating and Maintaining Organizational Success*. San Francisco: Jossey-Bass, 1989.

Krugman, P. *The Age of Diminished Expectations*. Cambridge, Mass.: MIT Press, 1992.

Langer, E. J. *Mindfulness*. Reading, Mass.: Addison-Wesley, 1989.

Larson, C. E., and Lafasto, F. M. *Teamwork*. Newbury Park, Calif.: Sage, 1989.

MacManus, S. "Budget Strategies Among Florida Local Governments." Technical report, University of South Florida, Tampa, 1992.

Marlowe, H. A., and Arrington, L. "The Governing Crisis." Speech presented to Florida Association of County Administrators 1992 Conference, Marco Island, June 1992.

Marlowe, H. A., and Nyhan, R. C. "Validation of the Organization Culture Index." Unpublished manuscript, Institute of Higher Education, University of Florida, 1992.

Moore, T. *Care of the Soul.* New York: HarperCollins, 1992.

Noel, A. "Magnificent Obsession: The Impact of Unconscious Processes on Strategy Formation." In M.F.R. Kets de Vries and Associates (eds.), *Organizations on the Couch: Clinical Perspectives on Organizational Behavior and Change.* San Francisco: Jossey-Bass, 1991.

Nyhan, R. C., and Marlowe, H. A. "Organizational Effectiveness Enhancement Under Total Quality Management in a Non-Manufacturing Setting." Unpublished manuscript, School of Public Administration, College of Urban and Public Affairs, Florida Atlantic University, 1992.

Osborne, D. "Beyond Left and Right: A New Political Paradigm." *Responsive Community,* 1992, *2,* 26-41.

Osborne, D., and Gaebler, T. *Reinventing Government.* Reading, Mass.: Addison-Wesley, 1992.

Ott, J. S. *The Organizational Culture Perspective.* Chicago: Dorsey Press, 1989.

Pammer, W. J. *Managing Fiscal Strain in Major American Cities: Understanding Retrenchment in the Public Sector.* New York: Greenwood Press, 1990.

Peterson, I. "Americans See Dimmer Prospects." *Miami Herald,* Nov. 4, 1991, p. 5a.

Schein, E. *Organizational Culture and Leadership.* San Francisco: Jossey-Bass, 1985.

Scitovsky, T. *The Joyless Economy: The Psychology of Human Satisfaction.* New York: Oxford University Press, 1992.

Senge, P. M. *The Fifth Discipline: The Art and Practice of the Learning Organization.* New York: Doubleday, 1990.

Sitkin, S. B., and Pablo, A. L. "Reconceptualizing the Determinants of Risk Behavior." *Academy of Management Review,* 1992, *17,* 9-38.

Spitzer, K. "Florida Local Government Review and Expenditure Forecasts, 1991-2000." Vol. 1. Tallahassee, Fla.: Florida Association of Counties, 1991.

Talbot, M. *The Holographic Universe.* New York: HarperCollins, 1991.

Van Maanen, J., and Barley, S. R. "Cultural Organization: Fragments of a Theory." In P. J. Frost and others, (eds.), *Organizational Culture.* Newbury Park, Calif.: Sage, 1985.

Walters, J. "The Shrink Proof Bureaucracy." *Governing,* 1992, *5,* 32-39.

Wildavsky, A. "Ubiquitous Anomie: Public Service in an Era of Ideological Dissensus." *Public Administration Review,* 1988, July/Aug., 753-755.

13

Conclusion: Improving the Self
Through Total Quality Management

Ralph H. Kilmann, Ines Kilmann

IN THE INTRODUCTORY CHAPTER of this book, we summarized the contents according to five fundamental questions: What is ego energy? What is its source? What is positive versus negative ego energy? How can positive ego energy be channeled to achieve organizational goals? Why must ego energy be managed now? The answers to these questions—as discussed throughout the book—represent what is currently known about ego energy. The purpose of this concluding chapter is to propose the next steps: what new avenues of research and practice would further develop our understanding and use of ego energy?

We, along with the other contributors, have frequently noted that rapid technological, political, social, and economic change generates uncertainty, anxiety, and fear—which is precisely why the subject of ego energy is so relevant at this time. Since most organizations must respond to all this incessant change by periodically transforming and restructuring themselves, employees must also regularly reexamine their self-concepts and reattach themselves to new surroundings. To learn how these ego assessments and adjustments can take place most effectively, we will make use of the evolving paradigm of total quality management (TQM). Indeed, the key principles and practices of TQM offer a provocative approach for describing, controlling, and improving a person's ego-defining processes—just as organizations do for their core business processes.

First we summarize the fundamentals for managing quality, which will suggest why this approach is becoming such a universal paradigm for improving organizations. Then we focus our attention on improving each employee's self-concepts (the results) by improving how these self-concepts are determined (the process). Moreover, drawing on recent advances in business process innovation and reengineering, we also suggest a novel approach for radically redesigning ego-defining processes in order to help employees dramatically improve themselves and their organizations.

The Essence of TQM

Although TQM is often confused with quality circles, statistical process control, or a particular set of quality tools, it is best viewed as a systemic—strategic—approach for improving organizations in an increasingly competitive, fast-paced, global economy. (See Dixon and Swiler, 1990; Evans and Lindsay, 1993; Feigenbaum, 1991; Garvin, 1988; Harrington, 1991; Imai, 1986.) At its core, TQM is a certain way of seeing, thinking, feeling, and behaving—which amounts to a *process view* of organizational life. In essence, the process of doing something is considered as more important than the results, simply because the process determines the results. And the desired result—the essential reason for being—is to satisfy (and delight) customers according to their needs and wants (including quality products and services; zero defects, errors, and failures; short delivery time; and low cost or price). Of course, other stakeholders must also be satisfied—governments, communities, employees, shareholders, suppliers, and so on—if one is to stay in business. But the quintessential stakeholder is the ultimate customer who uses the organization's products and services. According to the essential principles of TQM: If all members continuously improve their processes, the results will improve as well (Crosby, 1979; Schmidt and Finnigan, 1992).

A process is defined as a sequence of tasks and decisions that includes receiving inputs from suppliers and delivering outputs to customers. Figure 13.1 shows a *process cell* as the elementary building block of TQM. Thus all activity in an organization is intended to be a value-added process for customers (and other key stakeholders). Moreover, as shown in Figure 13.2, all employees (and work groups) can be linked along a *process chain* according to the outputs they hand off to one another. Although we show the process chain in a linear format for graphic convenience, it could also be shown as a closed loop: every process chain begins and ends by specifying and satisfying the needs of the customer (Denning, 1992).

Three kinds of feedback provide a variety of opportunities to

Figure 13.1. A Process Cell.

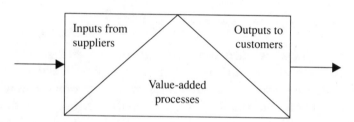

Figure 13.2. A Process Chain.

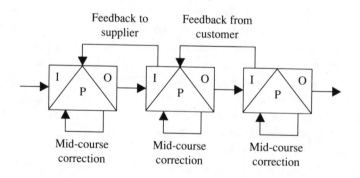

Note: I = Inputs; P = Process; O = Output.

revise the work being performed so that the ultimate customer is completely satisfied: (1) Every person in the process chain can assess the quality of his or her own work and make the necessary mid-course corrections before any output is given to someone else; (2) every person can actively facilitate customer feedback in order to provide what the customer requires; and (3) every person can specify what quality inputs are expected from suppliers so that processes add value all down the chain.

At this point, however, it is important to keep in mind the variety of possible dysfunctions in the formal and informal systems of an organization (and their corresponding dysfunctional manage-ment practices) that can prevent any value-added process on paper from working in practice. Unless all systemic barriers to success have been removed (or at least minimized), it is highly unlikely that employees will be able—or willing—to cooperate across work group boundaries in order to add value for their customers. Mistrust between functional departments, deficient communication and problem-solving skills, and a lack of cooperation between work units will surely get in the way of handoffs down the process chain. Nor can employees be expected to know what specific tasks and decisions will add the most value for customers if mixed strategic signals and conflicted priorities make it impossible for them to know who their ultimate customers really are and what they actu-ally want. Worse yet, what if the informal cultural norms and the formal reward system motivate employees to satisfy their bosses (up the hierarchy) instead of their customers (down the chain)? TQM is just not possible if systemic barriers to success are present.

Once systemic barriers have been identified and removed, however, processes must be described and controlled before they can be improved (Kilmann, 1993). As illustrated in Figure 13.3, pro-cesses are described with the use of flowcharts—starting with inputs from external and internal suppliers and ending with outputs to either intermediary or ultimate customers. By using rectangles to signify tasks and diamonds to signify decision points (including yes and no choices), organizational members can describe their core processes—both within and across work units. Moreover, by distin-guishing tasks and decisions that are value-added for customers (CVA), for other stakeholders (OVA), or for no stakeholders (NVA),

Figure 13.3. Describing Processes.

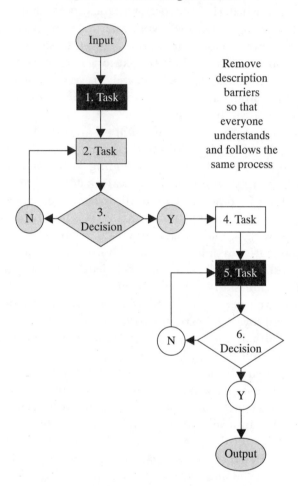

all members can identify the activities that should be streamlined (CVA), minimized (OVA), or eliminated (NVA). And by using different background colors or shadings to represent these various activities (for example, dark, medium, and light for CVA, OVA, and NVA, respectively), members develop a common language for describing processes throughout their organization. Thus, by drawing flowcharts, members can remove *description barriers:* not knowing who the customer is; not agreeing on who the customer is; making incorrect assumptions about what the customer really wants; not having an explicit, streamlined, and efficient value-added process; and not agreeing on the process that must be followed by all group members as the standard operating procedure (Harrington, 1991).

Once core processes have been described in theory, the next step is to learn how well each process works in practice. Translating customer requirements into numerical targets—the results—enables members to discover how consistently they are performing the process. Collecting data is the only way to determine if each process is under control (Montgomery, 1991): hitting the target (on average) with all data points within the UCL and the LCL (the upper and lower control limits, respectively). But if a process is out of control, something can now be done about it (Ishikawa, 1986). As illustrated in Figure 13.4, by plotting process control charts according to prod-

Figure 13.4. Controlling Processes.

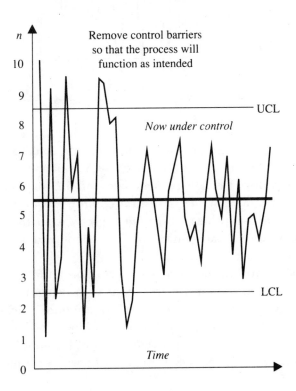

Figure 13.5. Improving Processes.

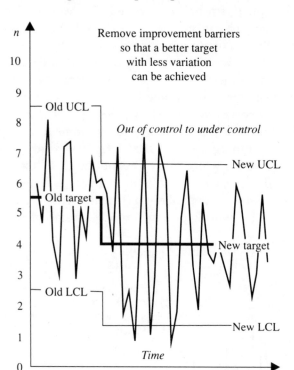

uct or service requirements, defects, errors, failures, cycle times, or process costs, work groups can learn to identify and then remove *control barriers:* not making the best use of available resources—including people, technology, materials, and information. Even if a process is brought under statistical control, however, does not assure that it is capable of providing exactly what the customer requires. A process that is under control but not capable, therefore, must be improved.

What satisfies customers today will not satisfy them tomorrow. Not only do customer expectations keep rising, but competitors continue to hit better targets with less variation. Benchmarking the best-known practices in other organizations and industries is often the quickest (and most effective) way of learning how to improve processes (Camp, 1989), rather than wasting time and resources reinventing the wheel and believing that "if it's not invented here, it doesn't apply and shouldn't be used." Once work units discover what indeed is possible, they can develop world-class performance goals. Next, as depicted by Dimancescu (1992), cross-functional teams can hold various meetings to identify and remove *improvement barriers:* not improving the use of old (or acquiring new) resources that primarily determine just what target and variation a process is capable of achieving. As illustrated in Figure 13.5, by retraining current employees, adding new technology, getting better materials from fewer suppliers, and providing more valid and timely information, the limits of any work-related process can be substantially altered (Deming, 1986; Juran, 1991).

People managing data is a key aspect of TQM: decisions and actions should be based on accurate information about suppliers, customers, and processes—not on guesswork, wrong assumptions, or wishful thinking. Since a lot of data are often gathered while describing, controlling, and improving processes, it is essential that these data are presented in a graphic (as opposed to a tabular) form: charts, plots, and diagrams, as shown in Figure 13.6, ensure that the forest will not be lost by seeing so many trees. Several quality tools are available to help organize data for group discussions and problem-solving efforts so that people will uncover the root causes of problems (and processes), focus their limited time on the most important things first (and the least important things last—or not at all), and assess whether their derived solutions, once implemented, have achieved the intended results (Ishikawa, 1986; Shigeru, 1988). Incidentally, these quality tools are not only invaluable for removing description, control, and improvement barriers, but also can help remove systemic barriers to success.

It is worthwhile highlighting two key statistical principles that have been featured by Shewhart (1931) and Deming (1986). The first principle emphasizes that all outcome variables (for example, product or service specifications, process costs, and cycle times) must be clearly defined and operationalized into valid measures before any described process can be brought under statistical control—and then improved. Specifically, if the process of measuring some attribute of quality is not under statistical control (including the instrument, the conditions of measurement, and the people in-

Figure 13.6. Some Quality Tools.

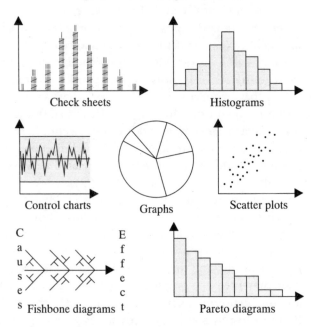

Check sheets   Histograms

Control charts   Graphs   Scatter plots

Fishbone diagrams   Pareto diagrams

volved throughout the measurement process), all subsequent efforts to control and improve the process for *producing* quality will be futile. Therefore, instead of making vague statements about improving quality, it is necessary to pinpoint what specific outcome variable is of interest (for example, cycle time) and then indicate exactly how this variable will be measured, by whom, and under what precise conditions—so that the measurement process is (and will remain) under statistical control.

A second key principle of statistical variation concerns the fundamental distinction between special causes and common causes (Deming, 1986). Special causes (which drive processes out of statistical control—similar to control barriers) can often be removed by the work group itself (for example, by ensuring that a described process is being followed by all group members as the standard operating procedure). Common causes (which render processes incapable of meeting customer specifications—similar to improvement barriers), however, can only be removed by those who have the resources and the authority to redesign—reengineer—the process itself. It seems very unreasonable, therefore, to hold the persons who perform a process accountable for deficiencies in the design of the process (which is evident if the process is not capable of meeting customer specifications and cannot be improved by the work unit). Practically and ethically speaking, employees should only be responsible for keeping a process under control—especially when the design of the process (including the allocation of resources) is beyond their sphere of influence.

The latest addition to TQM is termed business process redesign, process innovation, or reengineering (Andrews and Leventhal, 1993; Davenport, 1993; Davidow and Malone, 1992; Gunn, 1992; Hammer and Champy, 1993; Keen, 1991) and is primarily directed to removing the common causes (improvement barriers) that limit the performance of an organization's core business processes— enabled by advances in information technology. Although the proponents of this effort to achieve radical (order-of-magnitude) process improvements sometimes try too hard to distinguish their work from TQM and related approaches to gradual improvement, it is apparent that the foundation of all these approaches is a process chain leading to the complete satisfaction of the ultimate customer. Even though information technology can effectively be used to rethink and redesign business processes across all the traditional organizational, industry, and national boundaries, each process chain must still be explicitly described, precisely followed, validly measured, and then brought under statistical control before any potential (gradual or radical) improvements in quality, cost, and time can be achieved.

The real value-added contribution of reengineering, therefore, is not information technology per se (Davenport, 1993; Hammer and Champy, 1993) but helping organizations to examine—and then revise—their outdated assumptions about how work can best be organized, managed, and performed for today's, not yesterday's, world. Specifically, doing work in tall vertical structures according to the traditional business functions (marketing, finance, operations, human resources, and so on) is giving way to doing work in flat horizontal structures according to business processes (new product development and introduction, procurement and material handling, customer order fulfillment, customer service, and so forth). This latter, nontraditional approach to work often leads to dramatic structural change throughout the organization (Rummler and Brache, 1990), which can be assisted by computer hardware and software technology (Andrews and Leventhal, 1993; Tapscott and Caston, 1993). But beware the promise of *radical* improvement—if systemic barriers to success are present or members have not even learned how to manage (and adjust to) gradual change and continuous improvement (Kilmann, 1993).

In sum, then, when we strip away the peculiarities of terms, tools, techniques, and technologies, the foundation of the various approaches to TQM (including business process innovation and reengineering) is the explicit use of value-added process chains for the delight of the ultimate customer (and the satisfaction of other key stakeholders). By precisely defining and operationalizing variables, and by keenly appreciating the distinction between special and common causes of statistical variation, employees can provide the necessary value-added contributions for the long-term success of their organization. They can describe, control, and improve the core processes that determine—and thus improve—the desired results. Since total quality management is becoming an integrated approach for improving organizations, we now explore how these same essential principles and practices can also improve the self (Forsha, 1992).

Describing Ego-Defining Processes

In Chapter One we defined ego energy as each person's primitive struggle to know (both consciously and accurately) his or her identity (Who am I? What emotional investments should I make?), competency (How effective am I at being who I am? Are my decisions, actions, and investments ethical?), value (Have I contributed what others need or want? Is my organization benefiting from my decisions, actions, and investments?), worth (Am I a good or bad person? Do I deserve to be happy?), and responsibility (Who controls who I am, what I do, what emotional investments I make, and whether I am good or bad, happy or sad?).

In terms of TQM, a person's answers to these crucial questions are determined by ego-defining processes. In fact, each self-concept may be produced by a different process. The ego-identity process to establish the essence of "who I am," for example, may be quite different from the ego-investment process by which a person first detaches himself from a familiar work setting and then reattaches himself to a brand new job, department, and location (during organizational transformation or restructuring). And, based on TQM, if employees (and their organizations) wish to improve the self-concepts so that there is more positive ego energy available to achieve both personal and organizational goals (Ferris, Chapter Nine), the ego-defining process for each self-concept must be described—made explicit—before it can be controlled and improved. Exhortations by the self or others to improve ego energy (the results) are no more effective than pronouncements or slogans by senior executives to improve quality. Since the process *causes* the results, the only way to improve the results (such as more meaningful, functional, productive, and satisfying self-concepts) is to improve each process.

What would it be like for employees to describe their ego-defining processes in a specially designed workshop setting—under the conditions of free choice, psychological safety, and guidance by qualified facilitators? Keeping in mind the importance of precisely defining and operationalizing variables, each employee would first be asked to provide explicit answers to the various questions about each self-concept—to establish a baseline for subsequent improvement efforts. Then each employee would be asked to describe the process that he or she used to make each assessment: how did you determine your identity, competency, value, worth, and responsibility? We can only imagine what a powerful experience it would be for employees to flowchart (see Figure 13.3) the ideal value-added processes they should use to answer the questions about their self-concepts: the specific tasks and decisions in each ego-defining process. Of course, they would first have to address the TQM basics: who is the ultimate customer and who are the primary suppliers?

Each person's ultimate customer might ideally be himself—with family, friends, and the organization as the other key stakeholders. As it has been said many times before and in many ways, you can't satisfy others if you can't satisfy yourself. If employees have their own house in order (or their own act together), they can better serve their other key stakeholders—including their organization and its customers.

Each person's primary supplier should ideally be himself— with only a few carefully chosen others who provide accurate information, mastery experiences, emotional support, and stress reduction and serve as effective role models (Cianni and Romberger, Chapter Ten; Mone and Kelly, Chapter Five). Just as with TQM, the fewer the suppliers the better (especially when effective partnerships help ensure just-in-time, quality handoffs down the process chain). Recalling the fundamental distinction between special and common causes of statistical variation, employees would also be alert to the key implications of responsibility. (Who controls who I am, what I do, what emotional investments I make, and whether I am good or bad, happy or sad?) Basically, if employees allow multiple suppliers to determine who they are and what makes them valuable, then, by default, some of the common causes of their ego-defining processes are out of their immediate control (responsibility) and they are therefore at the mercy of others for determining (and later improving) their self-concepts—much like having an external locus of control (Marshall, Pitera, Yorks, and DeBerry, Chapter Eleven; Rotter, 1971). But if employees describe their ideal ego-defining processes so that they are fully responsible for who they are and what makes them valuable, both the control barriers (special causes) and the improvement barriers (common causes) are under their power. For better or worse, they are at the mercy of themselves—much like having an internal locus of control. An ideal ego-defining process, therefore, is when each person is his own primary supplier of identity, competency, value, worth, and responsibility— and deliberately regulates who has a say in defining his self-concepts.

The ideal ego-defining processes for defining the self-concepts can be contrasted with the actual processes that are now operating— either implicitly or explicitly. Using the basic flowchart symbols defined earlier and specifying whether a task or decision is customer value-added (CVA), other value-added (OVA), or no value-added (NVA) could reveal some fascinating insights. Imagine the case (just as many organizations have discovered) in which the great majority of activities (95 percent) are NVA or OVA—rather than being customer value-added (CVA) for the self. The worst possible case (from the standpoint of eventually enabling all members to improve their self-concepts) is any process that reveals: (1) unreliable, multiple suppliers of vital information and support for defining the self-concepts, (2) numerous customers other than the self as being the prime beneficiaries of whatever ego energy is available, and (3) most tasks and decisions as being NVA (not CVA or OVA). Indeed, people who have been described as experiencing chronically low self-esteem (Branden, Chapter Two; Allcorn, Chapter Seven) are, in all likelihood, habitually using such dysfunctional ego-defining processes—to the detriment of themselves and their organizations (including their families, friends, and communities).

The goal of describing processes, of course, is to close the gap between the actual and the ideal: to delight the right customer (the self) while satisfying other key stakeholders—by receiving the right inputs from one or only a few suppliers (accurate information and emotional support from oneself and carefully chosen others) and by performing only CVA and OVA tasks and decisions in the most efficient manner possible. Again, we wish to emphasize just how revealing it might be for employees to describe their ideal and actual processes for defining their self-concepts. Certainly the experience of describing business processes has often resulted in major breakthroughs for work group members who were at odds with each other with regard to who is their customer, what they should receive from their suppliers, and how they can add maximum value down the process chain via CVA and OVA tasks and decisions. But once these description barriers are clearly identified, they can be removed—thus closing the gap between the actual and ideal process.

Controlling Ego-Defining Processes

Once each employee has described the processes that should be used—at all times—to define his self-concepts (analogous to using each agreed-upon business process as the standard operating procedure), attention shifts to seeing if each process is under statistical control (with all data points between the upper and lower control limits). One might wonder whether a person's self-concepts are stable (and reliable) if they frequently fall outside the control limits and thus depict an out-of-control process—for example, when a person feels exceptionally good one moment, fine the next, and then completely worthless shortly thereafter.

While measuring the self-concepts is certainly a difficult task, it is nevertheless an essential step in controlling—and later improving—one's self-concepts. (See Hays, 1992, for guidelines and examples of measuring the equally elusive concept of customer satisfaction.) And if the same person is defining his self-concepts and measuring them under the same exact conditions, it is more likely that the measuring process itself will be under statistical control (which is an important requirement for TQM, as noted earlier). Also recall the importance of obtaining accurate self-appraisals (Bailey, Strube, Yost, and Merbaum, Chapter Six) and overcoming self-deception (Holmer, Chapter Three).

It is not our purpose here to provide the means by which the self-concepts can be measured, but it certainly is appropriate to intrigue the reader with the many possibilities. Imagine what it would be like for each work group member to develop a concise operational definition for his identity, competency, value, worth, and responsibility, and then, on a ten-point scale (from extremely low to extremely high), to assess each self-concept with a number (position) on the scale. Regarding the self-concept of responsibility, for example, each group member could ask himself: To what extent do I determine how good or bad I feel about myself? To what extent do I determine whether I am happy or sad? To what extent do I determine my emotional investments and attachments to my job? The person would then respond to each question on a ten-point scale (adjusting the endpoints of the scale to fit the nature of the question being asked—for example, from "completely" to "not at all"). One can also imagine just how difficult it would be to feel attached and secure in an organization if the ego-defining process were left implicit, which would also prevent it from being measured, controlled, and improved. The lessons learned from TQM are clear: A process that is neither described nor controlled cannot be improved and, worse yet, an implicit process cannot satisfy the changing needs—and rising expectations—of the customer.

Following the principles and practices of TQM, it is important for group members to measure their self-concepts on a regular basis (such as once every day or at least once every week) by responding to the same questions on the same scales. Then process control charts (see Figure 13.4) can be used to discover if the process for determining each self-concept is under control—after calculating the upper and lower control limits (Montgomery, 1991). Recall: It is an ego-defining process (along with a measurement process) that determines the placement of each data point (the result) on the process control chart. Next, for any process that is out of control, the various quality tools (see Figure 13.6) can be used to pinpoint the special causes—to see where and how the process of defining a self-concept has broken down. Finally, action steps can be planned and implemented in order to remove the identified control barriers (special causes)—thereby bringing each out-of-control process under control.

Once every ego-defining process is under statistical control, every employee should feel more stable and reliable in general. Also, with an in-depth understanding of statistical variation, each employee would know to squelch any temptation to remove random variation inside the control limits—since tinkering with random variation is not only misguided but can drive an under-control process out of control. Even if the processes for defining the self are under control, however, they may not be capable of satisfying the person and the organization. As noted earlier, a process that is under control but not capable must therefore be improved.

Improving Ego-Defining Processes

Almost all the material in this book has been concerned with unleashing, mobilizing, and channeling the ego energy that derives from each person's primitive struggle to define his self-concepts. But there has been little attention given to improving the self-concepts—the actual content or substance of ego energy (identity, competency, value, worth, and responsibility). Other than a few references to employee assistance programs for helping members with chronically low self-esteem (Allcorn, Chapter Seven), executive development programs for redirecting members' excessive ego energy (Kaplan, Chapter Eight), and redeployment (rightsizing)

programs to help employees reattach themselves to changed surroundings (Marshall, Pitera, Yorks, and DeBerry, Chapter Eleven;
Marlowe and Nyhan, Chapter Twelve), the actual content of the
self-concepts has largely been taken as a given.

Now we consider how people can improve their self-concepts
so they feel more unique, valuable, and better about themselves—
and thus have more positive energy for their organization. Naturally, some self-concepts (and their ego-defining processes) may be
more important to individuals and their organizations than others—depending on the person's goals, what is in most need of improvement, and the special challenges facing an organization.
Consequently, it may be worthwhile to prioritize the importance of
improving each self-concept by using Pareto diagrams (see Figure
13.6). Nevertheless, the discussion will proceed assuming that one
or more self-concepts have been chosen for improvement.

Imagine what it would be like for group members to set new
targets—stretching themselves to strive for improved results over
their earlier baseline definitions of the self-concepts. Each member
would ask: How much better do I want to be (or experience myself)
on each of the self-concepts—as measured by my responses to the
same questions on the previous scales (or on more challenging
questionnaires)? How much do I want to reduce the statistical variation around my self-concepts—so that I experience less variation
about who I am and what makes me valuable on a daily or weekly
basis? Once improvement goals have been established (guided, perhaps, by benchmarking what other people have accomplished with
respect to the self-concepts), group members can be asked to list
their improvement barriers—and then develop and implement action plans to remove them.

Recall: The more a person is his own primary supplier (and
carefully chooses whether to use other people's opinions to define
his self-concepts), the more the person can eliminate common
causes (improvement barriers) as well as special causes (control barriers)—without relying on any other person or organization. But the
more a person makes use of multiple suppliers, the more the common causes of his ego-defining processes will be determined by
others, which limits the extent to which the person can improve
himself—by himself.

As shown earlier in Figure 13.5, process control charts can also be used to see if each new target has been achieved (with less variation around the process mean). When a person first attempts to define himself differently, his new ego-defining process might initially be out of control (for example, regressing to old habits of seeing, thinking, and feeling about the self—while the improved process is still unfamiliar). Gradually, however, control barriers can be identified and removed (with the various quality tools shown earlier in Figure 13.6), which then brings the improved process under statistical control. The result? The members have improved their self-concepts (identity, competency, value, worth, and responsibility) so that there is more positive (and more reliable) ego energy for their organization to unleash, mobilize, and channel in functional ways. This result assumes, of course, that the external environment, leadership behavior, organizational systems, and management practices all enable the constructive use of ego energy.

Radically Redesigning the Self

The most recent enhancements to TQM—business process redesign, process innovation, and reengineering—take a more radical approach to organizational improvement. Rather than being satisfied with incremental or gradual change, the objective is to plan for and achieve order-of-magnitude improvement: the difference between a 10 percent improvement and a 100 or even a 1000 percent improvement. But it is still too early to tell what the long-term effects of reengineering will be and whether this extremely rational/technical methodology can effectively coexist with the deeply emotional/expressive needs of the human spirit (Deal and Hawkins, Chapter Four). The results have been mixed. There have been incredible success stories of reengineering at the one extreme and a 50 to 70 percent failure rate at the other (Hammer and Champy, 1993). Perhaps the process of reengineering is not yet under control; or systemic barriers to success are still operating in the failure cases (but are being ignored); or people have not yet learned to cope with gradual change and improvement and, therefore, neither understand nor accept the need for radical change. Nevertheless, process reengineering does seem to have the potential to achieve radical change under the right conditions. Perhaps redesigning the self might only be necessary (or advisable) if prior efforts to describe, control, and improve ego-defining processes gradually are now clearly insufficient to prepare employees for impending radical change (transformation, restructuring, or reengineering) that will severely threaten their emotional investments and attachments.

Notwithstanding the usual cautions about newly developed—radical—approaches to organizational change and improvement, it does seem appropriate in this concluding chapter to stretch the limits of what might be possible by radically improving the processes by which people define their self-concepts. As mentioned earlier in our review of the major principles and practices of TQM, the essence of reengineering is not the use of information technology per se—even though computer hardware, software, shared data bases, and various telecommunication systems certainly make reengineering possible. Rather, the major contribution of radical process improvement is a dedicated effort to confront—and then revise—outdated assumptions about how to organize, manage, and perform work. In an analogous manner, achieving radical improvements in the self-concepts also requires questioning—and then shattering—outdated assumptions about how people define themselves.

Assumptional analysis is a method that enables people to surface, classify, and synthesize their hidden assumptions behind their favorite conclusions (Kilmann, 1989). Starting with an initial conclusion (anything to be argued for, the best decision, or the right course of action), people are asked to list all the key stakeholders that are affected by their conclusion and can therefore affect the outcome of their decisions or actions. Some typical stakeholders are customers, suppliers, employees, competitors, communities, governments, and shareholders. Then people are asked to write assumptions about each stakeholder (what each stakeholder sees, values, and believes; how each makes decisions and acts) that would have to be true in order to argue, most convincingly, that the conclusion, as stated, is correct. This stage—surfacing assumptions—gives people the chance to see, face to face, what is really behind their conclusions, even if these assumptions were never examined before. For complex problems, tens or hundreds of assumptions could be surfaced to support initial conclusions.

The next stage—classifying assumptions—sorts all the sur-faced assumptions into four quadrants according to two key dis-tinctions: importance and certainty. First, the most important assumptions can be distinguished from the least important assump-tions by repeatedly asking the question: If I am wrong about this assumption, can I still argue for my conclusion? If a most important assumption were false, it would undermine my whole argument (and conclusion). But a least important assumption (being tangen-tial) would not stand in my way. Second, the certain assumptions can be distinguished from the uncertain ones by repeatedly asking these questions: Based on all my experience and knowledge, am I confident that this assumption, as stated, is either true or false (hence certain)? Or do I need to collect additional information be-cause I really don't know if this assumption is true or false (hence uncertain)? The critical region, as shown in the lower-right-hand quadrant of the matrix in Figure 13.7, contains the potentially most devastating assumptions. The assumptions in the critical region of the matrix are most important to the conclusion at hand (if a person is wrong about these assumptions he can no longer argue for his conclusion), yet he has no idea if these assumptions are true or false. The person is uncertain—a 50/50 gamble on the most important assumptions behind his most cherished conclusion.

Figure 13.7. The Assumption Matrix.

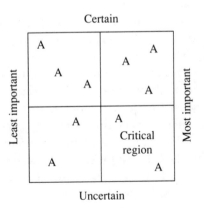

Now that the relevant assumptions about the key stakeholders to the initial conclusion have been surfaced and classified, they can be synthesized to reflect today's—not yesterday's—world. First, the most important assumptions that are known to be false (in the upper-right-hand quadrant of the matrix) can be reversed, since it is rather obvious (based on common knowledge and experience) what is actually true—now that these false assumptions have been made explicit. Second, the most important and uncertain assumptions (in the critical region of the matrix) can be further researched by collecting additional information to learn whether they are true or false—or something else altogether. Thus, these critical assumptions can also be revised as more is learned about what stakeholders value and believe or are inclined to do.

The last step in synthesizing assumptions is deriving a new conclusion to reflect the revised assumptions. In fact, the more that *false* certain/most important assumptions were detected (and then revised) and the more that new knowledge was acquired about the uncertain/most important assumptions (which caused them to be revised), the more that the new conclusion will be a radical departure from the initial conclusion—thus opening the doors to radical (and not just gradual) change and improvement.

Assumptional analysis is a rigorous, systematic approach for exposing—and then revising—outdated assumptions about any kind of initial conclusion. In terms of reengineering business processes, the method can be used to explore radically different approaches for organizing, managing, and performing work—so that the final synthesized conclusion will be based on the most up-to-date knowledge about all key stakeholders involved (in any way) in the performance of a business process. In terms of improving the self, assumptional analysis can be used not only for exploring radically different ego-defining processes but also for unleashing, mobilizing, and channeling more functional ego energy.

Imagine each member formulating different initial conclusions about radically different processes for defining his or her self-concepts. Each initial conclusion would then be subjected to an assumptional analysis. It would be interesting to discover the stakeholders who affect each different ego-defining process. It would be especially revealing to see the surfaced assumptions that would have to be true about each stakeholder in order to argue, most convincingly, that an ego-defining process will lead to the most meaningful, functional, productive, and satisfying self-concepts for the individual (and his or her organization). Once all the assumptions for each initial conclusion have been surfaced and classified, the most important assumptions that are known to be false can immediately be revised—while the most important/uncertain assumptions (in the critical region in the matrix) must be researched before they can be updated. Once all the out-of-date assumptions are synthesized and a radically new ego-defining process is designed and then implemented, each group member's self-concepts will be closer in touch with his or her inner being and the outside world. As a result, conjoint mental health for the individual and the organization is now possible to achieve—and sustain—so long as the radically new ego-defining processes are precisely described, statistically controlled, and continuously improved.

Prospects and Pitfalls

This chapter has sought to open new avenues of research and practice for better understanding and managing ego energy. Using the paradigm of total quality management (including the recent additions of business process redesign, process innovation, and reengineering), we have considered how ego-defining processes too can be described, controlled, and improved—both gradually and radically.

Although our discussion has been highly speculative, its logic is compelling. If a business process cannot be improved unless it is first described and controlled, what does it mean to empower members to improve their self-concepts? And knowing what it takes to make radical improvements in business processes, why would it be any different (let alone easier) to make order-of-magnitude improvements in the self-concepts? In either case, business process or ego-defining process, outdated assumptions are typically at the heart of all improvement barriers—especially when radical change is necessary or desirable in our fast-paced, global economy. Although the focus of TQM has been on the work-related processes outside employees, it may now be equally essential to manage the ego-defining processes inside every person. The better that members can describe, control, and improve their self-concepts, the better they will be able to focus their abundant energies and abilities on continuously—and radically—improving all their organizational processes.

Improving self-concepts has not been the traditional focus of in-house training and development programs—which tend to concentrate on enhancing employees' administrative, technical, and interpersonal skills. But driven by the increasingly competitive global marketplace, organizations are now expanding their search to identify and remove *all* improvement barriers (inside and outside their traditional boundaries) that stand in the way of gradual and radical process improvement—rather than defining any "common cause" as out of their reach. Because of the tremendous impact that ego energy and the self-concepts have on the functioning of organizations (especially during transformation and restructuring), organizational development programs that explicitly seek to improve employees' self-concepts are likely to be more extensively discussed and considered. Thus it is essential to alert the reader to the potential controversy behind any ego-based program: Does the organization have the right to ask employees to improve their psychological processes just as they are expected to improve their business processes? Although applying TQM to the self does not seem to resemble psychotherapy or other therapeutic approaches, discussions on ego and self-worth can be threatening (especially for people with chronically low self-esteem). We therefore encourage further debate on the ethics of personal and organizational change—as we proceed to manage ego energy.

References

Andrews, D. C., and Leventhal, N. S. *Fusion—Integrating IE, CASE, and JAD: A Handbook for Reengineering the Systems Organization.* Englewood Cliffs, N.J.: PTR Prentice-Hall, 1993.

Camp, R. C. *Benchmarking: The Search for Industry Best Practices That Lead to Superior Performance.* Milwaukee: ASQC Quality Press, 1989.

Crosby, P. B. *Quality Is Free.* New York: McGraw-Hill, 1979.

Davenport, T. H. *Process Innovation: Reengineering Work Through Information Technology.* Boston: Harvard Business School, 1993.

Davidow, W. H., and Malone, M. S. *The Virtual Corporation: Structuring and Revitalizing the Corporation for the 21st Century.* New York: HarperCollins, 1992.

Deming, W. E. *Out of the Crisis.* Cambridge, Mass.: MIT Press, 1986.

Denning, P. J. "Work Is a Closed-Loop Process." *American Scientist, 80,* July–Aug. 1992, 314–317.

Dimancescu, D. *The Seamless Enterprise: Making Cross Functional Management Work.* New York: HarperBusiness, 1992.

Dixon, G., and Swiler, J. (eds.). *Total Quality Handbook: The Executive Guide to the New American Way of Doing Business.* Minneapolis, Minn.: Lakewood, 1990.

Evans, J. R., and Lindsay, W. M. *The Management and Control of Quality.* St. Paul, Minn.: West, 1993.

Feigenbaum, A. V. *Total Quality Control.* (3rd ed.) New York: McGraw-Hill, 1991.

Forsha, H. I. *The Pursuit of Quality Through Personal Change.* Milwaukee: ASQC Quality Press, 1992.

Garvin, D. A. *Managing Quality: The Strategic and Competitive Edge.* New York: Free Press, 1988.

Gunn, T. G. *21st Century Manufacturing: Creating Winning Business Performance.* New York: HarperBusiness, 1992.

Hammer, M., and Champy, J. *Reengineering the Corporation: A Manifesto for Business Revolution.* New York: HarperBusiness, 1993.

Harrington, H. J. *Business Process Improvement: The Breakthrough Strategy for Total Quality, Productivity, and Competitiveness.* New York: McGraw-Hill, 1991.

Hays, B. E. *Measuring Customer Satisfaction: Development and Use of Questionnaires.* Milwaukee: ASQC Quality Press, 1992.

Imai, M. *Kaizen: The Key to Japan's Success.* New York: Random House, 1986.

Ishikawa, K. *Guide to Quality Control.* Tokyo: Asian Productivity Organization, 1986.

Juran, J. M. *Juran's New Quality Road Map: Planning, Setting, and Reaching Quality Goals.* New York: Free Press, 1991.

Keen, P.G.W. *Shaping the Future: Business Design Through Information Technology.* Boston: Harvard Business School, 1991.

Kilmann, R. H. *Managing Beyond the Quick Fix: A Completely Integrated Program for Creating and Maintaining Organizational Success.* San Francisco: Jossey-Bass, 1989.

Kilmann, R. H. *Workbook for Continuous Improvement: Holographic Quality Management.* New York: Xicom, 1993.

Montgomery, D.C. *Introduction to Statistical Quality Control.* New York: Wiley, 1991.

Rotter, J. B. "External Control and Internal Control." *Psychology Today,* June 1971, 37–42, 58–59.

Rummler, G. A., and Brache, A. P. *Improving Performance: How to Manage the White Space on the Organization Chart.* San Francisco: Jossey-Bass, 1990.

Schmidt, W. H., and Finnigan, J. P. *The Race Without a Finish Line: America's Quest for Total Quality.* San Francisco: Jossey-Bass, 1992.

Shewhart, W. A. *Economic Control of Quality of Manufactured Product.* New York: Van Nostrand, 1931.

Shigeru, M. *Management for Quality Improvement: The Seven New QC Tools.* Cambridge, Mass.: Productivity Press, 1988.

Tapscott, D., and Caston, A. *Paradigm Shift: The New Promise of Information Technology.* New York: McGraw-Hill, 1993.

Name Index

Subject Index

A

Alcoholics Anonymous (AA), 68; as personal transformation model, 66–69; principles behind, 68–69

Anxiety: basic versus neurotic, 4, 155; defense mechanisms for, 157–162; and ego energy, 7–8; ego psychology on, 154–155; lifestyle solutions to, 162–164; in psychodynamic organizational behavior model, 165, 166; separation, 8–9

Appraisal. *See* Self-appraisal; Self-evaluation

Arts. *See* Expressive activity

Assumptional analysis, 324–326

AT&T, 85, 115

B

Behavior: changing executives', 188–193; hypotheses on, in organizations, 176; with negative ego energy, 222; with positive ego energy, 218, 220; and self-esteem and self-efficacy, 106-109

Ben and Jerry's Ice Cream, 81, 93

"Bounded emotionality," 50, 57

C

Center for Creative Leadership, 194

Change. *See* Organizational change

Coaching, 245–246

Competency, 6; interpersonal, 56–57

Culture: ego energy and public organizational, 289–290; flexibility in corporate, 256–258

Customer confidence: loss of, in public organizations, 285–287; organizational redesign to regain, 290–294

D

Data General, 80

Defense mechanisms, psychologi-